Los Angeles County

A DAY HIKER'S GUIDE

For more of John McKinney's

hiking tips and trails, take a hike to www.thetrailmaster.com

Los Angeles County

A DAY HIKER'S GUIDE

by

JOHN McKINNEY

THE TRAILMASTER

SANTA BARBARA

Los Angeles County: A Day Hiker's Guide

Portions of this book appeared in the author's hiking column in the
Los Angeles Times, Westways and Sunset Magazines.

Cover illustration ("Malibu Creek State Park") by Gwen Meyer Pentecost
The Trailmaster Series Editor: Cheri Rae
Maps designed by Hélène Webb
Book Design and typography by Jim Cook

Published by: The Trailmaster Inc
www.TheTrailmaster.com
(805) 965-7200
Visit www.thetrailmaster.com for a complete listing of all
Trailmaster publications, products and services.

ACKNOWLEDGMENTS
For their cooperation, field- and fact-checking, the author wishes to thank the rangers and administrators of Angeles National Forest and Santa Monica Mountains National Recreation Area. Also thanks to the Los Angeles City and County parks departments, as well as to the Angeles District office of the California Department of Parks and Recreation. A special thanks goes to the Santa Monica Mountains Conservancy, an agency with an unmatched vision and dedication to the natural world in and around L.A. The Conservancy has preserved many of the parklands and pathways described in this book.

PHOTO CREDITS
Angeles National Forest, pp. 207, 214; Big Santa Anita Historical Society, p. 194; Brand Library, p. 77; California Department of Parks and Recreation, p. 266; California State Library, pp. 171, 173, 177; Richard Clinton, p. 14; Los Angeles City Recreation and Parks Department, p. 61; Pasadena Historical Society, 178; Rancho Santa Ana Botanic Garden, p. 251; Santa Clarita Valley Historical Society, p. 101; Santa Monica Mountains Conservancy, pp. 282. 287, 303; all other photos by John McKinney.

Cover painting from the collection of Marsha and David Moutrie; photo courtesy of Suzanne Ferguson.

LOS ANGELES COUNTY
A Day Hiker's Guide

CHAPTER 10: WHITTIER-PUENTE HILLS / 147

CHAPTER 11: SAN GABRIEL MOUNTAINS / 155

A Word from The Trailmaster

I've climbed many a mountain above the SoCal metropolis and contemplated the Southland. Sometimes it's the summit view that inspires, sometimes it's the hike itself or one of the region's lovely parklands I've experienced along the way, but always I return home with a slightly different perspective on Southern California.

Today in our frenzied modern world, often so separated from the natural world, this "hiker's perspective" is more important than ever. I know, hikers know, the benefits of climbing the aerie heights, the freedom of the footpath, the joys of experiencing nature. Hiking helps restore the sense of peace and tranquility that our souls require and our hearts desire.

So hike. Contemplate what makes you happy and what would make you happier still. Hike. Enjoy the company of friends and family or the pleasure of your own company. Hike. Delight in the beauty of this world. Hike. Get fit and lift your spirits. Hike. Think about what you can do to expand your life and what you can do to simplify it. Hike.

See you on the trail,
John McKinney
THE TRAILMASTER

The First Great Hiking Era

The Second Great Hiking Era

On Hiking L.A. County

WHEN THE SANTA MONICA MOUNTAINS National Recreation Area was created in 1978, it was done so with the same traditional purposes as other national parks, such as conserving natural and cultural resources.

To these noble purposes, Congress had one more in mind for these magnificent mountains, unique among all other parklands: the mountains that extend across Los Angeles would serve as an "airshed," that is to say as lungs for Los Angeles, as a kind of oxygen therapy for the citizenry.

Breathing space. That's exactly what the Santa Monica Mountains, San Gabriel Mountains and Verdugo Mountains offer, as do the seventy-five miles of coastline and a hundred parks and preserves that comprise wild L.A.

Breathing space. Helping you find some breathing space, helping you find a tranquil place in Los Angeles County, that's what this book is all about.

I'm delighted for the opportunity to share my favorite places, trails and experiences with you. More accurately, this book reflects your favorite places. Thanks to your generous feedback in response to previous books and seventeen years of weekly hiking columns in the *Los Angeles Times* and your many recommendations and suggestions, I've been able to craft a book that reflects the very best of wild Los Angeles.

It's quite satisfying to hear from readers who have hiked to a fabulous vista, conquered a high peak, sighted a rare bird, admired waterfalls and wildflowers. Even more rewarding, though is listening to hikers rhapsodize about their experience in L.A.'s big wild—the solitude or camaraderie, the connections among family members and friends that have been strengthened on the trail.

It's personally very satisfying to write about the natural world and point hikers in the right directions. Wild L.A. is wonderfully diverse and I never get tired of hiking about it, or writing about it. And I know L.A. hikers, whose ranks grow with each passing weekend, appreciate the unique landscape at their feet.

Increasingly, though, I have come to value the time-off every bit as much as the terrain. And judging by all the feedback I get from hikers, you feel the same way.

Parents rejoice in the "quality time" spent with their children in nature. Couples find—or rekindle—romance on the trail. Just about everybody who hikes anywhere comes back a little more refreshed and often greatly rejuvenated.

To be sure, there are still some misguided souls who claim that the Missing Persons song lyric "nobody walks in L.A." is fact. Puhhhhlease, that attitude is soooo '70s, so over. And no more whining about L.A.'s car culture. Sure we hikers love our cars; they help us get to the trailhead!

Years ago I did experience a curious anti-L.A. walking bias from the Department of Motor Vehicles when I applied for the custom license plate: WALK LA. The DMV rejected my request for "Configuration Meaning Unknown or Unclear" and "Possibly Obscene."

I appealed the DMV's decision and in time received my license plates. Without an explanation. Guess I'll never know who thought WALK LA was an unknown concept or possibly obscene statement. Or why.

Optimistic nature-lover that I am, I believe the only reason it might seem that nobody walks in L.A. is that everybody hikes. Every singles ad seems to mention that the searcher for love loves to hike. Movie stars, talk show hosts, SoCal opinion leaders of all kinds, everybody likes to hike in L.A.'s big backyard.

Okay, maybe not everybody. But a lot of people, enough to spawn The Great Hiking Era II. Yes, together we're going to. . . . Well, maybe I better contain my enthusiasm for a moment and tell you about the first Great Hiking Era.

At the dawn of the 20th century, when the automobile was still regarded as a noisy novelty, Los Angeles has a great vogue for hiking. Hordes of hob-nailed boots headed for the San Gabriel Mountains, the Santa Monica Mountains, the Hollywood Hills.

Thousands of hikers rode the city's Red Cars to Sierra Madre, then disembarked and walked up Mt. Wilson Trail to the popular rustic resort at Orchard Camp. Forty thousand people passed over the trail in the peak year of 1911. (Don't worry, solitude-seekers, it's nowhere near as popular today!)

Now, a century later, the Great Hiking Era II has begun. Hiking is the most popular form of outdoor recreation in America, and some 30 million Americans describe themselves as "frequent hikers."

L.A. hikers are not just following a trend; they're leading the way. The Sierra Club's Angeles Chapter has the largest membership nationwide, with the most extensive schedule of organized hikes. Angelenos on the hoof have made the Angeles National Forest the most hiked of any of America's national forests.

The benefits of all this hiking are immeasurable and fit in with our Southern California lifestyle—physical fitness, improved health, stress relief, a natural experience that can't be beat.

That golden glow and sense of well-being from time on the trail—even if it's only once a month—has a kind of tonic effect that sustains the hiker between hikes.

I've resided in many parts of Los Angeles County: Hoover Boulevard near USC, Topanga Canyon, Whittier, Downey, Venice, East L.A. West L.A., Silverlake, Santa Clarita and Santa Monica. I've lived in neighborhoods where the people were as bland as the whitewashed walls of their neat stucco homes, and in neighborhoods where the sights and sounds reflected the full cultural diversity of the county. I've lived in some of the most park-poor parts of the metropolis as well as in some of its greenest parts with a nature trail only a five-minute walk from my front door.

Wherever I've lived—and where I haven't—I've hiked, getting to know the splendidly diverse landscapes of Los Angeles County. There's a lot of land, 4,000 square miles worth, to get to know. I've always been impressed—and occasionally even overwhelmed—that we L.A. County hikers can choose a path to explore from among a dozen sets of hills and ranges of mountains. Pathways lead through more than a hundred intriguing canyons and arroyos, through state parkland, national parkland, a large national forest and dozens and dozens of parks, preserves and special places.

Its many parklands and thousands of miles of trail would make L.A. County a hiker's paradise were it not for one major fact: ten million people live in the county. The population of metro L.A. alone is nearly four million. Add in the populations of a hundred or so incorporated and unincorporated cities spread across the basin and from the desert to the sea. Thus, the urban-suburban-exurban population has a paucity of parks and pathways per person. What would be a rich diversity of parkland and open space for a metropolis of two million is an often crowded, green space-challenged environment for ten million.

I wrote this book in order to share some of my favorite respites from city life: quiet canyons, peaceful forests, mountaintop retreats, and romantic beaches. And I had another purposes in mind as well. As a writer and hiking expert, I've worked locally, nationally, and even internationally to address what we in the field call "Nature Deficit Disorder." This disconnect with nature has profound effects on us as individuals and as a society. One prescription to combat NDD is to take a hike. I've suggested more than 150 cures, er, hikes in this book.

Know that some of L.A. County's green spaces and tranquil places are closer than you think. Here's a sampling:

MOUNTAINS: The Verdugo Mountains bound the L.A. Basin on the southwest. Trending northwest to southeast. The mountains separate the San Fernando Valley on the western margin from La Crescenta Valley to the north and the San Gabriel Valley to the east. A sister range—the San Rafael Hills—bound the basin on the southwest.

Because the crest of the range is so steep, the upper parts of the Verdugos (topping out at 3,077-foot Verdugo Peak) have been isolated from human impact. The crest of the range and a dozen of its upper canyons offer fine hiking with terrific metropolitan views.

What you see when you look up at the Santa Susana Mountains depends on where you stand. North-facing slopes are covered with coast live oak woodland and grassland, and even some big-cone Douglas fir while the south-facing slopes present panoramas of coastal sage scrub and grassland. The upper ramparts of the range have an unusually rich population of the valley oak. One of many great places to hike in the range is O'Melveny Park, second-largest city of Los Angeles park.

The San Gabriel Mountains are the only major mountain range in California that is considered a Transverse Range; that is, extending east-west across the state. The San Gabriels are divided lengthwise into a steeper southern front range and a taller northern range by a series of east-west trending canyons. For more than a century, the front range of the San Gabriels has delighted Southland residents seeking quiet retreats and easy-to-access tranquil trails. The mountain high country, crowned by 10,064-foot Mt. Baldy, towers over the City of the Angels and offers the hiker the most challenging trails in the range, much of which is included within the Angeles National Forest.

"The slopes are exceptionally steep and insecure to the foot and they are covered by thorny bushes from five to ten feet high," was how the great naturalist John Muir described the chaparral, the dominant plant community of the mountains. Higher elevations have a wealth of taller trees: oaks, pines, incense cedar and spruce.

Other front range attractions are arroyos. These boulder-strewn washes may seem lifeless on the bottomland; however, a hiker following an arroyo's course upward may soon find lush creekside flora, including ferns and wildflowers, shaded by sycamore, alder and antiquarian oaks.

It is in the San Gabriel Mountains where Great Hiking Era I was born, and it is here where Great Hiking Era II is in full swing with the Angeles National Forest having the distinction of being one of the most heavily hiked national forests in America.

The Santa Monica Mountains are the only relatively undeveloped mountain range in the U.S. that bisects a major metropolitan area. They extend from Griffith Park in the heart of Los Angeles to Point Mugu, fifty miles away. The range is twelve miles wide at its broadest point and reaches an elevation of a little over 3,000 feet.

One of the few east-west trending ranges in the country, the Santa Monica Mountains can cause a little geographic confusion to the first-time visitor. The Santa Monica Bay and Malibu coastline also extend east-west alongside the mountains so that the mountain explorer actually looks south to view the ocean and heads west when heading "up the coast."

The mountains are a Mediterranean ecosystem, the only one in the country under National Park Service protection. Large stretches are open and natural, covered with chaparral and oak trees., bright in spring with wildflowers. Oak woodland and fern glens shade gentle seasonal creeks.

The famed Hollywood Hills are the eastern end of the Santa Monica

Mountains and share a similar ecology to the range's taller and wilder peaks to the west. The differences between the two ends of the range have more to do with human settlement than natural history; the Hollywood Hills are by far the most developed part of the mountains. The hills separate the San Fernando Valley from Hollywood, Beverly Hills and parts of Los Angeles. They present a dramatic picture from afar, not because of their height which varies from 800 to 1,600 feet, but because the steep canyons of the hills make them look particularly rugged.

The Hollywood Hills comprise the wild side of Griffith Park and include the park's famed high point, Mt. Hollywood. That famed international symbol of Tinseltown, the Hollywood sign, is perched on Mt. Lee,

VALLEYS: The densely populated San Fernando Valley is rectangular in shape, measuring twenty-four miles east to west and about twelve miles north to south. The valley holds restored stretches of the Los Angeles River and some botanical preserves. To really get a feel for the Valley, you need to take a look at the surrounding mountains that wall off the Valley from the rest of the county. It's in the mountains surrounding the Valley—the Santa Monica Mountains, San Gabriel Mountains, Simi Hills and Verdugo Mountains—where hikers discover the best traces of the natural and human history of the region.

The San Gabriel Valley may not seem very valley-like to the commuter speeding along the Foothill Freeway; however, the valley, as a geographic entity, is apparent to the hiker standing on high. The San Gabriel Mountains border the valley on its northern edge, Puente Hills on the south and southeast, the San Rafael Hills on the west. Extending along the base of the San Gabriel Mountains, from Pasadena to Glendora, this former orange-growing empire is now thoroughly suburbanized. The nature that remains is preserved in canyons, along waterways and in some hillside retreats.

COAST: While millions flock to the sand strands of the county beaches, few realize that at the right time and in the right place there's some great beach hiking to be found along the county's seventy-five miles of shoreline. Rocky Palos Verdes Peninsula's fifteen miles of reefs, tide pools, coves and crescent beaches will surprise those energetic enough to hike them. The hills of PV anchor the south end of crescent-shaped Santa Monica Beach, a series of wide sandy beaches extending thirty miles from Redondo Beach to Malibu.

The northern part of the county's coastline, beginning about Malibu, is decidedly different from the south. The Santa Monica Mountains veer toward the coast, creating a series of bluffs, rocky points, coves, and sandy beaches. Zuma Beach is one of the county's largest sand beaches, and one of the finest sand strands in California. Above the beach soars Pt. Dume, a good place to watch for migrating California gray whales.

Best Hikes . . .

For Watching Migrating California Gray Whales:
Pt. Dume above Zuma Beach

For Sunset-Viewing
Mt. Hollywood in Griffith Park • Sunset Peak in San Gabriel Mountains

To a Classic Peak
Mt. Wilson • Mt. Baldy • Mt. Lukens • Mt. Lowe • Mt. Hollywood

For Views
Baldwin Hills • Getty View Trail • Mulholland Gateway • Mt. Hollywood,
Inspiration Point • Will Rogers State Park • Palos Verdes Peninsula
Cucamonga Peak

For Fishing
West Fork, San Gabriel River

For Romance
Any beach walk!
Moonlight Walk to Mt. Hollywood • Descanso Gardens
Henninger Flats • Charmlee Wilderness Park

Featuring Waterfalls
Los Pinetos Falls • Sturtevant Falls • Santa Ynez Canyon Falls
Fish Canyon Falls • Switzer Falls • Escondido Falls
Eaton Canyon Falls • Millard Canyon Falls

Very Best Waterfall Hike
San Antonio Falls, a three-tiered, 60-foot cascade
tumbling from the shoulder of Mt. Baldy

For Tree-Huggers
Baldwin Hills (Olympic Forest) • TreePeople Headquarters, Coldwater Canyon
Cheeseboro Canyon (Oaks) • Elysian Park (Palms)
East & Rice Canyons (Big-cone Douglas fir)
Cooper Canyon (Incense cedar, Jeffrey pine, sugar pine)

ALONG GARDEN PATHS
Descanso Gardens • Theodore Payne Foundation • Orcutt Ranch
Rancho Santa Ana Botanic Garden • South Coast Botanic Garden

ON THE BEACH
Malibu Lagoon
From Malaga Cove to Rocky Point, Palos Verdes Peninsula, Palos Verdes
Point Dume

TO FIND WILDFLOWERS
(Best spring blooms and flowering plants near metro L.A.
are in the Santa Monica Mountains)
Reagan Ranch area, Malibu Creek State Park
Paramount Ranch
Nicholas Flat area, Leo Carrillo State Park
Charmlee Wilderness Park

FOR AUTUMN COLOR
Liebre Mountain • Placerita Canyon
Upper Arroyo Seco

INTO HISTORY
Mt. Lowe Railway Trail • Santa Susana Pass • Corriganville
Griffith Park's Western Heritage • Arroyo Seco
Will Rogers State Historic Park

TO TAKE GUESTS FROM OUT-OF-TOWN
Mt. Hollywood • The Overlook, Pacific Palisades • Big Santa Anita Canyon
Malibu Beach

BEST HIKES WITH DOGS
Arroyo Seco • Franklin Canyon • Runyan Canyon • Verdugo Mountains

BEST HIKES WITH KIDS
O'Melveny Park • Placerita Canyon • Cabrillo Beach
Charmlee Wilderness Park • Malibu Creek
Ferndell, Griffith Park

GETTING THE MOST FROM HIKING L.A. COUNTY

There are two tried-and-true approaches to selecting a hike. One is by mood and the other by scenery.

First decide on the kind of hike you'd like to enjoy. A walk for the whole family? A long lonely trek where you can be alone to think? An after-work workout? A first-date excursion? A scout or youth group outing?

Decide where you want to hike. About 150 hikes plus some options are described in this guide so it may be quite a challenge to select one.

Want some help narrowing the field? Check out my recommended "Best Hikes". Unsure of what to expect from the Santa Monica, San Gabriel or Verdugo Mountains? Read the chapter introductions.

Pick a walk in your geographical area of interest. Next, turn to the corresponding trail description in the main body of the book.

Beneath the name of the trail is the distance from the trailhead to various destinations. Mileage, expressed in round trip figures, follows each destination. The hikes in this book range from one to fourteen miles. Gain or loss in elevation follows the mileage.

In matching a hike to your ability, consider both mileage and elevation, as well as the condition of the trail, terrain and season. Hot, exposed chaparral or a trail that roller-coasters steeply up and down can make a short walk seem long.

Use the following guidelines:

• A hike most suitable for beginners and children is under five miles of length and requires an elevation gain less than 700 to 800 feet.

• A moderate hike is one in the five- to eight-mile range, with less than a 2,000-foot elevation gain. You should be reasonably fit for these. Pre-teens often find the going difficult.

• A hike longer than eight miles, particularly one with an elevation gain of 2,000 feet or more, is for experienced hikers in at least average condition. Those hikers in top form will enjoy these more challenging excursions.

Season is the next item to consider. Although Los Angeles County is one of the few regions in the country that offers four-season hiking, some climactic restrictions must be heeded. You can hike some of the trails in this guide all of the time, all of the trails some of the time, but not all of the trails all of the time.

Snow closes the trails to Mt. Baldy and trails in the San Antonio Canyon area, and sometimes pathways on Mt. Wilson. Angeles Crest Highway is sometimes closed after a heavy snowfall. Those more-than-a-mile high trails and trailheads located in the San Gabriel Mountains high country are often inaccessible during winter.

Heavy rains can lead authorities to close trails to public use. State park rangers and rangers at the county's regional parks often close park trails after a heavy rain in order to protect the pathways from erosion by trail users—hikers and particularly mountain bikers.

For the hiker venturing out into flatland and mountain parks, heat, not moisture, is a more common challenge. Park authorities rarely close parks or trails in the summer so you won't be prevented from taking a hike; the question is: "Should you hike in the heat?"

Early mornings and late afternoons are the times for warm-weather jaunts in the low-elevation mountains and foothills, as well as in the county's various parks and reserves.

Years ago, portions of the Front Range of the San Gabriel Mountains (in Angeles National Forest) were closed automatically in the summer for fire-safety reasons and did not re-open until the first rains of the following rainy season. While fire closure is no longer a common Forest Service policy, do remember that low elevation trails in the San Gabriel Mountains are often too hot and dry to offer comfortable summer hiking.

Beneath the name of the hike at the top of the page is the trail name, plus the starting point and one or more destinations. Mileage, expressed in round trip figures, follows each destination. The hikes in this guide range from two to twenty miles, with the majority in the five to ten mile range. Gain or loss in elevation follows the mileage. In matching a hike to your ability, you'll want to consider both mileage and elevation as well as condition of the trail, terrain, and season. Hot, exposed chaparral or miles of boulder-hopping can make a short hike seem long.

My introductions to the hikes describe what you'll encounter in the way of plants, animals and panoramic views and outline the natural and human history of the region. I'll also point out the good, the bad and the ugly and tell you straight out what's hot and what's not about a particular trail.

DIRECTIONS TO TRAILHEAD take you from the nearest major highway to trailhead parking. For trails having two desirable trailheads, directions to each are given. A few trails can be hiked one way, with the possibility of a car shuttle. Suggested car shuttle points are noted.

THE HIKE describes the hike. The hike write-ups note important junctions and point out major sights. Options allow you to climb higher or farther or take a different route back to the trailhead. These trail descriptions, in combination with the superb maps created by my long-time collaborator at the Los Angeles Times, Hélène Webb, will help you stay oriented and get where you want to go. We haven't described and mapped every single feature, though; we've left it to you to discover the multitude of little things that make a hike an adventure.

Additional maps: The Automobile Club of Southern California publishes several maps useful to the hiker including: Los Angeles County Mountains & Deserts (The Trailmaster's favorite), San Fernando Valley, Santa Clarita Valley, Simi and Conejo Valleys, Central and Western Area, San Gabriel Valley and Southern Area (Long Beach).

Add to these city/county maps: Angeles National Forest (U.S. Forest Service map). I particularly recommend Tom Harrison's maps of the San Gabriel Mountains and Santa Monica Mountains.

BEFORE YOU GO
FEES

ANGELES NATIONAL FOREST: The National Forest Adventure Pass is a parking permit that can be purchased for an annual fee that allows parking in Southern California's four National Forests: Angeles National Forest, San Bernardino National Forest and Cleveland National Forest. The annual pass currently costs $30 a year or $5 per day and can be purchased at Forest Service offices, outdoor retailers and local outlets near or within the boundaries of the national forests.

An Adventure Pass is required for parking at "High Impact Recreational Areas" which covers most locales along the main forest highways and all the most popular trailheads. Many of the trailheads in the San Gabriel Mountains within Angeles National Forest require an Adventure Pass for parking at a trailhead. For more information call Angeles National Forest at (626) 574-5200.

COUNTY PARKS: Devil's Punchbowl, Eaton Canyon, Bonelli, Kenneth Hahn, Placertita, Schabarum and other parks have day use fees. The vehicle entry fees for the county's regional parks begin at $3 per vehicle entry.

STATE PARKS: Day use entry fees for California State Parks begin at $5 per vehicle. An Annual Day Use Pass is also available and The Trailmaster heartily recommends getting one—a very good deal for state park enthusiasts.

For an extensive discussion
of hiking techniques, apparel,
trail safety, and much more,
visit my website at

www.thetrailmaster.com

• The 10 essentials
• Hiking equipment
• Footwear and apparel
• Precautions and hazards
• Park contact information
• Nature essays and travel stories
• Lots more hikes from across the nation
and around the world

Inspiration for the Trail

San Gabriel Mountains

"Hither come the San Gabriels lads and lassies to gather ferns and dabble away their hot holidays in the cool waters, glad to escape their common-place palm gardens and orange groves,"

—John Muir, *The Mountains of California*, 1877

San Gabriel Valley

"It would be difficult to suit a pleasure-seeker, who could not be satisfied in this land—this veritable land of milk and honey, where Nature pours out her bounties and her beauties in lavish abundance, and the air of heaven conspires with the cunning of man to confirm health and to sanctify happiness."

—Jeanne C. Carr, *West of the Rocky Mountains*, 1888

Hollywood Hills

"Then there are the hillsides, laced with meandering public paths and stairways tunneling through profusions of wild vegetation and presenting, from raw crests and mélanges of balconies, breathtaking views of Hollywood and the city beyond."

—Sam Hall Kaplan, *L.A. Follies*, 1989

The Coast

"Looking eastward from the cliff on which I stood, I could see the long wharf at Santa Monica, and beyond, a long curve of shore that ran to Palos Verdes and the promontory of Point Fermin, The roar of the sea close by met me with a sort of boisterous friendliness, like the welcome of some tremendous massif."

—Joseph Smeaton Chase, *California Coast Trails*, 1913

Santa Monica Mountains

"The copper-hued men who roamed these hills not so long ago were very likely better tenants than you and I will be. And when we are gone, as we will go, a few unnoticed centuries will wipe out our bravest scars, out most determined trails."

—John Russell McCarthy
Those Waiting Hills, the Santa Monicas, 1924

CHAPTER ONE

Downtown

Located midway between the mountains and the sea,
downtown Los Angeles offers some surprisingly green spaces
and quiet places for the urban adventurer.
The hills of Elysian Park and the Montecito Hills of
Debs Park, for example, provide parkland with dramatic views
of the downtown skyline. And thanks to the untiring efforts of
conservationists who have worked to establish greenbelts,
jogging paths and nature trails along the
Arroyo Seco and the Los Angeles River, with the
promise of even more riverside preserves.

🌿 ELYSIAN PARK

PORTOLA TRAIL
5 miles round trip with 200 feet of elevation gain

Elysian Park, close to downtown Los Angeles, is a 575-acre retreat from urban stress. Although the park has been cut by many roads, it's possible to follow trails that will immerse you in greenery.

Although near the central city, Elysian Park is usually uncrowded and has a remote feeling—possibly because access is a bit confusing. The park appears to be everywhere and nowhere at the same time. Motorists see it while motoring along the Golden State and Pasadena Freeways, and pass through it on the way to Dodger Stadium; to commuters and Dodger fans, it's a familiar sight. But when you explore the park on foot, it somehow seems as if it's in the middle of nowhere. More than 10 miles of hiking trails and dirt fire roads lead through some surprisingly wild terrain.

Elysian Park's hilly acreage is an undeveloped remnant of the original 17,172-acre Spanish land grant from which Pueblo de Los Angeles grew. Part of the park, along with Pershing Square, are among the lands set aside for public use at the founding of Los Angeles in 1781.

Portola Trail takes you through shady glens, over grass carpets and past rare palms. You can picnic under imported rubber trees or native oaks and enjoy the views of the Big Basin offered by the park's promontories.

The trail and the historical marker at the trailhead honor explorer Don Gaspar de Portolá who led the first overland expedition to California. Capt. Portolá's party camped on the banks of the Los Angeles River near what would soon become Pueblo de Los Angeles.

DIRECTIONS TO TRAILHEAD: From downtown Los Angeles, head north on North Broadway through Chinatown. Turn left on Park Row Drive and park along the road. The trail begins at the historical landmark commemorating Portolá's campsite.

THE HIKE: Head uphill on wide Portola Trail, which soon crosses Park Row Drive. You'll pass among oak and eucalyptus trees, top a grassy knoll, then descend to Park Row Drive, which you'll join and follow over a bridge that spans the Pasadena Freeway.

Beyond the freeway bridge is a junction with a dirt fire road on your right.

The next mile of travel is through the most tranquil part of the park. Portola Trail winds through a zany mixture of trees: eucalyptus, walnut, oak, pine and palm. Cross East Park Drive and continues on a narrow hillside path. Periodically, you will emerge from the greenery and look down at the metropolis in miniature: freight yards, Glendale, Interstate 5.

As the trail descends toward Stadium Way, the cacophony of urban life is gradually overwhelmed by birdsong. Mockingbirds, jays, red-tailed hawks, bushtits, Audubon's warblers, red-shafted flickers, house finches and many more birds have been spotted in Elysian Park. In 1940, the California Audubon Society dedicated the park as a bird sanctuary.

You'll enjoy views of Dodger Stadium, which occupies Chavez Ravine in the southwest corner of the park. During pueblo days, indigents were buried in a "potter's field" in the ravine, and as a quarantine area during 19th-century small-pox epidemics. The name belongs to Julian Chavez, city councilman circa 1850 and the original owner of the canyon.

Portola Trail reaches a junction with Elysian Park Drive and Stadium Way. On the west side of Stadium Way is a wide grassy area for picnicking. Within easy walking distance are other park attractions: Palm Hill, the fountain and stream of Grace E. Simons Lodge, the Arboretum and Elysian Fields. Those wishing to extend their walk will join a bridle trail from the grassy knoll of Palm Hill and climb south for views of Dodger Stadium and the Los Angeles skyline.

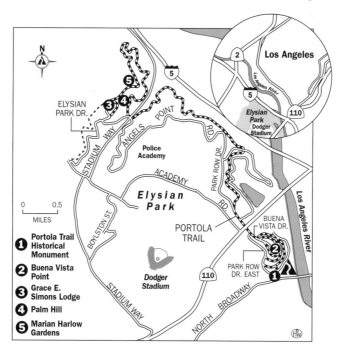

❀ LOS ANGELES RIVER

WEST BANK TRAIL
From Riverside Drive to Fletcher Drive is 5 miles round trip; to Loz Feliz is 7.5 miles round trip

Viewed in the soft light of a winter rain, and from its most verdant vantage point, this river inspires the plein-air painter—a low, slow, but steady flow past sculpted sand bars and several tiny isles, by willow-lined banks and driftwood-strewn beaches. Musical accompaniment is offered by croaking bullfrogs, the rusty-hinge sounding call of the red-winged black bird, and by the river itself, bubbling over its cobble bed.

When the rain stops and the misty curtain parts, L.A.'s namesake river is a different picture indeed. In harsher light, and from most vista points along its 51-mile length, the river looks just like what it is—a concrete channelized viaduct built with the same aesthetics, environmental consciousness and sensitivity to neighborhood integrity as the freeways that cross and parallel it.

This hike explores one of the best sections of the Los Angeles River Greenway, with numerous natural areas and parks en route. If it's been a few years since you took a walk along the river, you will be delighted, perhaps even astonished, by the habitat restoration efforts in, and alongside, the river. Trees, lots of them, and an abundance of native plants, line the riverbanks and cover lush islands in the stream. The riparian vegetation, including reeds and willows, attracts abundant bird species, resident and migratory. River-side hikers will see many a mallard, plus white egrets and great blue herons.

I strongly suggest a visit to the Los Angeles River Center and Gardens before or after your hike. Walk past the brick circular driveway and through arched wrought iron gates and you'll find classic Mission style-buildings, a lovely patio, reflecting pool, fountains, and a multitude of flowers. The visitor center has exhibits illustrating the river's history, restoration efforts and visions for its future.

Difficult as it is for Angelenos or anyone else to believe, the Los Angeles River was once a real river on which the city was founded. In 1781, a weary group of colonists from Sonora, Mexico, settled on the river's west bank. For more than a hundred years, the Los Angeles River was the sole source of water for the city.

Surprisingly, in this land of too little rain and too many people, it was not the need to capture more water but the need to dispose of it during the rainy season that led local politicians and the Army Corps of Engineers to cement most of the river channel in the late 1930s. A river plan of that era created by the Olmsted brothers, famed landscape architects, imagined the river as a greenway, linking parks like a string of pearls; this plan sank into oblivion and the river de-evolved over the decades into a flood control channel lined by freight yards and the ugliest of industry.

Re-visioning and restoration efforts have been led by Friends of the Los Angeles River, who have championed the notion that urban rivers are what you make of them: they can be barriers or connections. As a result of their efforts the river now has many loyal friends including the National Park Service with its Rivers, Trails and Conservation Assistance Program, enlightened politicos at City Hall, and most importantly the now eco-politically empowered residents who live along the river. North East Trees, an organization that employs local youth, has created numerous mini-parks and planted thousands of trees along the river.

DIRECTIONS TO TRAILHEAD: To reach the Los Angeles River Center and Gardens from the Golden State Freeway (5) southbound, take the Pasadena Freeway/Los Angeles off-ramp (the first exit after Stadium Way). Stay left and take the Figueroa exit. Turn right onto Riverside Drive, which leads over a bridge and your road becomes Figueroa Street. After two blocks of travel, turn left on Avenue 26 and drive a block and a half to the entrance of the center on the left.

From the Golden State Freeway (5) northbound, take the Pasadena Freeway off-ramp (the first right exit after Broadway). Stay to the right and exit on Figueroa. Turn left on Avenue 26 and drive a block and a half to the entrance of the center on the left.

To reach the trailhead, return to Figueroa Street, turn right, and follow Figueroa as it curves under the freeway and resumes as Riverside Drive. Look for the first street parking you find on the right. A couple of landscaped access points (Egret Park) put the river bike path in easy reach.

THE HIKE: The first thing you'll notice is the green—all those trees in the river bed are easy on the eye. Then you might notice the quiet. The L.A. River might not be Amazonian in size, but is big enough to provide a lot of "white noise" to drown out the sounds of auto traffic and of the trains on the opposite bank.

The view north, away from the river, isn't quite so inspiring—backyards, junkyards topped with razor wire, the backsides of industrial buildings, but is looking better with each passing year and the community has been much enhanced with the addition of numerous pocket parks.

Pause at Steelhead Park, with steelhead trout decorating wrought iron fencing, and read interpretive displays about the Juan Bautista de Anza National Trail. And check out the new Marsh Park in Elysian Valley, billed as "the Los Angeles River's first clean water natural park."

On approach to Fletcher Drive, the hiker passes under the Glendale Freeway, then through Rattlesnake Park and the Great Heron Gates, an inspiring interpretation of river wildlife. Carefully cross at the light, follow Ripple Street for a short distance, and resume passage on the bike path.

The path leads under Glendale Boulevard and to the Sunnynook Pedestrian

Bridge, from which the hiker can contemplate the river's past, present and future. Cross the bridge to join the East Bank Trail (see following hike description). Another pedestrian bridge leads from the West Bank over the Golden State Freeway—an unusual pedestrian experience to say the least!

Continue to a crossing of Los Feliz Boulevard on the Baum Bicycle Bridge and the best turnaround point for all but the most dogged river-walkers. North of Los Feliz, the trail continues too close to the freeway for my taste, but if you're game, stick it out to Colorado Street, and even all the way to Victory Boulevard.

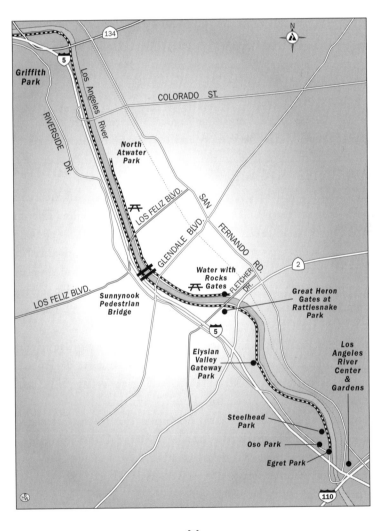

✿ LOS ANGELES RIVER

EAST BANK TRAIL

Los Feliz Boulevard northbound to North Atwater Park is 2 miles round trip; southbound to Sunnynook pedestrian bridge is 1 mile round trip

The eastside riverside revival is underway. More parks, more pathways, more people accessing the river from the east bank. Friends of Atwater Village is one organization active in river restoration efforts. Atwater, and other neighborhoods east of the river had, over the years, walled itself off from the waterway, but now is embracing the east bank as a greenway and as a community asset.

At Fletcher Drive, the east bank hiker is welcomed with the Zen-named "Water with Rocks" park and a decorative gateway that interprets that theme. At Glendale Boulevard, the pedestrian encounters Red Car River Park. This park pays homage to the Pacific Electric Red Cars Glendale/ Burbank line that carried passengers to and from downtown L.A. and via a trestle that spanned the L.A. River. From the park, you can look out and see six large concrete pillars that once supported this passageway across the river.

Plan a pre-hike breakfast or post-hike meal at Eatz located at 3207 Los Feliz Boulevard just steps from the river. The café is known for its old-fashioned milk-shakes, the best in the city, claim some ice cream devotees.

DIRECTIONS TO TRAILHEAD: From the Golden State Freeway (5) in Los Angeles, exit on Los Feliz Boulevard. The Los Angeles River is just east of the freeway. The trailheads for both southbound and northbound river hikers are at pocket park bordering Los Feliz.

THE HIKE: Northbound hikers herd upriver alongside the Los Feliz Golf Course. A dirt path parallels the paved one. Reaching the end of the links, you'll then see—and smell—the Atwater stables and related equestrian facilities. It's quite a sight to see horses cantering about within sight of downtown high-rises.

L.A. hikers should rally behind L.A. riders, who've long advocated for a new equestrian/pedestrian bridge that would link north Atwater Village with Griffith Park. Currently, horseback riders descend a dirt berm and ford the river.

A good turnaround point, where the dirt path ends, is North Atwater Park.

From Los Feliz Boulevard, southbound hikers cross the little park and follow the paved path past Atwater Village homes to the Sunnynook Pedestrian Bridge. Continue a bit farther to Glendale Boulevard (where passage from river to boule-vard is sometimes problematic) and Red Car River Park

Nothing much beckons the eastside sojourner along the one mile of river between Glendale Boulevard and Fletcher Drive.

MT. WASHINGTON

JACK SMITH TRAIL
4 miles round trip with a 400-foot elevation gain

Sometimes called "the poor man's Bel-Air," Mt. Washington manages to be both in the city and off the beaten track at the same time. Most motorists speeding north on the Pasadena Freeway have no clue to the charms of the hill to the left of the freeway, or to the northeast of Dodger Stadium.

Mt. Washington has much to offer the urban hiker. Follow the historic path of a streetcar line to the old Mt. Washington Hotel, now headquarters for the Self-Realization Fellowship. Wander the mountain's bucolic lanes, visit a nature preserve (Rainbow Canyon) and that long-standing institution—the Southwest Museum.

Like the flat lands surrounding it, Mt. Washington was used for sheep and cattle raising in the 19th century. But some city residents enjoyed hiking and picnicking on its slopes.

Mt. Washington was subdivided by realtor Robert Marsh and electrical products manufacturer Arthur St. Claire Perry, who built a two-car incline railway to carry passengers up the mountain. The developers hoped that people riding the railway would be inspired to buy lots and homes on the hill.

The ploy worked. As the March 7, 1909, the *Los Angeles Times* enthused about Mt. Washington: "Now right here in our own Los Angeles, the man of even moderate wealth may build his home on a charming, sun-kissed eminence that commands a vista of snow-capped mountains, several cities and the blue ocean—not surpassed on either hemisphere."

Located at the top of the railway was the Mt. Washington Hotel, completed in 1908. Visiting socialites, as well as sports and entertainment celebrities, were attracted to the hotel.

After World War I, the hotel and railway fell upon hard times. The hotel served as a convalescent hospital for wounded soldiers, then closed in 1916. Citing unsafe operating conditions, the Board of Public Utilities closed down the railway three years later.

In 1925, Paramahansa Yogananda, a monk of the ancient Swami Order, acquired the hotel and converted it into an international headquarters for his Self-Realization Fellowship. The handsomely landscaped grounds have long been a quiet place to meditate for both members and the visiting public.

Mt. Washington today is a socially and ethnically diverse community whose residents cherish the hill's semi-rural flavor. With the help of city and county

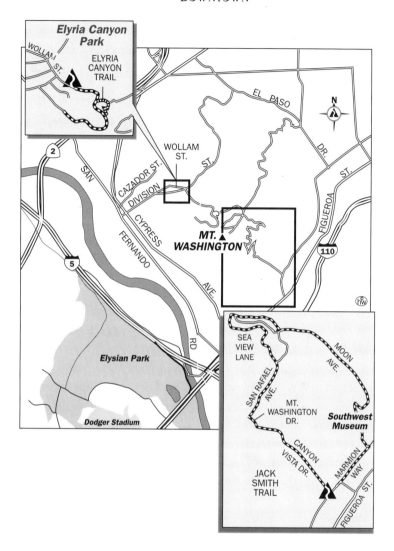

government, as well as the Santa Monica Mountains Conservancy, residents recently united to preserve Rainbow Canyon, a ravine filled with native California walnut trees.

A walk up Mt. Washington offers great clear-day views of the city. This trail honors the late *Los Angeles Times* columnist Jack Smith who often wrote about the peculiarities of the mountain he called home.

Also located on Mt. Washington is the Southwest Museum, one of the most complete collections of native Californian artifacts, including basketry, tools and other evidence of cultures that one flourished in the Southland and throughout the Southwest.

DIRECTIONS TO TRAILHEAD: Exit the Pasadena Freeway on Avenue 43, head west to Figueroa Blvd and turn right. Turn left onto Avenue 45, then make another left onto Marmion Way and park. Begin this walk at the flight of stairs that ascend west from the west side of Marmion Way, just north of Avenue 43.

THE HIKE: From Marmion Way, march up the stairs to Canyon Vista Drive. You'll be walking in the tracks (torn up in 1919) of the Mt. Washington railway. Two cars, the Florence and the Virginia, were pulled by a cable running under wooden planking. The conductor would ride up on one car and collect the fare then, when the two cars met, would jump across to the other and collect money for the descent.

After a stiff, 0.5 mile climb, Canyon Vista merges with Mt. Washington Drive. You bear right, continuing your ascent via a white fence-lined walkway on the left side of the road. After a couple of curves along Mt. Washington's namesake drive, you'll reach San Rafael Avenue and turn right.

You're now walking close to the crest of Mt. Washington (elevation 940 feet). You'll see the huge iron gates of the Self-Realization Fellowship. Stroll the serene grounds and contemplate the city at your feet.

Meditations completed, continue along San Rafael Avenue past the Mt. Washington School and turn left onto Sea View Lane. Until the 1930s, the lane was a dirt road known as Central Terrace; after winter rains, its adobe surface was infamous for trapping autos. After 0.25 mile you'll reach pavement's end and begin a U-shaped traverse around one of Mt. Washington's more rustic knolls. On clear days, the dirt portion of Sea View Lane lives up to its name, offering vistas of Santa Monica Bay, Palos Verdes Peninsula and Catalina Island.

After 0.25 mile, Sea View Lane resumes as a paved road and returns you to San Rafael Avenue. Bear left, then right onto Moon Avenue. Now you begin your descent along roads that wander like lost children. Moon leads to Crane Drive, which descends to Museum Drive. Bear left and descend another 0.5 mile to the entrance to the Southwest Museum. After touring Casa de Adobe, continue on Museum Drive to its junction with Marmion Way, where you began this hike.

❦ ELYRIA CANYON PARK

ELYRIA CANYON TRAIL
1 mile or so around Elyria Canyon

Like the flat lands surrounding it, Mt. Washington was used for sheep and cattle raising in the 19th century. But many city residents enjoyed hiking and picnicking on its slopes. And many still do.

Just three miles from City Hall, on the southwest slopes of Mt. Washington, is a small nature preserve, a living example of the Los Angeles of two hundred years ago.

"The protection of wild land is always satisfying, but preserving a place like Elyria Canyon in the heart of the city is deeply gratifying," relates Clare Marter-Kenyon, one of the many determined conservationists who, aided by the funds and tactical skills of the Santa Monica Mountains Conservancy, saved the canyon land from becoming condo-land.

Highlight of Elyria Canyon Park is an impressive black walnut woodland. The height and girth of the walnut trees, along with the tree-sized stature of toyon and blue elderberry bushes, suggest the canyon has not burned in several decades.

Botanists in particular are thrilled by the canyon's remnant communities of native flora—walnut woodland, coastal sage scrub, chaparral and grassland. Native plant lovers are especially delighted by patches of purple needlegrass (once bountiful in Southern California); the native grass has survived despite being surrounded by such aggressive aliens as oats and black mustard.

A red barn in the canyon bottom has been restored and is now being transformed into a nature center. Elyria Canyon hosts weekday visits by school children and weekend visits by families.

DIRECTIONS TO TRAILHEAD: From the Glendale Freeway 2 (near its junction with the Golden State Freeway (5) exit on San Fernando Road and drive south a few blocks to Cazador Street. Turn left, then make an immediate right onto Cypress Street and a right onto Division Street, which you follow to Wollam Street. Turn right and drive to road's end at the new parking lot for Elyria Canyon Park.

THE HIKE: Some two miles of trail meander to and through Elyria Canyon Park. The paths visit the black walnut woodland and offer a bird's-eye view of the Los Angeles River, Griffith Park Observatory, and much more.

❁ ARROYO SECO PARKWAYS

ARROYO SECO TRAIL
From Heritage Square to Avenue 60 is 4 miles round trip;
through Arroyo Park to the border of Pasadena is 8 miles round trip

Construction of a superhighway between Los Angeles and Pasadena was a dream that began with the motoring age. Arroyo Seco Parkway, the nation's first freeway, opened to traffic the day before the 1941 Tournament of Roses Parade.

But before Arroyo Seco became a parkway, it became a park. In the 1920s, a sand and gravel company was digging up the arroyo near Avenue 43 and an irate local citizenry demanded that Los Angeles buy the riverbed and convert it to a park. Arroyo Seco Park was constructed from 1927 to 1930.

The Chamber of Commerce and City Council next decided a "parkway" leading through the park would be a wonderful asset to the city. Depression-era WPA workers helped build the first stretch of road, about six miles long, which extended from Pasadena to Avenue 22 in Los Angeles. The financial cost? The then-remarkable sum of a million dollars a mile. Motorists came from all over the Southland just to drive back and forth on the parkway, free of stop signs and stop lights.

The environmental cost of the parkway? Few citizens back then were asking such questions. Arroyo Seco Parkway not only made automotive history, but environmental history as well: the Arroyo Seco was the first instance of parkland lost to, or cut up, by a freeway.

Today much of the green around the arroyo is picnic grounds and ball fields, though conservationists have proposed "greening" efforts similar to those undertaken to restore the Los Angeles River.

Hikers with an architectural interest will enjoy glimpses of Craftsman-style brown-shingled bungalows near the arroyo. Look for isolated jewels in the Highland Park area and a treasure trove of the period in Pasadena. Heritage Square, trailhead for this ramble up the arroyo, displays a number of significant structures of Victorian Southern California.

El Alisal, the Lummis Home and Garden, is also located near the beginning of this walk at 200 East Avenue 43. The house was built by writer Charles Fletcher Lummis, founder of "Arroyo Culture," and promoter of all things Southwest and Southern Californian. Built of concrete and arroyo stone, the house has Pueblo Indian, Spanish and Craftsman architectural features.

DIRECTIONS TO TRAILHEAD: From the Pasadena Freeway (formerly the Arroyo Seco Parkway!), exit on Avenue 43. Head south on the residential street east of the freeway—Homer Street—and drive to its end at Heritage Square.

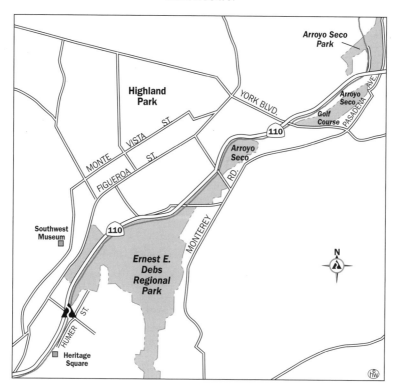

Park along Homer or in the lot bordering the arroyo just outside the gates to Heritage Square.

THE HIKE: Walk along Homer Street to Avenue 43 and turn left. Visit the Lummis House now, or continue your walk by turning right on Mosher Avenue and following it a block to its end at the ball fields and picnic ground of the Montecito Heights Recreation Center.

Join the bike path that leads down into the arroyo. Across the arroyo—and the freeway—is Sycamore Grove, popular picnic ground of the 1920s and 1930s. The path stays by the arroyo, curving slowly eastward around the Montecito Hills; the undeveloped slopes are part of Debs County Park. The bike path emerges from the arroyo briefly in Arroyo Seco Park, then heads back down the channel again and enters South Pasadena. Just short of the par 3 Arroyo Seco Golf Course, you'll abandon the arroyo for a bridle path that climbs a brushy slope along the eastern edge of the course, passes a driving range, then crosses under the freeway and leads to Arroyo Seco Park. Another bridle trail leads alongside the park road, Stoney Lane, crosses San Pasqual, then heads behind a stables and above the arroyo.

(To extend your walk along Pasadena's portion of the Arroyo Seco and ramble to the Rose Bowl, see the Arroyo Seco hike in the San Gabriel Valley chapter of this book.)

❧ MONTECITO HILLS

MONTECITO HILLS TRAIL
2-mile loop with a 300-foot elevation gain

Many urban residents view this park from their homes in Lincoln Heights and from the heights of Mt. Washington, as well as from Highland Park and South Pasadena. Thousands of motorists whiz by it on the Pasadena Freeway. And yet this park, glimpsed daily by so many, remains unknown to most city dwellers.

Ernest E. Debs Regional County Park, as it's officially known, occupies a small range of hills called the Montecito Hills. The 300-acre park is on the east side of the Pasadena Freeway, more or less opposite Mt. Washington. The park includes a family picnic area with barbecue facilities, and plenty of lawn for play, but the greater part of the park is brush-covered hillsides. Trails and fire roads loop through the park.

DIRECTIONS TO TRAILHEAD: From the Pasadena Freeway (110) in Highland Park, exit on Marisol Avenue and head right (west). (Marisol Avenue separates Debs Park on your right from Arroyo Seco Park on your left.) When you reach Monterey Road, turn right and proceed 0.75 mile to the park entrance. Turn right and follow the park road 0.5 mile past picnic sites to its end at a parking lot.

THE HIKE: Join the asphalt fire road at the north side of the parking lot. The road leads steeply north up a hillside to the park's high point. Views from the road include downtown, Elysian Park, and Mt. Washington. The front range of the San Gabriel Mountains, including Mt. Baldy, as well as much of the San Gabriel Valley is also part of a clear-day panorama.

Just left of the road is the park's small lake. Continue on the road, which soon passes a huge shade shelter. Pass a junction with a dirt fire road on your left, then approach a turnaround at road's end. Join a dirt fire road on your right and follow it along the ridgetop. Next pick up a trail, which at first descends through some eucalyptus trees toward Monterey Road. The trail soon swings north and drops to a fire road, which offers views of the Arroyo Seco, Pasadena Freeway and Pasadena as it turns west. Another good view of the arroyo is offered at a viewpoint on the westernmost curve of the fire road. That striped stretch of asphalt you see below you is an old soapbox derby track.

Stay on the fire road which brings you back up to the park's paved road near the shade shelter. Or join a steep, but distinct, shortcut trail that does likewise. If you're hiking at day's end, the park lake is the place to watch the sun set over the metropolis.

☙ BALDWIN HILLS

LA BREA, BALDWIN HILLS TRAILS
La Brea loop is 2 miles round trip with 200-foot elevation gain;
main park loop is 3 miles round trip with 300-foot elevation gain

From a distance, the Baldwin Hills appear to have little attraction for the hiker. Oil wells work on slopes that have been scarred by roads and bulldozers. But the oil is petering out, the hillsides are being ecologically rehabilitated, and parkland is being created.

Located in the west-central part of Los Angeles, Kenneth Hahn State Recreation Area was named for the longtime Los Angeles County Supervisor and is operated by Los Angles County. The park encompasses the hills and canyons between La Brea and La Cienega Boulevards.

The clean, well-kept, developed part of the park is no secret to nearby residents, who enjoy weekend picnics and barbecues on the expansive lawns. However, the park is completely unknown to most hikers, as well as to most everybody else in the Southland.

Two walks in the park beckon hikers. A new trail leads through the park's undeveloped "La Brea Extension," a former oil drilling site on slopes along La Brea Boulevard. Master trail-builder Ron Webster and a trail crew of Sierra Club volunteers built connector trails and linked existing dirt roads to create a two-mile loop.

Another loop leads through the park's Olympic Forest. The forest includes at least one tree for each of the 140 nations that participated in the 1984 Olympic Games. View sea hibiscus from Seychelles, oleander from Algeria, sweet bay from Greece and the Cajeput from Papua New Guinea. You'll probably be able to figure out which countries are represented by the Italian stone pine and Cedar of Lebanon.

Los Angeles also hosted the Olympics in 1932, at which time the Baldwin Hills park site served as the Olympic Village hosting the athletes. An interpretive display near the forest describes the trees and gives some history of the Olympic Games.

While the Baldwin Hills are only 500 feet high, the park's summits offer the hiker dramatic, clear-day vistas of the Santa Monica Mountains, the whole sweep of Santa Monica Bay, the San Gabriel Mountains and much of the metropolis.

DIRECTIONS TO TRAILHEAD: From the Santa Monica Freeway (10) in Los Angeles, exit on La Cienega Boulevard and drive south a few miles to Kenneth Hahn State Recreation Area. Follow the park access road to the lot at the top of the park.

Oasis in the city.

THE HIKE: From the south end of the parking lot, join the service road as it leads over a grassy hilltop. Tables are positioned to offer picnickers marvelous views north and east. Vistas of L.A.'s Westside and the ocean are framed by working oil wells.

The old road bends east, descends gradually toward La Brea Boulevard, then turns north, paralleling the boulevard. Your route travels terrain that's partly landscaped and partly native brush to the park's north boundary.

Join an old paved road on a moderately steep ascent north past a beige-colored Los Angeles Department of Water and Power Chlorinating Station and continue to the top of the park. What was once the east bank of the Baldwin Hills Reservoir is now the perimeter of a grassy field. To complete this loop, turn left and walk south a hundred yards back to the parking area.

For an intriguing second loop, stroll over to the road coming up from the developed park. Join a paved path, which parallels this road, and descend a landscaped hillside to the main park picnic area. Improvise a route past a pond, a bubbling brook and picnic grounds toward the Olympic Forest.

From the interpretive displays posted at the edge of the parking lot, take the path into the Olympic Forest. The "forest" is divided into a half-dozen habitats, including desert, tropical and temperate environments. Contemplate the paper mulberry from Tonga, the carob from Cyprus, the date palm from Egypt.

After your around-the-world tree tour, ascend a path leading to some palms and a landscaped oasis, where a waterfall cascades into a little grotto. Continue your ascent on trail and dirt road to a pine grove and a picnic ramada perched on the hilltop.

The view from the summit includes the Wilshire corridor, Century City, Westwood and the Hollywood sign. Look for sailboats tacking this way and that

44

as they head out to sea from Marina del Rey and get an air traffic controller's view of the amazing number of jets zooming in and out of LAX.

A dirt road crosses the hilltop plateau and passes more picnic ramadas. Enjoy the striking views of Palos Verdes Peninsula and Catalina Island. The road, then a footpath, follows a fence beside some power lines.

The trail passes near the site of the old Baldwin Hills Dam, which failed in 1963. Some 300 million gallons of water cascaded down the hills, drowning five people, destroying homes and causing a water shortage for a half-million city residents.

The reservoir was subsequently filled with earth and landscaped with the grass and trees you view as you return to the trailhead.

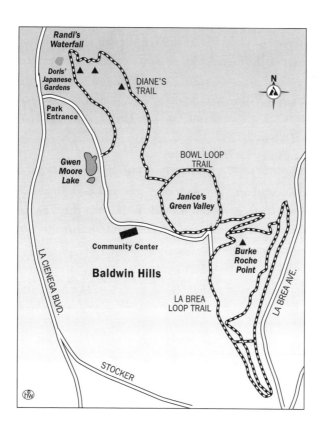

✹ VISTA PACIFICA

VISTA PACIFICA TRAIL
To Vista Pacifica is 1 mile round trip with 300-foot elevation gain

Imagine a lovely park entrance, where visitors board a tram for a lift up slopes carpeted with native grasses and wildflowers to a nature center, where they join a ranger-led hike up to a magnificent viewpoint.

Welcome to newest enclave in the Baldwin Hills, Vista Pacifica, where the landscape of the imagination may just be the most important landscape of all. Right now the Baldwin Hills resemble a conservationist's nightmare more than a dream, but park agency professionals and citizen-activists imagine—and are planning for—something different.

Conservationists say the Baldwin Hills area is the last, large, undeveloped open space in the urbanized portion of Los Angeles County. About a million people live within five miles of the hills.

A recent feasibility study considers the expansion of Kenneth Hahn State Recreation Area from 1,200 to 3,000 acres and the inclusion of all, or a substantial portion of the hills in the park. Places to heed the call of the wild are few and far between in this part of the metropolis, so locals are certain to support an expanded park.

Check out the new Vista Pacifica portion of the state recreation area and get a great overview of what might become a large (bigger than Griffith Park) park with lots of hiking one day.

Bring a picnic. And your imagination.

DIRECTIONS TO TRAILHEAD: Exit the Santa Monica Freeway (10) on La Cienega Boulevard and go south to Rodeo and turn right. Drive south to Jefferson, turn left and proceed about 0.3 mile to Hetzler Road on your left. I suggest you begin your Baldwin Hills walk from here. Or, turn left and follow the road up the hill until you come to the park office, which is a small brown construction trailer located next to a large water tank.

THE HIKE: A half-mile ascent brings you to Vista Pacifica, a homely looking viewpoint with stunning, 360-degree panoramic views of the megalopolis, several mountain ranges and Santa Monica Bay.

CHAPTER TWO

Hollywood Hills

The Hollywood Hills, separating the San Fernando Valley
from Hollywood, Beverly Hills and other parts of Los Angeles,
may be some of the most famous hills in the world.
Not because of their natural attractions, but because of the
Hollywood sign nestled on the rugged slopes dotted with the
toyon – or California holly – that gave the hills their name.
A quiet retreat from the bustling metropolis,
the Hollywood Hills offer cinematic views of the steep canyons
and the dream homes of moguls, perched on stilts
high above the city's dream factory.

⊤ HOLLYWOOD SIGN

MT. LEE TRAIL
3 miles round trip with 500-foot elevation gain

To make sure everyone knew about the new Beachwood Canyon real estate development, the developers, including *Los Angeles Times* publisher Harry Chandler, ordered a huge wooden sign built atop Mt. Lee. HOLLYWOODLAND read the sign.

The Beachwood Canyon residence were advertised as "above the traffic, congestion, smoke, fog, and poisonous gas fumes of the lowlands." Looking back now, it's hard to believe Angelenos were worried about pollution in the early 1920s.

Never kept in the best repair, letters-particularly the "H" frequently blew down. In 1923, a depressed actress leaped from the sign. During a 1949 gale, the sign lost its LAND. Finally, in 1978, celebrities-among them Alice Cooper, Hugh Hefner and Gene Autry-pledged $27,777.77 a letter to restore the HOLLYWOOD sign, sans LAND, to its former glory.

Besides the sign, 1,640-foot Mt. Lee has another claim to fame: L.A.'s first television signals were broadcast from the peak in the 1940s.

Mt. Lee Trail offers a visit to the world renowned Hollywood sign as well as views north of the San Fernando Valley and south to Tinseltown. The intrepid walker can also trek a rough trail to nearby Cahuenga Peak, at 1,820 feet the king of the Hollywood Hills. As the story goes, the Shoshone tribe had a village called Kawi located on the banks of the Los Angeles River near present-day Universal City. Some have speculated that Cahuenga, which names a pass, a peak, and a boulevard, originated from the village Kawi, combined with the Indian word for village, *nga*; that is, Kawi-nga.

DIRECTIONS TO TRAILHEAD: In Hollywood, from the corner of Franklin Avenue and Beachwood Drive (Beachwood is one short block east of Gower), turn north and proceed up Beachwood into the Hollywood Hills. After 1.7 miles, you'll spot Hollyridge Drive on your right. Park in a safe and courteous manner along Beachwood Drive near its intersection with Hollyridge. You'll see a

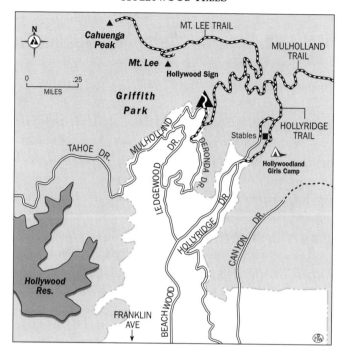

sign for Hollyridge Trail just outside the entrance to Sunset Ranch, which offers horse boarding and rentals.

THE HIKE: The signed Hollyridge Trail to Mt. Lee begins by following the paved lane into Sunset Ranch. Look for signed, dirt Hollyridge Trail on your right. the path climbs a ridge just east of the stables. Your views of the Hollywood sign begin almost immediately. Off to the right, looking very sci-fi from this angle, is the dome of the Griffith Park Observatory.

Ignore the bridle path on your left coming up from the stables, and continue your ascent to an unsigned junction with Mulholland Trail. A right would lead into Griffith Park and intersect Mt. Hollywood Drive, but you turn left on the fire road and wind west to an intersection with Mt. Lee Drive.

As you ascend paved Mt. Lee Drive, you'll enjoy excellent clear-day views of Forest Lawn, beautiful downtown Burbank, and the Valley beyond.

(Just short of the summit, as the trail makes a sharp left bend, look for a rough, narrow trail leading westward. Cahuenga Peak Trail climbs steeply 0.25 mile to the summit. After more good views, the trailheads along the ridge, then switchbacks down to Wonderview Drive.)

You can't stand right on top of Mt. Lee because a locked gate keeps you out. (There's a civil defense communication facility on the summit.) But you can-and will-enjoy the views from your perch above the Hollywood sign. Resist the urge to climb over the fence in order to have your picture taken next to the sign; it's strictly illegal.

⊤ HOLLYWOOD RESERVOIR

LAKE HOLLYWOOD TRAIL
4-mile loop around the lake

Nestled in the Hollywood Hills, this lovely lake is one of the quietest and most secluded bodies of water in the city. The pathway around the lake is a favorite exercise circuit for film industry folks.

If you experience a déjà vu while walking around the reservoir, don't be surprised. Scenes in *Chinatown*, the 1974 movie that showed the slimy side of Los Angeles water and power struggles, were shot around the lake. In another 1974 film, *Earthquake*, the reservoir dam collapsed and flooded the city below.

Hollywood Reservoir was built in 1925 by city water commissioner William Mulholland as part of the city's gigantic waterworks program designed to secure, ship, and store water for the rapidly expanding population of Los Angeles. Compared to some of the city's other, more utilitarian-looking reservoirs, Hollywood gets an A for aesthetics.

Less concerned with aesthetics than with evaporation, pollution and possible sabotage, the Los Angeles Department of Water and Power periodically makes noises about covering the top of L.A.'s reservoirs, and invariably is confronted by outraged citizens who prefer their lakes remain topless.

DIRECTIONS TO TRAILHEAD: From the Hollywood Freeway (101) in Los Angeles (Universal City area) exit on Barham Boulevard and head north a short ways to Lake Hollywood Drive. Turn right and do your best to stay on the Drive as it winds east through a residential area, then turns south toward the reservoir. Park along the Drive near the gate to the reservoir.

The path is open from 6:30 to 10 A.M. and 2 to 7:30 P.M. daily, and 6:30 A.M. to 7:30 P.M. weekends. During winter, the reservoir sometimes opens later and closes earlier.

THE HIKE: The pine-shaded service road soon isolates you from the noise of the city; unfortunately a chain link fence and high vegetation precludes more than an occasional glimpse of the lake. The effect is rather like that of moving through a green tunnel.

Lake views are dramatic, however, when you cross over to the other side of the reservoir via the top of Mulholland Dam. The view includes the Hollywood sign, reflections on the lake above and the metropolis below.

The reservoir service road doesn't completely make a circle, so you'll have to follow Lake Hollywood Drive back around to your starting point.

⊤ RUNYAN CANYON PARK

RUNYAN CANYON TRAIL
3-mile loop with 500-foot elevation gain

No Man's Canyon was the earliest name given to the deep arroyo that nature sculpted in the Hollywood Hills. A century and a half ago it was the wild domain of birds and rabbits, coyotes and lizards. Amazingly, it still is.

Runyan Canyon Park in the heart of the Hollywood Hills is a wildlife preserve and quite a contrast from the wild life associated with nearby Hollywood and Sunset Boulevards.

Coal magnate Carmen Runyon bought the canyon in 1919 and built a hunting lodge. But it has been mostly Runyan Canyon ever since, usually spelled with an "a," not an "o." Actor-singer John McCormick, just after his appearance in the hit movie *Song of My Heart,* purchased Runyan Canyon in 1929. He built a mansion called San Patrizio, after St. Patrick, and began extensive landscaping projects in the canyon. Wallace Beery, John Barrymore and Basil Rathbone were frequent guests.

In 1942, McCormick sold his property to millionaire Huntington Hartford, who renamed the estate "The Pines." He commissioned Frank Lloyd Wright and Wright's son, Lloyd, to draw up plans for a futuristic resort hotel perched on the canyon walls overlooking the city. While Hartford definitely left his mark on the cultural life of Southern California, he was unable to build the Huntington Hartford Play Resort.

The city of Los Angeles, with funding provided by the Santa Monica Mountains Conservancy, purchased Runyan Canyon and it was proclaimed a city park in 1984. Today, the Friends of Runyan Canyon, a volunteer group, works to keep the canyon clean, as well as interpret the area's rich architectural and natural history.

Runyan Canyon Park offers a great after-work leg-stretcher. Anyone interested in Hollywood's faded glory will enjoy exploring the ruins of the old McCormick estate. Clear-day vistas from the canyon overlooks encompass Hollywood, downtown and many a civic landmark.

DIRECTIONS TO TRAILHEAD: From the Hollywood Freeway in Hollywood, exit on Highland Avenue and head south to Franklin Avenue. Turn west on Franklin to Fuller. Turn right and proceed a short distance on Fuller to road's end at "The Pines" entrance gate to Runyan Park. Please respect the quiet and privacy of the residents near the park.

THE HIKE: From the wrought-iron gate inscribed "The Pines," enter

Runyan Canyon Park and encounter the ruins of the great estate San Patrizio. Angle left at the first opportunity and join the asphalt road ascending north along the west canyon wall (This walk is a clockwise tour of Runyan Canyon.) Runyan Canyon Road (closed to vehicles) climbs through a chaparral community of chamise, ceanothus, buckwheat and sage. Castor bean, tree tobacco, sugar bush, toyon and golden yarrow are also part of this community.

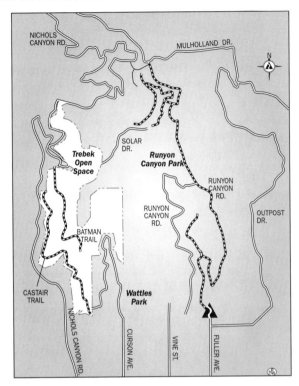

Nearing the head of Runyan Canyon, the road intersects a dirt road that leads down the east wall of the canyon. (Paved Runyan Canyon Road continues north to a park entrance or exit as the case may be at Mulholland Drive.) Near the intersection is a viewpoint offering great clear day vistas of the Griffith Park Observatory, the Hollywood sign and the San Gabriel Mountains.

Bear right on the narrow dirt road and descend along the steeply pitched east wall of the canyon. The trail gets quite steep (use caution) as it descends to Inspiration Point and the ruins of the Lloyd Wright designed pool house, occupied by Errol Flynn from 1957 to 1958.

From here you get good views of the rooftop pools of Hollywood hotels, the pagoda of Grauman's Chinese Theatre, Century City, the high rises of Wilshire Boulevard, and much more. Your path turns up canyon for a short distance, passes a tennis court overgrown with vines, and reaches the canyon bottom. Leave the road at a huge cactus and wander the canyon bottom trail under pines, palms and eucalyptus, to the stone and cement ruins of several structures. Returning to the dirt road, head down canyon past more ruins to the trailhead.

T WILACRE PARK

DEARING MOUNTAIN TRAIL

From Wilacre Park to Coldwater Canyon Park is 2.5 miles round trip with 500-foot gain; to Fryman Overlook is 6 miles round trip with 700-foot gain

Wilacre Park and Fryman Overlook, Coldwater Canyon Park and Franklin Canyon Ranch contribute some much-needed breathing room to the San Fernando Valley side of the Hollywood Hills.

Dearing Mountain Trail connects Fryman Overlook with both Coldwater Canyon Park and Wilacre Park. The trail begins in the wilds of Studio City in Wilacre Park, the former estate of silent movie cowboy Will Acres. The land was saved from the bulldozer by environmentalists and the Santa Monica Mountains Conservancy in 1982.

The trail continues to Fryman Overlook on Mulholland Drive, where valley vistas are terrific. From the overlook, you can follow a footpath and a suburban street back to Wilacre Park.

Between the panoramic viewpoints is Coldwater Canyon Park, headquarters of the TreePeople. The group's well-publicized tree-planting campaign has con-tributed a great deal to the greening of Los Angeles. Learn about the Treepeople's work by visiting their exhibits, landscaping display, nursery and headquarters. And learn about the trees themselves by taking Magic Forest Nature Trail, which winds through the preserve. Benches and drinking water welcome the weary hiker.

Along Dearing Mountain Trail, you'll observe two man-made alterations of the landscape. One alteration is botanical; many exotic trees and shrubs grow on the steep slopes of Coldwater and Fryman canyons. TreePeople Headquarters was once a fire station.

Look up at some truly astonishing residences: homes on stilts, homes built stairstep-like down precipitous canyon walls, homes that seem certain to slide down to Ventura Boulevard after the first good rain.

DIRECTIONS TO TRAILHEAD: From the Ventura Freeway (101) in Studio City, exit on Laurel Canyon Boulevard and drive south 1.5 miles to Fryman Canyon Road. Turn right and park in the good-sized lot provided by the Santa Monica Mountains Conservancy. The trail begins at a vehicle gate.

THE HIKE: Ascend the asphalt road past bay laurel and towering toyon, walnut trees and assorted planted pines. The road retires to dirt and soon proffers clear-day vistas of the San Fernando Valley.

At a wide spot in the road, a bit more than a mile from the trailhead, you'll intersect Coldwater Canyon Park's Magic Forest Trail. You may continue on

Dearing Mountain Trail, still a dirt road at this point. For a little break, detour right on the park's nature trail. Ascend one of the handsome stone staircases, built by the WPA in the 1930s, to the domain of the TreePeople. After learning about the group's tree-planting efforts, rejoin Dearing Mountain Trail.

A half-mile descent on the trail brings you past the backside of some homes, a yellow vehicle gate, and down to Iradell Street. Walk 50 yards on the street and rejoin Dearing Mountain Trail at another yellow gate. After a hundred yards the trail junctions. Stay left and begin a short, but very steep ascent up a terraced slope. The trail then descends to the head of a ravine that's watered by a seasonal creek and shaded by towering eucalyptus. Frogs provide musical accompaniment to the path, which traverses the canyon wall, then dips again to the bottom of another ravine.

The trail ascends moderately up the chaparral-covered south wall of Fryman Canyon to Mulholland Drive and Fryman Overlook. From the overlook, much of the San Fernando Valley is at your feet. Beyond the valley, smog-free views also take in the Verdugo, Santa Susana and San Gabriel mountain ranges.

Those physical fitness buffs not content with the workout afforded by this hike will proceed to Fryman Overlook's exercise course for a round of hip flexor stretches, side bends and gluteus stretches. The less energetic will head for home.

Return a short distance on Dearing Mountain Trail to a junction; instead of descending the way you came, keep straight and follow the sage- and toyon-lined path as it heads east below Mulholland Drive. The trail turns north then east again and soon junctions. Take the left fork and descend steeply down a mustard-cloaked hillside to a dirt fire road. Turn left on the fire road, which after a hundred yards continues as a cement path and descends to a yellow gate at the corner of Dona Maria Drive and Fryman Road. Follow Fryman Road 0.75 mile to the trailhead at Wilacre Park.

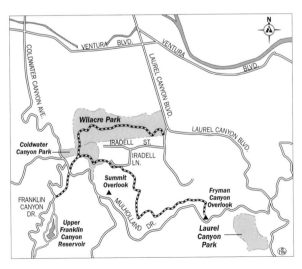

⊤ FRANKLIN CANYON

HASTAIN LOOP TRAIL
From the Visitor Center through the canyon is 2.5 miles round trip with a 400-foot elevation gain

Despite frequent invasions of Hollywood film crews, Franklin Canyon on most days offers hikers, bird-watchers and nature lovers a tranquil retreat. The canyon is protected by Franklin Canyon Ranch, a National Park Service preserve perched atop the hills above Beverly Hills.

It's appeared in your living room a hundred times, but you probably don't know its name.

The many faces of Franklin Canyon can be seen almost daily on television. Moviemakers have found the canyon to be a convincing substitute for a wide variety of locales ranging from High Sierra forest to jungle lagoon. "Bonanza," "Andy of Mayberry," and countless other television shows have used the canyon as a stage.

Franklin Canyon and its visitors benefit enormously from interpretive efforts provided by the William O. Douglas Outdoor Classroom (WODOC), named for the Supreme Court justice and environmentalist whose eloquence on behalf of America's wildlands will long be remembered. WODOC offers a hike/nature experience for almost everyone. Each year, docents conduct thousands of schoolchildren through the canyon. Leading through the canyon are special trails for senior citizens, the disabled and the blind. Aerobic walks, moonlight hikes, bird walks and map-and-compass walks are offered regularly.

The upper part of the canyon centers around Upper Franklin Reservoir, which was constructed in 1910, then improved and expanded in the 1930s. After the 1971 earthquake, the earthen dam was declared unsafe, so the reservoir is no longer part of the Southland's far-reaching waterworks system. Today the reservoir—now more lyrically referred to as Franklin Lake—is home to bass, catfish, ducks and coots. The nine-acre lake is an important stop-over for migratory birds. More than 90 different species of birds have been sighted in the canyon.

Hastain Trail explores the lower part of Franklin Canyon. It ascends the eastern ridge of the canyon and offers fine views of both the San Fernando Valley and the westside of Los Angeles.

You can pick up a trail map at the visitor center/outdoor classroom headquarters.

DIRECTIONS TO TRAILHEAD: From the westside of Los Angeles, proceed through the intersection of Beverly Drive and Coldwater Canyon Drive

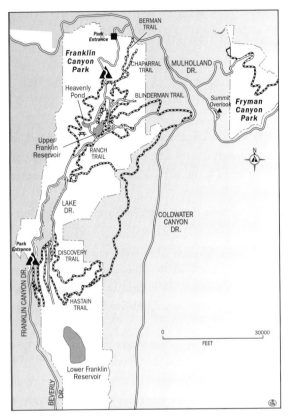

and follow Beverly Drive north for 1.2 miles. Turn right onto Franklin Canyon Drive and continue 0.8 mile to Lake Drive. Make a sharp right for 0.7 mile to the outdoor classroom headquarters, Franklin Canyon Ranch House. Park along Lake Drive.

From the San Fernando Valley: Exit the Ventura Freeway (101) on Coldwater Canyon Drive. Head south past Ventura Boulevard to the top of Coldwater Canyon Drive and Mulholland Drive. Cross Mulholland and proceed south on Franklin Canyon Drive. After a mile, the pavement ends. Continue 0.8 mile on a dirt road past Upper Franklin Reservoir to a junction and bear left onto Lake Drive. Parking is available on Lake Drive near the outdoor classroom headquarters.

THE HIKE: From the Visitor Center, you may walk up Lake Drive to the start of Hastain Trail or cross Lake Drive to the Canyon Trail, which winds beneath live oaks and sycamores and through a chaparral community on the west slope of the canyon. A rightward fork of Canyon Trail returns you to Lake Drive, which you'll follow a short distance to a fire road (Hastain Trail).

Hastain Trail ascends sage-, bay laurel- and chamise-covered slopes. Notice the outcroppings of Santa Monica slate, the oldest rock in the Hollywood Hills/Santa Monica Mountains. The slate is geological evidence that the mountains were once beneath the ocean.

A bit more than a mile's walk brings the hiker to an overlook where there's a good view of Beverly Hills and the Wilshire corridor. (The fire road, Hastain Trail, continues climbing to good views of Upper Franklin Canyon and the San Fernando Valley.) Turn right onto the distinct trail that descends to the nature center/outdoor classroom headquarters. Walk back up Lake Road to your car.

⊤ SEPULVEDA PASS

GETTY VIEW TRAIL
From Sepulveda Boulevard to East Sepulveda Fire Road is 2.5 miles round trip with 500-foot elevation gain; to Casiano Road is 3.5 miles round trip

Here's how to see the Getty Center without reservations or crowds: Take a hike on the Getty View Trail.

While you won't see any art en route, you will get an inspiring view of the world's most expensive art facility from a ridgetop above Sepulveda Pass. You'll also get a bird's-eye views of two of the world's priciest neighborhoods, Bel-Air and Brentwood.

The view has changed immeasurably since the 1840s when Francisco Sepúlveda, rode through this gap in the Santa Monica Mountains and over his 30,000-acre Rancho San Vicente y Santa Monica. Today, the San Diego Freeway extends through the pass, which connects the Los Angeles Basin and the city's westside with the southern San Fernando Valley.

Constructed by the Mountains Recreation and Conservation Authority with funding by the Santa Monica Mountains Conservancy, the path is surely one of the most freeway-convenient in the Southland. Instead of idling along in heavy traffic, frustrated commuters could exit on Sepulveda and take a hike. From the top of the trail, hikers can gather their own traffic reports; the view down of the San Diego Freeway rivals that of what a helicopter news crew can see. When that San Diego Freeway SigAlert ends, you can return to civilization, such as it is.

Getty View Trail switchbacks up the brushy slopes east of Sepulveda Pass to meet dirt East Sepulveda Fire Road. No doubt such fire roads are crucial to fire-fighting efforts in the steep terrain surrounding Bel-Air's pricey real estate. On November 6, 1961, a wind-driven wildfire destroyed some $24 million worth (an extraordinary figure for that time) of homes.

Getty View Trail delivers on the promise of its name from the southern end of the fire road. Other views from the ridge-hugging fire road include the Santa Monica Mountains, San Gabriel Mountains, the Wilshire corridor and the Pacific Ocean.

Views the trail delivers, peace it does not. Given the path's proximity to the freeway, tranquility would be too much to ask of this trail, so don't. At times, the trailside traffic noise is more intense than anything you experience as a motorist in the lanes below.

DIRECTIONS TO TRAILHEAD: From the San Diego Freeway take the Getty Center exit and follow the signs directing you down Sepuleveda

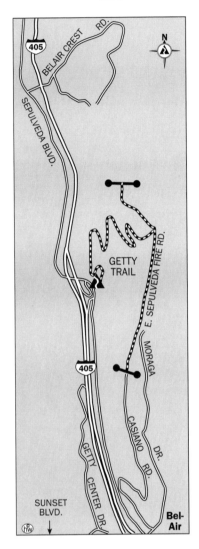

Boulevard. Just as Sepulveda crosses under the San Diego Freeway, look left for the signed Getty View Trail and a small parking area. The landscaped trailhead includes a toilet and a couple of picnic tables.

THE HIKE: The path ascends past a few handsome sycamores (the only shade en route) and climbs northeast above Sepulveda. The powerful din of the freeway seems to vibrate the very landscape. Switchback by switchback, more and more of Sepulveda Pass is revealed.

Getty View Trail tops out on a ridgeline where it meets the wide, dirt East Sepulveda Fire Road. For a fine view, angle north on a trail that leads a bit above the fire road to a lone oak. If you continue north on this trail it will drop back down to the fire road.

A ten-minute walk north on the fire road leads to its end at Bel-Air Crest, a gated community located on the opposite side of the freeway from Mountaingate Country Club. Here signs warn of DANGER RATTLESNAKES and NO TRESPASSING. A security card-key system allows estate owners through a gate onto the fire road and prevents hikers from wandering in.

If you head south on the fire road from its junction with Getty View Trail, you'll soon get grand views to the west of Getty Center, and a surprising view to the east—an undeveloped canyon! East Sepulveda Fire Road ends at Casiano Road on the far west side of Bel-Air.

CHAPTER THREE

Griffith Park

The nation's largest municipal park was donated to the city by Colonel Griffith J. Griffith in 1896. Today it attracts an estimated ten million visitors each year. Some enjoy the landscaped urban park featuring golf courses, picnic areas, a train museum, observatory and the L.A. Zoo—and others enjoy the wild mountain park complete with more than fifty miles of hiking trails. With its chaparral-covered hillsides, fern canyons and even a redwood grove, Griffith Park offers a diversity of environments and experiences.

❧ FERNDELL

FERNDELL TRAIL (see map on page 63)
From Ferndell Canyon to Griffith Observatory
is 2.5 miles round trip with 500-foot elevation gain

In well-named Ferndell, a brook bubbles through a woodsy, fern-lined glen. The brook waters a grove of coast redwood that thrives in the bottom of the dell. The redwoods complement the native sycamore and alder, which shade this oasis in the heart of the Hollywood Hills.

Hopefully, your sense of surprise upon discovering ferns and redwoods won't be lessened when you discover that human engineering, not Mother Nature, is responsible for the life-giving brook that waters Ferndell. Recycled water from Griffith Observatory's cooling system is released from the top of the hill and sent merrily on its way down to the dell.

Still, the urban mountaineer can be grateful for the brook, which attracts numerous birds, including brown towhees, robins and jays. Around sunrise and sunset, Griffith Park's deer often descend from the hills for a drink.

The trail climbs to Griffith Observatory, where you can tour a little museum and catch the planetarium show. More ambitious hikers can continue to the top of Mt. Hollywood, highest peak in the park, for great views of the metropolis. (See Mt. Hollywood hike description.)

DIRECTIONS TO TRAILHEAD: This day hike begins at the south end of Griffith Park off Los Feliz Boulevard. One way to go: Exit the Hollywood Freeway (101) on Sunset Boulevard and head east to Western Avenue. Turn left and follow Western north until it jogs right onto Los Feliz Boulevard. Turn left on Ferndell Drive and park alongside the drive. If parking is scarce, continue up the road a little farther to Ferndell Picnic Area.

THE HIKE: Join the path to the east of Ferndell Drive. Large sycamores shade the trail which ascends alongside the moss-covered banks of a brook, past tiny waterfalls, to Ferndell Picnic Area. The picnic ground has plenty of tables and is a great place for a post-hike lunch stop.

As you walk toward the redwoods and past the picnic area, stay to the right, east, side of the brook.

(Two other trails that ascend from Ferndell should be noted. One trail follows the left, west, bank of Ferndell Brook. A second trail, which departs from the end of the picnic area where Western Canyon Road makes a wide left turn, climbs to an intersection with the trail that connects Mt. Hollywood with the Observatory; this path is a good, optional return route.)

Fern-filled Ferndell.

Your trail lingers for a time alongside the east bank of Ferndell Brook, then begins to climb out of the dell. Gaps in the eucalyptus and chaparral allow good views of the Hollywood sign above and the city below. About 0.75 mile from Ferndell is an unsigned junction. The trails ascend to the Observatory, but the one to the right was closed at its upper end during the restoration of the Observatory.

From viewpoints near the Observatory, enjoy clear-day views of Hollywood and its hills, Century City, the Wilshire corridor and downtown, as well as the beach cities to the south and west.

Those hikers bound for Mt. Hollywood should walk toward the north end of the Observatory parking lot, where a handsome trail sign points the way to Mt. Hollywood.

❧ MT. HOLLYWOOD

MT. HOLLYWOOD TRAIL
To Mt. Hollywood is 3 miles round trip with 500-foot elevation gain

Griffith Park's most popular trail is the path from Griffith Observatory to the top of 1,625-foot Mt. Hollywood, the park's second highest peak. Mt. Hollywood is not the mountain crowned by the historic Hollywood sign; you can, however, see the sign quite well as you near the summit.

On clear days the entire basin is spread out before you from the San Gabriel Mountains to the Pacific Ocean. Sometimes mounts San Gorgonio, Baldy and San Jacinto can be seen. Viewed from the peak, sunsets are terrific.

En route you'll want to pause at the curiously named Dante's View. Some hikers, climbing to Dante's during a smog alert, look out over the smoky metropolis and conclude that the viewpoint must have been named for the 14th-century Florentine, Dante Alighieri, and his version of the "Inferno." The more romantic, no doubt inspired by a clearer day, hypothesize that some jilted young man wandered about these hills to this promontory in a search similar to Dante's quest for his fair, lost Beatrice. Actually, Dante's View was named for 20th-century artist-writer Dante Orgolini. Orgolini, an immigrant of Italian descent, was a mural painter during the Depression. In his later years, he put his artistic energies into planting a two-acre retreat of pine, palm and pepper trees high on the south-facing slope of Mt. Hollywood.

DIRECTIONS TO TRAILHEAD: From Los Feliz Boulevard, take Vermont Avenue through a residential area into the park. Follow signs to the observatory and park in the north end of the lot farthest from the observatory, near the signed Charlie Turner trailhead leading to Mt. Hollywood.

In 2003, the Griffith Park Observatory was closed for extensive renovation. The parking lot was closed as well. Access to the Mt. Hollywood Trail will improve when the Observatory reopens.

THE HIKE: A brief ascent brings you to the Berlin Forest to the left of the trail. Among the young trees planted by L.A.'s German sister city officials, is a whimsical sign pointing northeast to Berlin, 6,000 miles away.

The trail, a wide fire road, winds up the brushy shoulder of Mt. Hollywood, swinging west, then east. A mile from the trailhead, the fire road forks; the left branch loops around the west side of Mt. Hollywood, the right around the east side.

The right (east) branch of the Mt. Hollywood Trail climbs to Dante's View, where a water fountain and picnic tables suggest a rest stop for hikers.

Continue the short distance to the top of Mt. Hollywood and enjoy the view, then either return the way you came or descend the western loop of the Mt. Hollywood Trail past Captain's Roost, a eucalyptus-shaded rest stop, to a junction with the east loop of the Mt. Hollywood Trail.

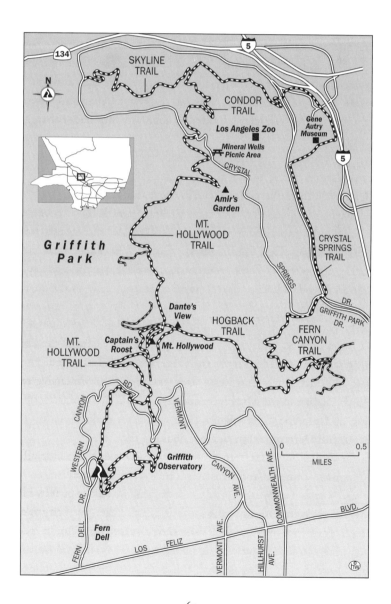

ꙮ ALL AROUND THE PARK

MT. HOLLYWOOD, HOGBACK, FERN CANYON, CRYSTAL SPRINGS, SKYLINE, CONDOR AND OTHER TRAILS (see map on page 63)
13-mile loop with numerous 400 to 800-foot elevation gains

Many veteran Griffith Park hikers have devised their own special 'round-the-park routes and, with more than 50 miles of trail weaving through the park, the scenic options are numerous. One of my favorite ways to go is a counter-clockwise circuit that begins and ends at Ferndell. This grande randonée of Griffith visits, or provides good vistas of, most of the park's most favorite attractions: Mt. Hollywood, the Hollywood sign, the Observatory, Greek Theater, the Zoo and much more.

The café at the Gene Autry Western Heritage Museum (open Tuesday through Sunday, closed Monday), located at about the midpoint of this hike, is a good place to stop for lunch.

This is not a hike for the directionally challenged or the first-time Griffith Park hiker. Few trails are marked, none of the many junctions are signed. Having issued this warning, let me add that hikers who like to improvise a bit, customize their own route, and see a lot of the park in one day, will enjoy circling the park. To hike around the park in a single day is to be impressed at how much is still preserved in its wild state.

DIRECTIONS TO TRAILHEAD: Take Western Avenue north to its end at Los Feliz Boulevard. Curve right onto Los Feliz, then almost immediately make a left on Ferndell Drive. Travel north about 0.4 mile to the main parking area on the left side of the road.

THE HIKE: Join unsigned Mt. Hollywood Trail as it travels the bottom of Western Canyon for 0.5 mile, then curves upward and eastward to a vista point and meeting with the road leading to the Observatory. Cross the road and resume climbing on the trail which soon crosses over the top of the Mt. Hollywood Drive tunnel. As you head toward Mt. Hollywood, you'll likely be joined by lots of hikers walking up from the Observatory. Bear right at a major junction to Dante's View, a beautifully landscaped garden overlooking the city.

From the garden, 2.5 miles from the start, leave the wide trail and join the narrow unsigned Hogback Trail that roller-coasters a mile down a narrow ridge. Toward the end of the trail, just as it widens, a signed connector trail invites hikers to scale Glendale Peak. Henry's Trail leads 0.2 mile to the summit, which offers grand city views.

Hogback Trail ends at Vista Del Valle Drive, which you should follow rightward (south) for 200 feet to pick up unsigned Fern Canyon Trail on the left side of the road. Descend 0.25 mile east with this path to a five-way junction, and continue left with Fern Canyon Trail as it descends a mile into the canyon. Fork right and walk the bridle trail alongside the merry-go-round access road. Shortly before reaching Crystal Springs Drive, the trail crosses over to the left side of the road. Just across the drive is the Griffith Park Ranger Station, which welcomes the hiker with water and restrooms.

Now with five miles under your boots, walk an easy mile north on Crystal Springs Trail, a wide path extending alongside the east side of Crystal Springs Drive. This popular exercise trail also doubles as the Griffith Park "Walk of Lights" during the holiday season.

When you reach the zoo parking lots, the path bends right (east) for 0.2 mile to the Gene Autry Museum, the suggested lunch stop for those who aren't brown-bagging it. From the museum, continue north on the trail that closely parallels the Golden State Freeway. The trail enters an underpass below the park's freeway offramp, then curves westward around the zoo parking lot. Next you pass through two more equestrian/pedestrian underpasses.

Emerging from the second underpass, you join unsigned Skyline Trail as it begins a westward ascent. The trail climbs one mile along the backside of the zoo to unsigned Condor Trail, which branches left.

Join Condor Trail for a steep, mile-long descent to the Mineral Wells Picnic Area. Pick up Mineral Wells Trail, which extends along the right side of Griffith Park Drive and descend 0.25 mile to a junction with an unsigned trail. Turn right and ascend 0.5 mile to Amir's Garden.

After relaxing at Amir's tranquil oasis, resume your ascent. You'll soon see the results of Toyon Canyon Land Reclamation Project. Efforts to rehabilitate the onetime dumpsite have been considerable.

After hiking a bit more than 0.5 mile from Amir's Garden, you'll ignore the right-forking trail leading toward Toyon Canyon and join Mt. Hollywood Trail, which crosses Vista Del Valle Drive then climbs south over the shoulder of 1,582-foot Mt. Bell.

At a major junction, continue straight to climb Mt. Hollywood, park high point. After enjoying the views, take the path descending the west side of the mountain to Captain's Roost, a small picnic area with a water fountain.

From the Roost, a short descent brings you the same four-way junction above the car tunnel that you encountered early in your hike. If you've had enough directional changes for one day, retrace your steps two miles to the trailhead. Those determined to make the full circle will head straight for the Observatory.

To return to Ferndell, join the pathway descending from the left (east) side of the Observatory. At the first junction bear right and at the second, bear left to return to Ferndell in about a mile.

❧ BEACON HILL

FERN CANYON, UPPER BEACON, COOLIDGE AND LOWER BEACON TRAILS

4-mile loop around Beacon Hill with 600-foot elevation gain

Long before Los Angeles International Airport was constructed, Glendale's Grand Central Airport was the Southland's main terminal. During the teens and twenties, bankers, businessmen, politicians and Hollywood stars (commercial air travel was not for the masses in those days) boarded planes on the runways next to San Fernando Road. Flying to the east coast was a several day, multi-stop journey.

Atop Beacon Hill was a beacon, illuminated at night to warn approaching aircraft of the high Hollywood Hills near the airport. The beacon is long gone, but you can still get a pilot's-eye view of Los Angeles from the summit of Beacon Hill.

This 4-mile workout could be a delightful way to unwind for downtown workers. Take off a wee bit early from work, or take advantage of the longer summer daylight hours and head for the Griffith Park hills. From atop Beacon Hill, you can survey your commute route—the Pasadena, Golden State and Ventura freeways. The tranquil trail around the hills is a nice way to wait out rush hour.

DIRECTIONS TO TRAILHEAD: From the Golden State Freeway (5) just north of downtown Los Angeles, exit on Los Feliz Boulevard and head west a short ways to Griffith Park's Crystal Springs Drive. Turn right and continue to a junction with the park's ranger station on your right (where you can stop for a map and trail information). From this junction, turn left on the road leading to the park's merry-go-round. Park in the lower lot below the merry-go-round.

THE HIKE: Walk up the short asphalt road below the parking lot. The first trail on your left that you'll spot, signed "No Bicycles Allowed" will be your return route from Beacon Hill. Ignore a second trail on your left, the Fern Canyon Nature Trail (a wonderful side trail but not part of this hike) and walk 40 yards along the bridle trail to a three-way junction at a large eucalyptus tree.

Bear left on unsigned Fern Canyon Trail and ascend the wide path into the brushy hills. Clouds of ceanothus accent the sandstone cliffs. You'll soon cross an old stone bridge and climb through a mixture of pine, oak and eucalyptus, which frame clear-day views of the San Gabriel Mountains.

As you climb, you get a good view of Fern Canyon with the city's suburbs beyond and below. It's a woodsy journey, with the wind blowing through an assortment of pines and the chattering birds offering relief from the din of the city.

At a five-way trail junction, you'll take the left-most trail and ascend a short

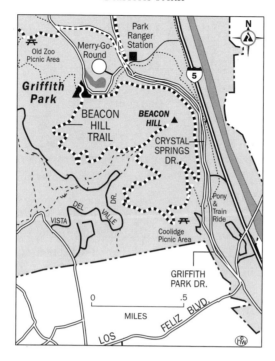

distance along a brushy ridge to the top of Beacon Hill. Nowadays it takes some imagination to realize how Los Angeles must have looked to the pilot of 1920: No freeways, no dramatic skyline. Not much there, there, then.

Today, you'll get great clear-day vistas of downtown, Elysian Park, Silver Lake Reservoir, freeways and freightyards, and the big bold "G" etched into the hill above Glendale. You'll also get a grand view of the Los Angeles River, once a real river before being channeled for flood control. Contemplate the conservationists' notion of creating an urban greenbelt and restoring the river to something like its natural state, something like the pilots of old saw when they swooped in for a landing at Grand Central Airport.

Retrace your steps back to the five-way junction and stay left. Follow unsigned Coolidge Trail on a pleasant one-mile descent. Stay left at a fork (the right fork leads down to Coolidge Picnic Area and the train and pony rides) and continue along unsigned Lower Beacon Trail, which parallels Griffith Park Drive. You'll descend toward the noisy Golden State Freeway, and toward the park's ball fields, before the path deposits you back at the trailhead, just opposite the merry-go-round parking area.

🦅 THE PARK'S WILD WESTERN HERITAGE

SKYLINE, MINERAL WELLS, ECKERT, CRYSTAL SPRINGS TRAILS
8-mile loop with 1,000-foot elevation gain

"A rock is a rock, a tree is a tree. Shoot it in Griffith Park."

This was an oft-repeated dictum of cost-conscious movie producers during the 1920s, 1930s and 1940s, and resulted in many film companies heading for the "wilds" of Griffith Park.

The brushy hills of the park, laced with bridle trails, were a particularly popular locale for Westerns. For this reason alone, it seems fitting that the Gene Autry Western Heritage Museum is located in the northeast corner of Griffith Park.

Cowboy movie lore is part of a permanent exhibition that the museum calls "The West of the Imagination." Most of the museum, however, is devoted to interpreting the "real" West, with paintings, artifacts and audio-visual material.

Taking a hike in the morning, picnicking in the park or lunching at the museum's café, then touring the museum in the afternoon add up to a fine way to spend the day.

DIRECTIONS TO TRAILHEAD: From the Golden State Freeway (5) or Ventura Freeway (134) exit on Zoo Drive and follow signs to the Los Angeles Zoo parking lot and over to the Autry museum parking lot.

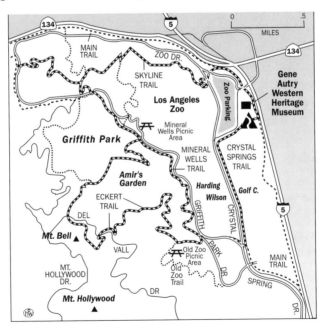

THE HIKE: Walk across the lawn on the south side of the museum toward the Golden State Freeway and bear left (north) on the bridle trail. The trail enters an underpass below the park's freeway offramp, then curves westward around the zoo parking lot. A line of eucalyptus filters some of the freeway din.

Next you pass through two more pedestrian/equestrian underpasses. Emerging from the second underpass, you join unsigned Skyline Trail as it begins a westward ascent. How this trail got its name is anybody's guess. The only visible skyline is that of Glendale, and this skyline emerged relatively recently—long after the trail was built and named.

The trail climbs above the back side of the zoo. (Smile. The zoo's video surveillance cameras are watching you.) Continue past Condor Trail, which branches left. About two miles from the trailhead, just as you pass the right fork of Rattlesnake Trail, you'll join the left fork and descend 0.25 mile to Oak Canyon and Griffith Park Drive.

Cross Griffith Park Drive and bear left on the trail paralleling the road. Half a mile's travel takes you to Mineral Wells Picnic Area and a trail junction. Turn right and ascend, moderately to steeply, 0.5 mile to Amir's Garden.

You'll leave behind the din of the Ventura and Golden State freeways and find an eclectic collections of pine and pepper trees, asparagus fern and spider plant, as well as a host of succulents.

After catching your breath, leave Amir's and climb again for another 0.5 mile to a junction near a water tank. To your right you'll spot what remains of Toyon Canyon, formerly a landfill, now a mountain of earth-covered, landscaped, compacted trash. Bear left onto Mt. Hollywood trail and continue your ascent.

The trail crosses paved Vista Del Valle Drive and soon comes to another junction. (A right turn will take you around 1,582-foot Mt. Bell, just a bit smaller than 1,625-foot Mt. Hollywood, highest peak in the park.) Bear left, then soon make another left onto Eckert Trail, which leads back down to Vista Del Valle Drive. Walk down the paved drive 100 yards or so and rejoin the dirt road on the left.

You'll soon begin a long, looping descent. Below are two of the park's golf courses, the museum and the Los Angeles Zoo. Either a left or a right on the trail will eventually lead you to Griffith Park Drive; or, simply improvise a route through the picnic area, crossing Griffith Park Drive and making your way to Crystal Springs Drive. On the far (east) side of the drive is Crystal Springs Trail. Follow this trail as it leads north by the golf courses. A bit more than a mile of level walking on the bridle trail returns you to the museum.

⚜ AMIR'S GARDEN

AMIR'S TRAIL
From Mineral Wells Picnic Area to Amir's Garden
is 1 mile round trip with 250-foot elevation gain

"My secrets to a healthy and happy life . . . " the late Amir Dialameh revealed to me one day as he tended his garden in the aerie heights of Griffith Park. "Being out in nature at least five days a week, staying away from doctors and lawyers, and hiking, lots of hiking."

The Iranian immigrant began fashioning his namesake two-acre oasis in 1971 following a severe fire that ravaged the brushy slopes above the Mineral Wells Picnic Area. Dialameh hiked in the park and worked his garden nearly every single day. He passed away in 2003 at the age of 71. His slogan was "In the land of the free, plant a tree." Today, volunteers inspired by his example, tend Amir's Garden with his spirit in mind.

Amir's Garden is a perfect rest stop for the hiker on a longer journey or an easy goal for the walker desiring a quick escape from city life.

DIRECTIONS TO TRAILHEAD: From the south side of the park on Los Feliz Boulevard, turn north on Griffith Park Drive and follow it just past Harding Golf Course clubhouse and driving range to Mineral Wells Picnic Area. Park in the picnic area and look for a three-way trail junction at the extreme lower end of the picnic ground, close to where the road splits to go around the picnic area.

THE HIKE: At the unsigned junction of three bridle trails, join the middle trail and ascend moderately to steeply a half-mile to Amir's Garden. You'll leave behind (some of) the din of the Ventura and Golden State freeways and find an eclectic collection of pine and pepper trees, asparagus fern and spider plant as well as a host of succulents.

Amir Dialameh, happy in nature.

❧ GLENDALE PEAK

ABERDEEN, HENRY'S TRAILS
From Vermont Canyon Tennis Facility to summit of Glendale Peak is 2.5 miles round trip with 500-foot elevation gain

What Glendale Peak lacks in name recognition, it makes up in terrific, clear-day vistas: downtown L.A., as well as panoramas from the San Gabriel Valley all the way to the sea.

Of course, the views of Glendale from atop its namesake peak are excellent, too. This Glendale-born writer likes to climb Glendale Peak on occasion in order to check out the old hometown.

Located literally and figuratively in the shadow of world famous Mt. Hollywood, Glendale Peak is an overlooked destination ignored by all but a handful of hikers. Most maps don't show the peak, which is located about one mile east of Mt. Hollywood in the southeast corner of the park.

What little recognition Glendale Peak does enjoy comes from the late, popular Sierra Club leader Henry Shamma, who delighted in leading hiking groups to the summit and sharing the fabulous views. In recognition of Shamma's efforts to

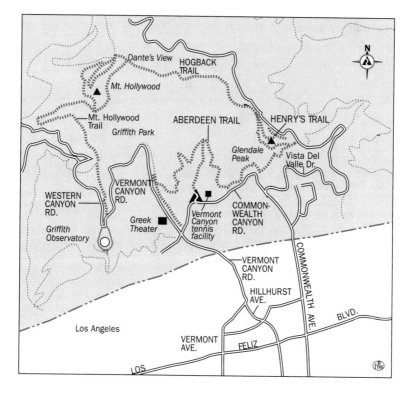

maintain the park's gardens and trails, grateful Sierra Club members and park officials dedicated "Henry's Trail," a pathway that leads to Glendale Peak.

DIRECTIONS TO TRAILHEAD: Exit the Hollywood Freeway on Vermont Avenue and head north a couple of miles to Los Feliz Boulevard. Continue north on what becomes Vermont Canyon Road for 0.7 mile to Commonwealth Avenue. Turn right and drive 0.2 mile east to the signed entrance for the Vermont Canyon Tennis Facility on the left. Park in the lot just below the tennis courts.

THE HIKE: Ascend north on a trail between the tennis courts for a quarter mile to an unsigned junction with Aberdeen Trail. Go right on the wide path, which bends south, then east again.

The trail dips into Aberdeen Canyon then climbs again to a junction with paved Vista Del Valle Drive. Just before this junction, at a green shed housing a pumping station, you'll swing sharply left onto the signed "Bridle Trail" and ascend west then north for another quarter-mile to the signed junction with Henry's Trail. Hogback Trail beckons ambitious hikers to tackle the narrow ridge leading up to Dante's View and the shoulder of Mt. Hollywood, but those bound for Glendale Peak will ascend Henry's Trail along the summit ridge to the top of the peak.

🦅 BRUSH CANYON

BRUSH CANYON TRAIL
From Canyon Drive to Bat Cave is 0.5 mile round trip;
to Mt. Hollywood is 4.5 miles round trip with 800-foot elevation gain

"To the Bat Cave, Robin." With that cry, Batman and Robin of TV fame hopped into the Batmobile and sped off to their hideaway. The dynamic duo's underground lair was not, as you might guess, a movie set built on a studio back lot, but a real cave in the southwest corner of Griffith Park.

"Batman" was not the only TV show to make use of the area known as the Bronson Caves. About every Western from "Gunsmoke" to "Bonanza" used the caves as a hideout for desperadoes. "Star Trek," "Mission Impossible" and many more shows were filmed here.

Long before moviemakers discovered the caves, the rocky walls of the canyon were quarried by the Los Angles Stone Company. During the early years of the 20th century, the crushed rock from the quarry formed the railbed for the Pacific Electric Transit System. In later years, the crushed stone from the quarry was used to pave such thoroughfares as Sunset and Wilshire boulevards.

Brush Canyon Trail also offers a moderate workout to many of Griffith Park's most popular destinations—Captain's Roost, Dante's View and Mt. Hollywood. The trail is much less traveled than other routes to Mt. Hollywood and offers the same great clear-day views of the metropolis.

DIRECTIONS TO TRAILHEAD: From Franklin Avenue, on the southern boundary of Griffith Park, turn north on Bronson Avenue or Canyon Drive (the streets soon join and continue as Canyon). Follow Canyon Drive a winding mile through the hills into Griffith Park. You an park alongside the road near a picnic area or in a small parking lot by the trailhead at road's end.

THE HIKE: Those heading directly for the Bat Cave will look to the right (east) side of Canyon Drive for a red wall, a white pipe gate and a Griffith Park locator sign that reads "49." You'll join a fire road and head south a short distance to the Bronson Caves. Heed the NO CLIMBING signs on the steep canyon walls above the caves.

Those hikers bound for Mt. Hollywood will join the unsigned fire road (Brush Canyon Trail) at the end of Canyon Drive. The lower stretch of this trail is popular with dogs and dog walkers.

The trail passes handsome sycamores that line the canyon bottom. In autumn, the sycamores, cloaked in yellow, brown and rust-colored leaves, provide a welcome burst of color.

Once the trail begins climbing northeast and leaves the trees behind, Brush Canyon begins to live up to its name. The brush includes the usual chaparral plants plus fennel and toyon.

A mile's walk from the trailhead brings you to an unsigned junction with Mulholland Trail. Head right, and ascend to a turnout alongside Mt. Hollywood Drive. Turn left, walk a short distance along Mt. Hollywood Drive and rejoin Mulholland Trail on your right.

After a short ascent up Mt. Bell, Mulholland Trail will continue east around the mountain, but you'll bear right on a narrower trail. From graffiti-splattered Water Tower No. 52, you'll join a narrow footpath and descend first moderately, then steeply, to a junction with Mt. Hollywood.

Junctions with various fire roads let you head toward Dante's View or Captain's Roost, but Mt. Hollywood-bound hikers will head straight for the picnic tables atop the peak and take in the famed views.

Most hikers will want to return the same way. The very experienced, armed with a good park map, can use Mt. Hollywood Trail and the extremely steep and washed-out trail dropping southwest off Mt. Hollywood Drive to make a loop trip back down to the caves and Canyon Drive.

CHAPTER FOUR

The Verdugo Mountains

This range of mountains—thirteen miles long and three miles wide—is surrounded by millions of people who live in metropolitan Los Angeles, yet few have ever discovered its charms. Wildflower-dotted grasslands, coastal shrub- and chaparral-covered slopes and shaded canyons, along with highly fractured metamorphic rocks await the hiker who ventures into this virtually undiscovered land. This historic former ranchland, once owned by the Mexican Governor of California, José Maria Verdugo, offers hikers the promise of year-round solitude in a close-to-home setting.

🌺 BRAND PARK

BRAND TRAIL
From Brand Park to Verdugo Overlook is 6.5 miles round trip
with a 1,300-foot elevation gain

"Have you been to Glendale?" This was the question posed in full-page advertisements that ran every Sunday in Los Angeles newspapers during the early 1900s. The man who placed these ads was civic booster and real-estate tycoon Leslie C. Brand, often referred to as "The Father of Glendale."

Born in St. Louis, Brand moved to the Southland in 1898 and did quite well in the insurance business, becoming president of Guarantee Title and Trust Company of Los Angeles. By 1902, he owned one thousand acres in the Verdugo Mountains.

At the base of the mountains Brand built El Mirador, a 5,000-square-foot mansion. El Mirador, with its elegant white exterior, horseshoe arches and bulbous domes is a unique example of Saracen architecture—a mixture of Spanish, Moorish and Indian styles.

Brand died in 1925, his widow in 1945, after which, by the terms of his will, Brand's property was deeded to the city of Glendale for use as a park. El Mirador is now Brand Library.

Brand Park, shaped a little like Italy, preserves a portion of the Verdugo Mountains back of Glendale. Brand Trail is a fire road that offers a moderately steep ascent from El Mirador, through Brand Park to the ridgeline of the Verdugos. From Verdugo Overlook (fine valley views), the intrepid can easily extend their hike by joining one of several fire roads that travel the rooftop of the Verdugos.

DIRECTIONS TO TRAILHEAD: From the Golden State Freeway (5) in Glendale, exit on Western Avenue and head northeast on the palm-lined avenue 1.5 miles to Brand Library.

THE HIKE: Join the asphalt road to the left of the library that leads past the "Doctor's House," an 1880s Victorian home in the Queen Anne-style that was occupied by a series of four doctors. Citizens saved this historical treasure from the wrecking ball and moved it to its present site.

A bit past a pipe gate that closes the road to vehicle traffic you'll encounter Canary Island pines, palm trees and other tropical vegetation gone wild. These trees and various tropical shrubs are what's left of Brand's estate grounds, once a fairyland of waterfalls, fountains and exotic flora.

A half-dozen roads crisscross this area. Stay on the main, widest one. A mile from the trailhead you'll pass a less attractive scene—a small sanitary landfill.

Leslie Brand, Glendale's founding father

Beyond the landfill, the road, now dirt, returns to a more natural setting. You pass a sycamore-lined canyon and reach a signed junction. Keep left on "Brand" and don't stray onto "Brand Lat."

Those parts of the hills where tilted rock outcroppings don't predominate are covered with the chaparral and coastal sage communities. Lemonade berry, toyon, ceanothus, sage, buckwheat, manzanita and tree tobacco are among the more common flora.

Two miles of ascent brings you to an oak tree, which offers the only shade en route. Keep climbing another long mile to the overlook.

A clear-day view takes in much of the San Fernando Valley and part of the Los Angeles Basin, including downtown. You can see the southeast end of the Santa Monica Mountains, the Hollywood Hills and Griffith Park.

From the overlook, you can travel left (northwest) 2 miles along the ridgetop to 3,126-foot Mt. Verdugo, highest peak in the range.

🌸 STOUGH CANYON NATURE CENTER

STOUGH CANYON, VERDUGO FIRE ROAD, LINK TRAILS
From Stough Canyon Nature Center to Fire Warden's Grove, return via
Wildwood Canyon is 7.2 mile loop with 1,500-foot elevation gain

Hiker awareness of the range's many attractions is increasing thanks to a new
nature center in Stough Park in the hills above Burbank. Stough Canyon Nature
Center boasts some fine nature and Native American history exhibits and its
docents lead an ambitious variety of interpretive hikes: full moon evening hikes, a
bird walk, a fitness walk and much more.

The hike from Stough Canyon Nature Center to Fire Warden's Grove
(blackened by a recent wildfire) offers an excellent introduction to the Verdugos.
It's the shortest (but not the easiest route to the crest), and is a loop hike to boot.

From the nature center, the trail ascends out of Stough Canyon onto brushy
slopes blanketed with sage, scrub oak, toyon, monkeyflower, and lemonade berry.
An eastward climb leads to Fire Warden's Grove, a mixed stand of conifers planted by the Los Angeles County Department of Forestry in the 1930s. The department's fire wardens patrolled the Verdugos until 1953 when the agency was combined with the Los Angeles County Fire Department.

From the ridge just above the grove, hikers enjoy great views, particularly to
the south, of Griffith Park, the Santa Monica Mountains and downtown Los
Angeles. On a clear day, even the Palos Verdes Peninsula, Los Angeles Harbor and
Catalina Island are visible from this vantage point.

Link Trail extends from the ridge to De Bell Golf Course. (I thought this
path should have been named Links Trail for its golf course connection, but then
discovered its true purpose was a link between Wildwood Canyon and Stough
parks.) Unfortunately for hikers, the link is broken by the golf course, meaning
hikers are required to walk 1.2 miles on paved roads and sidewalks to complete a
loop hike. No wonder Mark Twain defined golf as "a good walk ruined".

DIRECTIONS TO TRAILHEAD: From the Golden State Freeway (5)
in Burbank, exit on Olive Avenue. Head northeast (toward the mountains) 1.2
miles to Sunset Canyon Drive. Turn left and drive 0.7 mile to Walnut Drive,
turn right, and proceed north another mile to road's end and the parking lot below
Stough Canyon Nature Center.

THE HIKE: Walk north on the dirt fire road, which climbs the brushy
west wall of Stough Canyon. A half-mile ascent brings you to a junction. The fire
road continues north while a footpath bends west. Take the path, first to an overlook of Burbank Airport and the San Fernando Valley (as well as the not-so-

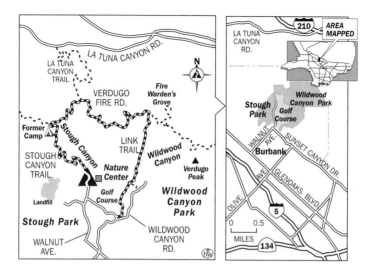

inspiring Stough Landfill). Continue ascending another 0.5 mile to the foundation and chimney ruins of a 1920s-era youth camp. (Park rangers hope to build a
new camp here one day soon.)

Past the ruins, the trail climbs briefly and bends west to meet Verdugo Fire
Road. Turn right, and you'll soon pass a fire road on your right—the east leg of the
Stough Canyon loop. (Return to the nature center on this fire road for a family-
friendly 2.5 mile round trip hike.)

After passing a junction with left-branching La Tuna Canyon Trail, you'll
ascend another two miles to fire-ravaged Fire Warden's Grove.

The road splits just as you approach the grove. Verdugo Fire Road continues
east into the main part of the grove. Take the right fork south to the base of a
communications facility and the signed Link Trail, a footpath.

Link Trail begins a knee-jarring descent down a ridgeline on tight switchbacks and stairsteps. Ignore a couple of left-branching connector trails that lead
down to Wildwood Canyon Park and continue to trail's end near the intersection
of Wildwood Canyon Road and Harvard Road. Hiker amenities here include
tree-shaded picnic tables, a drinking fountain and a porta-potty.

Walk west on Harvard Road 0.2 mile to De Bell Drive, turn right and walk
(carefully, there's no shoulder) 0.5 mile past De Bell Golf Course to Walnut
Avenue. Turn right and walk the sidewalk north 0.5 mile back to Stough Canyon
Nature Center and the trailhead.

🌿 ACROSS THE VERDUGO MOUNTAINS

VERDUGO FIRE ROAD (BACKBONE ROAD)
13 miles one-way; 1,900-foot elevation gain

Thirteen-mile long Verdugo Fire Road, sometimes called Backbone Road, travels almost the whole length of the Verdugos. It traverses the spine of the range and offers grand mountain and city views.

The west-east walk described below is more difficult than traversing the mountains from east to west. By all means, feel free to hike the Verdugos from either direction.

DIRECTIONS TO TRAILHEAD: From the Golden State Freeway (5) in Burbank, exit on Hollywood Way. Head north to Penrose Street (one block south of La Tuna Canyon Road) and proceed to Village Avenue. Turn right and follow it to road's end at the trailhead.

To reach this long walk's end point, exit the Glendale Freeway (2) on Mountain Street. Head west a short distance to Verdugo Road, turn right, then fork left onto Canada Boulevard. Turn left on Colina Drive. Follow the Drive, continuing onto Sunshine Drive, to the trailhead—Los Flores Fire Road.

THE HIKE: From Erdmore Place, the road wastes no time ascending. After a mile, you'll note the trail coming up from Village Avenue. This is one of the few

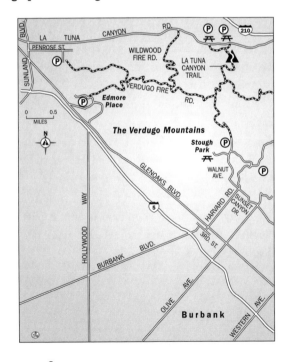

trails—as opposed to fire roads—in the Verdugos and it offers another way to begin your journey.

The road ascends to the head of Cabrini Canyon, passes a junction with Wildwood Fire Road and three miles along passes the junction with Stough Canyon Fire Road coming up from the south. You're above 2,000 feet in elevation now, and you'll stay this high, or higher, for quite a few more miles.

Rising sharply to the east is Verdugo Peak and its radio towers, and Fire Warden's Grove; it's two more miles of ridge walking to the welcome shade of the Grove. Continuing east on Verdugo Fire Road, you'll pass the second-highest peak in the Verdugos, an unnamed 3,120-foot-antennae-topped summit. You pass a junction with Hostetter Fire Road, which drops north off the ridge, then pass mighty Verdugo Peak. The road drops a bit, rises again, then drops for good, passing Whiting Woods Fire Road and reaching the "hub" of the Verdugos, where roads come up from Brand Park and Sunset Canyon.

Take a seat on the only bench for miles around, then continue down Verdugo Fire Road, passing a junction with Beaudry North Fire Road, ascending 0.5 mile to a viewful peak crowned by candy-striped radio towers, then descending again past the junction with Beaudry South Fire Road. Now you drop sharply off the west end of the range on Las Flores Fire Road, descending two zigzagging miles to the fire road's junction with Sunshine Drive.

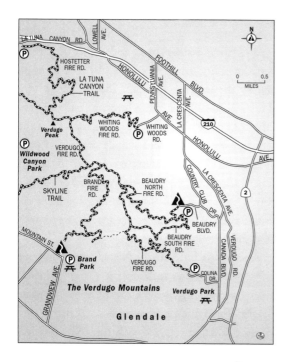

❧ BEAUDRY CANYON

BEAUDRY FIRE ROAD, VERDUGO FIRE ROAD,
WHITING WOODS FIRE ROAD (see map on page 81)
Loop around Beaudry Canyon is 6 miles round trip with 1,300-foot elevation gain; from Beaudry Canyon to Henderson Canyon is 7.5 miles one way

This walk on the eastern side of the Verdugo Mountains offers a number of options, including a 6-mile loop, a ridgeline ramble, and the chance to climb the range's 3,126-foot signature summit, Verdugo Peak. A clear-day walk to the top of the eastern crest offers a great geography lesson.

DIRECTIONS TO TRAILHEAD: From the Glendale Freeway (2) in Glendale, exit on Mountain Street (Verdugo Road) and head west a short distance to Verdugo Road. Turn right (north), forking to the left onto Canada Boulevard. Just before the Oakmont Country Club, turn left onto Country Club Drive, then left onto Beaudry Boulevard. Park near the trailhead at the intersection of the boulevard and Beaudry Terrace.

If you'd prefer a one-way walk through the Verdugos, arrange a car shuttle to Whiting Woods trailhead: From the Foothill Freeway in La Crescenta, exit on Pennsylvania Avenue and head south. Just as Pennsylvania bends southeast, continuing as Honolulu Way, look right for Whiting Woods Drive and follow it to road's end.

THE HIKE: Begin along a paved length of fire road, pass a vehicle barrier, and continue on dirt road 0.25 mile to a fork in the road. Bear right on unsigned Beaudry North Fire Road. The road ascends a steep mile and passes a narrow ravine on the left. A rough path enters the ravine which is watered by a little creek.

Another mile's ascent brings you to the mountains' main road—Verdugo Fire Road. Loop hikers will turn left and ascend 0.5 mile toward a forest of radio towers. From the antennae-covered peaklet, the road descends another 0.5 mile to a fork; the right branch drops down to Glendale's Sunshine Drive, but you descend left to the junction 0.25 mile short of the trailhead, then retrace your steps to your starting point.

Those hikers bound for Henderson Canyon will turn right on Verdugo Fire Road. The road levels for a bit and in a half mile brings you to a major intersection, perhaps the "hub" of the Verdugo's trail network. Here two trails drop south off the mountain crest—to Brand Park and to Sunset Canyon.

Continue on Verdugo Fire Road a long mile to Whiting Woods Road on your right. (If you want to visit Verdugo Peak, it's another mile up the road.) Whiting Woods Road switchbacks down the ridge separating Sheep Corral Canyon to your left and Henderson Canyon to your right. Two winding miles of descent brings you to the bottom of Henderson Canyon and trail's end at paved Whiting Woods Road.

🌿 LA TUNA CANYON

LA TUNA CANYON TRAIL (see maps on pages 80-81)
From La Tuna Canyon Road to Horny Toad Ridge is 6 miles round trip with 1,000-foot elevation gain; to Fire Wardens Grove is a 9 miles round trip with 1,700-foot gain; returning via Hostetter Fire Road is 10.5 miles round trip

La Tuna Canyon Trail visits some quiet oak- and sycamore-lined canyons and ascends to the range's principal feature—and its main attraction for hikers—its ridgetop, which extends the length of the range. The ridgetop offers grand clear-day views of the San Fernando Valley, San Gabriel Mountains and downtown Los Angeles.

La Tuna Canyon Trail, constructed in the spring of 1989, is the first foot trail built in modern times to explore the Verdugo Mountains. The trail was built by the Los Angeles Conservation Corps, under the leadership of Ron Webster. The Santa Monica Mountains Conservancy provided funds for the project.

Hikers who have hiked a lot of trails will be delighted with the look and feel of La Tuna Canyon Trail. The hand-built trail follows the lay of the land and is not at all obtrusive.

DIRECTIONS TO TRAILHEAD: From the Foothill Freeway (210) in Tujunga (between the communities of La Crescenta and Sunland), exit on La Tuna Canyon Road. As you head west, look sharply left, and you'll spot what looks like a frontage road paralleling the freeway. This road, closed to vehicular traffic, is the road you'll be descending from the ridgetop if you elect the longer loop option of this hike.

One mile from the freeway exit, you'll spot a turnout on the south side of the road. (A short trail leads to a grotto and a seasonal waterfall.) Continue another 0.3 mile to a second turnout on your left and park.

THE HIKE: The unsigned trail descends into the mouth of a narrow canyon, then promptly ascends the canyon wall to a little wooden overlook. The path switchbacks out of the canyon, tops Horny Toad Ridge, then descends holly-leaved cherry-covered slopes into a second, unnamed canyon. (Not only are the charms of the Verdugos undiscovered, they're also unnamed.) Reaching the bottom of the canyon, the trail visits an oak- and sycamore-shaded glen. Beneath the trees are ferns, tangled vines and plenty of poison oak.

At the canyon bottom, the trail joins a very steep, crumbling dirt road. Below the road are a couple of old pickup trucks; one guesses their owners drove them down the steep grade, but couldn't get them back out of the canyon. The road climbs at a 25 percent grade for a half-mile, then joins Horny Toad Ridge, so-named by the trail builders for the abundance of spiky-looking, brown, tan, and cream-colored horned toad lizards found here. Another half-mile's ascent along the ridge brings you to a junction with Verdugo Fire Road. Looking sharply to the east, you can see the hike's next destination—the radio towers and pine plantation near Verdugo Peak.

Turn left (east) on Verdugo Fire Road, sometimes called "Backbone Road," and begin a moderate ascent. Enjoy the great ridgetop views of the San Fernando Valley. Near the top of the range, you'll reach Fire Warden's Grove, planted by the Los Angeles County Department of Forestry more than a half-century ago. The department's fire wardens patrolled the Verdugos until 1953 when the agency was combined with the Los Angeles County Fire Department. The mixed stand of conifers planted by the fire wardens offer some welcome shade.

From the ridge just above Fire Warden's Grove, enjoy the views, particularly to the south, of Griffith Park, the Santa Monica Mountains and downtown Los Angeles On a clear day, even the Palos Verdes Peninsula, Los Angeles Harbor and Catalina Island are visible from this vantage point.

From Fire Warden's Grove, continue east on the ridge road, and you'll soon pass the second-highest peak in the Verdugos, a 3,120-foot-antennae-topped (again we have a shortage of names here) peak. Continue toward Verdugo Peak, and you'll soon reach a junction; Verdugo Fire Road continues along the top of the range, then descends to Glendale, but you turn left and begin descending on unsigned Hostetter Fire Road toward La Tuna Canyon. As you descend the north slopes of the Verdugos, and look north, particularly prominent is Mt. Lukens—bristling with antennae—the highest peak within the city limits of Los Angeles. You'll also get a good look at the Glendale Freeway and narrow Verdugo Valley, which separates the mountains from its smaller sister range, the San Rafael.

A bit more than a mile's descent from the top brings you to a water tank, and two miles along to an apiary. The Foothill Freeway comes into view, the road turns to asphalt, and you'll travel the frontage road one-half mile to La Tuna Canyon Road. Here you'll head west (use caution when walking on the road shoulder) 1.3 miles back to the trailhead.

🌸 DESCANSO GARDENS

DESCANSO TRAIL
1 mile or so round trip through the gardens

Native oaks of the Old West meet a camellia forest of the Far East in Descanso Gardens, an eclectic collection of flora tucked away in a natural bowl in the San Rafael Hills.

Sitting pretty in Descanso

Descanso is the Spanish word for "rest." The aptly named garden is a most restful place from its oak-shaded camellia garden (featuring 600 varieties, said to the be the world's largest) to its bird observation station overlooking Descanso Pond. Paths and hiking trails explore flora, native and exotic.

The camellia gardens began as landscaping around the mansion built in 1938 by F. Manchester Boddy, owner of the *Los Angeles Daily News*. He named his property, known as Rancho San Rafael since Spanish days as Rancho del Descanso.

More than 100,000 camellias, indigenous to the mountainous valleys of eastern Asia, thrive in the gardens. Many of the shade loving (native oaks provide the shade) plants stand more than 20 feet tall–a veritable forest. Complementing the camellias are pools and landscaping created by L.A.'s Japanese-American community.

Six miles of garden paths as well as hiking trails in an adjacent watershed area beckon the walker. Two rose gardens–an historical one with varieties dating back to 1200 B.C. and a modern garden devoted to All-American Rose selections–are popular walking destinations, as is a lush fern collection.

DIRECTIONS TO TRAILHEAD: From the Glendale Freeway (2), just south of its junction with the Foothill Freeway (210) exit on Verdugo Boulevard. Head west a short distance to Descanso Drive, then turn right and follow the oak-line street to Descanso Gardens. Open daily 9 A.M. to 5 P.M.; closed Christmas.

THE HIKE: Hikers who want to go native can wander among California cactus, shrubs and succulents. Nature trails meander creekside through oak woodland and past stands of pine. I particularly recommend Chaparral Nature Trail.

On the west side of Descanso is a bird observation station, which overlooks a small lake. More than 150 kinds of land and water birds have been sighted from the station.

❧ CHERRY CANYON

OWL, LIZ'S LOOP, CERRO NEGRO TRAILS

From Cherry Canyon Open Space to Lookout Tower 1.5 miles round trip with 400-foot elevation gain; return via Liz's Loop is 2.5 miles round trip. To Hospital Overlook and Descanso Gardens (no entry) is 5 miles round trip. More options available.

Every community should be so hiker-friendly. Footpaths and fire roads link La Cañada Flintridge with the Arroyo Seco and the Rose Bowl, as well as to the extensive trail system of the San Gabriel Mountains. An ambitious LaCF (as locals abbreviate it) resident could conceivably hike on trail from the 'burbs to the top of Mt. Baldy.

The lower reaches of the San Rafaels have been settled—"mansion-ized," as some long-term residents grouse—while the upper ramparts have been left untouched. During the 1990s, local conservationists thwarted developers intent on building dozens of huge haciendas atop the crest of the hills.

Cherry Canyon is a good place to begin a short hike into the San Rafael Hills. The trail system hereabouts is in good shape and features first-rate signage thanks to the efforts of the City of LaCF and the LaCF Trails Council.

DIRECTIONS TO TRAILHEAD: From the Glendale Freeway (2), just south of its junction with the Foothill Freeway (210) in La Cañada Flintridge, exit on Verdugo Boulevard. Turn right (east) and drive 0.3 mile to Descanso Drive, turn right and proceed 0.7 mile to Chevy Chase Drive. Turn right, then soon make another right onto Hampstead Road, which you'll follow on a 0.5 mile ascent to the signed turnoff for Cherry Canyon Open Space. Park alongside the preserve's access road near signed Owl Trail.

THE HIKE: Owl Trail meanders up oak- and sycamore-shaded Cherry Canyon. You'll soon encounter a short (200-foot) connector trail with a signed offer to take you over to Cerro Negro Trail. Decline this offer for now and continue on Owl Trail which all too soon leaves the cool recesses of the canyon and ascends onto brushy and still-fire blackened slopes.

About 0.3 mile from the trailhead, you'll reach a signed junction with Cerro Negro Trail, which contours south over to the Lookout Tower. For a more direct route to the top, continue straight with Owl Trail on a steep 0.2 mile ascent to the main dirt fire road on the ridge crest. You'll spot the Fire Lookout, bear left, and hike south toward it.

The faded green tower, perched on steel framing, must have given the fire lookouts of yesteryear quite a good view when they walked 'round the catwalk: the

San Rafael Hills, Verdugo Mountains, San Gabriel Mountains, the San Gabriel Valley and more. At 1,887 feet, the unnamed peak where the now retired tower rests, is only two feet shorter than Flint Peak, high point of the hills.

After enjoying the view, double-back north on the fire road, past the Owl Trail to a major signed junction that offers the opportunity to travel 0.9 mile to the Descanso Gardens rear gate or 1.1 miles to the Verdugo Hills Hospital Overlook. This option travels along the ridgeline past the Glendale police firing range and offers excellent valley views. It's also a road to nowhere: the garden gate is locked tight and the hospital overlook puts you at roof level of the hospital.

A better bet is to continue on the main fire road to signed Liz's Loop, which honors longtime trails activist Liz Blackwelder, President of the La Cañada Flintridge Trails Council. This pleasant path swings east, then southwest as it loops 1.2 miles through the burn zone back to Cherry Canyon Fire Road. Walk down the fire road to the trailhead.

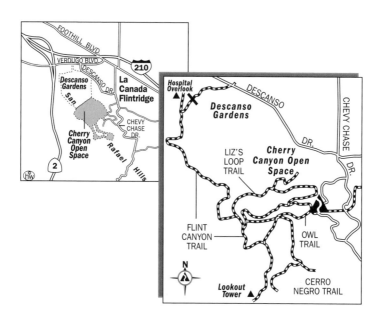

🐾 FLINT PEAK

SENATOR FLINT TRAIL
1 mile round trip with a 200-foot gain

Historically, politicians have more often been known for campaign trails rather than hiking trails, but one turn-of-the-19th-century California politician, Senator Frank Flint, left us a namesake town, peak and path.

The path to Flint Peak, like politics, is not always pretty, but it does have its rewards. Hike it on a brisk fall or winter day. The 1,889-foot peak, one of the more noteworthy peaks of the San Rafael Hills, offers fine clear-day city views.

After becoming a successful attorney, Flint served as a superior court judge and U.S. District Attorney. Flint, a Republican, was elected to the United States Senate in 1904 and served one term. As a Senator, he was involved in some of the behind-the-scenes maneuvering to bring Owens Valley water to Los Angeles.

Flint's small place in history comes not from his political career but from his real estate career. Flint is remembered as one of the major builders of urban and suburban Los Angeles.

Flint was well aware that Los Angeles had a housing shortage and that good roads would soon be extended from downtown to the La Canada-Glendale area, so he began buying up hundreds of acres of foothill land.

Astride his horse, Flint rode over his property and designed the street plan for his new suburb. He envisioned a quiet community of luxury houses built on large lots, scattered seemingly at random on the wooded hills.

Flint's development—dubbed Flintridge—was a huge success. Frank Flint was an outdoors enthusiast, and he designed his suburb with more than twenty miles of riding–hiking trails, for which we hikers are grateful.

DIRECTIONS TO TRAILHEAD: From the Ventura Freeway (134) in Glendale, exit on Glendale Avenue. Head south and turn left at the first light—onto Lexington Avenue. Proceed 0.5 mile to Verdugo Road. Turn right, then make an immediate left onto Chevy Chase Drive, which you'll follow on a winding ascent to Linda Vista Road. Turn right and drive a mile to Figueroa Road. Turn right again and follow Figueroa to its end. The unsigned trail, a fire road, begins at a locked gate.

THE HIKE: Follow the fire road, which ascends steeply for the first fifty yards, then proceeds at a more moderate incline toward the peak.

The top of the antennae-covered peak is fenced. If the gate at the end of the dirt road is locked, you'll have to peer through the brush to get the best view of the metropolis.

CHAPTER FIVE

San Fernando Valley

A world unto itself, the San Fernando Valley is more often
thought of as endless suburbia than a natural enclave.
But one of the finest stretches of the Los Angeles River,
a couple of botanical gems and historical treasures—along with
a surprising waterfall—are just some of the attractions that
beckon the hiker who wants to explore the real world
of the so-called Valley girl. The hidden trails of the valley
feel as far away from the mall as you can get.

ᛉ THEODORE PAYNE FOUNDATION

THEODORE PAYNE TRAIL
0.75-mile loop around the grounds

The Theodore Payne Foundation, dedicated to educating us about the culture and uses of native plants, is a great place to learn about local flora. A walk around the foundation's gardens is most informative; the short hike up Wildflower Hill, inspiring.

Located in Sun Valley—an apt location if only for the name—is the Theodore Payne Foundation for Wildflowers and Native Plants, which carries on the work of its founder, botanist Theodore Payne.

Payne, who studied the nursery and seed business in his native England, moved to Southern California in 1893, where he continued to practice his trade. The botanist soon became interested in preserving the natural flora of his new home, particularly the wildflowers that were being lost to development even then.

He cultivated the seeds of nearly 500 native shrubs, trees and flowers, and sold his plants at a succession of nurseries, which he owned and operated for nearly sixty years. He wrote articles and lectured on the subject of preserving wildflowers and native plants.

The facility named for Payne includes a nursery, a growing yard, nature trails, and an alder- and sycamore-canopied picnic area.

DIRECTIONS TO TRAILHEAD: From Interstate 5 in Sun Valley, exit on Sunland Boulevard and head north 0.5 mile to Tuxford Street. Turn right and proceed two blocks to the entrance of the Theodore Payne Foundation. Follow the dirt driveway to the parking lot. Open 8:30 A.M.-4:30 P.M. Tuesday-Saturday, Oct. 1 through June 30; open Thursday-Saturday during the summer.

THE HIKE: Begin at the gift store and stroll through the landscaped grounds around the offices, which feature many of the natives available for purchase in nursery. Next, enter the nursery, where you'll find 600 (!) varieties of native plants.

As you walk through the grounds, watch for Payne's favorite California native, the Matilija poppy, as well as many varieties of lilacs. Several rare and endangered native species are preserved here, including a variety of manzanita that is now extinct in nature.

After your walk through the grounds, join the footpath ascending Wildflower Hill. During spring, the aptly named hill displays a colorful array of at least 25 native wildflowers. The easy zigzag hike up the hill offers a delightful assortment of blooms, including poppies, lupine, owl's clover, cream cups and many more.

❦ Sepulveda Dam Recreation Area

LOS ANGELES RIVER TRAIL
3 miles round trip

The Los Angeles River, which drains the San Fernando Valley at its southeast corner, is very much a part of the Valley's history and geography. Prior to the valley's subdivision and suburbanization, sand-filled arroyos extended across the valley. Winter storms filled the arroyos which in turn, swelled the river. Flooding has been a problem since recorded history.

Today, the Golden State Freeway parallels the cement-lined river channel as it crosses the Valley. But before extensive flood control measures were taken, winter and spring rains would wash out the trans-valley roads. Most travelers preferred journeying from the valley to downtown via Cahuenga Pass (now the site of the Hollywood Freeway), a higher, drier route.

In 1941 the U.S. Army Corps of Engineers rimmed the Sepulveda Basin with a three-mile long earth-filled dam. Today the city leases some 2,000 acres of the the basin from the Army Corps of Engineers and established the Sepulveda Dam Recreation Area, complete with golf courses, sports fields and bike paths. Sepulveda Basin flooded—just as flood control engineers had designed—when the Los Angeles River overflowed in the winter of 1992.

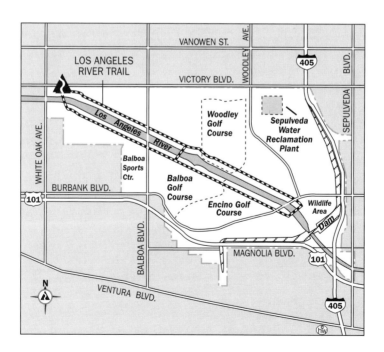

One of the few semi-natural stretches of the Los Angeles River (and the only one along which the authorities encourage walking) flows through the basin.

The river attracts lots of bird life. Finding the reeds, willows and cattails of the river to its liking is the red-winged blackbird. Look for its distinctive red and yellow banded wings and listen for its call—often described as "a rusty hinge."

Friends of the Los Angeles River and other conservation groups have called for the "Sepulveda Wildlife Reserve."

DIRECTIONS TO TRAILHEAD: From the Ventura Freeway (101) in Encino, exit on Balboa Boulevard. Head north 0.5 mile, crossing a bridge on the Los Angeles River and looking right for a drive leading to parking area for Sepulveda Dam Recreation Area.

THE HIKE: Begin walking on the dirt road by the river. Not long from the start you'll notice a river crossing. You can boulder-hop across the river on the return trip, if you want. The ol' river looks pretty good along this stretch. Plenty of riparian growth and yeah, a few shopping carts.

You can make you way down to the river for a closer look and even bush-whack your way up-river through the jungle that thrives on the riverbanks.

You'll cross the river on the Burbank Boulevard bridge and resume walking on the other side. (Across Burbank Boulevard you can take a path to the foot of the Sepulveda Dam, but it isn't exactly a thrill a minute.) Your route passes two golf courses and leads you back to the aforementioned river crossing or, alternately if the river is up, to Balboa Boulevard, which you can follow back to the entrance of the recreation area and the beginning of your walk.

¥ SERRANIA RIDGE

SERRANIA RIDGE TRAIL
2.5 miles round trip with 500-foot elevation gain

Not much open space remains on the south rim of the San Fernando Valley. True, the Santa Monica Mountains are located nearby, but this range sometimes seems a world apart, more connected to the ocean side than the valley side of Los Angeles.

So it's with some relief that the eye travels over the valley's south rim and finds a little green space that's not a golf course. That little green space in Woodland Hills is Serrania Ridge, a pocket of parkland on the suburban edge.

The ridges's name—and its geography—seem to be in limbo. Serrania Ridge, which is part of the hills of Woodland Hills is also called Woodland Ridge. (Woodland Hills itself was formerly known as Girard after its subdivider, Victor Girard.) Certainly the geographer could also place Serrania Ridge in the Santa Monica Mountains, which rise directly behind it. Last, but maybe not least, could Serrania Ridge be part of the Chalk Hills located a stone's throw northeast?

Hikers can contemplate these and other questions of geography as they climb the ridge for far-reaching valley views.

DIRECTIONS TO TRAILHEAD: From the Ventura Freeway (101) in Woodland Hills, exit on De Soto Avenue and head south. After crossing Ventura Boulevard, the avenue continues as Serrania and you proceed a mile to Serrania Park

THE HIKE: Join the path along the far eastern edge of the park and begin ascending south. The steep trail roller coasters up and down, but mostly up, offering one rise and then another from which to partake of the view.

West of the path is Woodland Hills Country Club and the hillside suburbs of Calabasas and Hidden Hills. Just east are—or once were—the Chalk Hills; so graded, contoured, terraced, plumbed and engineered for haciendas have the hills become, it's difficult to discern what was once there.

Your path climbs some more and eventually finds Mulholland Highway, your turnaround point.

☀ ORCUTT RANCH HORTICULTURE CENTER

ORCUTT RANCH TRAIL
0.5 mile or so around the ranch

Rancho Sombre del Roble (Ranch in the Shadow of the Oak) was once a 200-acre estate owned by William Warren Orcutt. Orcutt, a geologist with Union Oil Company, is credited with the discovery of the La Brea Tar Pits. His shady retreat in the valley remains a haven for ancient oaks and groves of oranges.

Tucked away at the western end of the San Fernando Valley, is a delectable slice of valley history, served up in the prettiest of surroundings—amidst a rose garden and ancient oaks.

Orcutt Ranch began as the vacation retreat of Los Angeles residents W.W. and Mary Orcutt in 1914. Orcutt, a well-respected geologist, is remembered not only for his considerable contributions to modern geology, but for his discovery of a fossil ground sloth in the La Brea Tar Pits; his discovery prompted great public and scientific interest, to say the least.

The Orcutts built a beautiful Spanish-style home and planted hundreds of acres of citrus and walnut groves. Many of the valley oaks and coast live oaks on the property were preserved.

In 1966, the Los Angeles City Parks Department purchased the estate and gardens and opened them to the public. Much of the "1920s look" has been preserved.

The large adobe house, the former Orcutt residence, is surrrounded by several gardens decorated not only by interesting collections of varied plant species, but attractive fountains, statues and sundials as well.

DIRECTIONS TO TRAILHEAD:
From the Ventura Freeway, exit on Topanga Canyon Boulevard and head north to Roscoe Boulevard. Turn west and drive to the park entrance, at 23600 Roscoe, a few blocks past Fallbrook. Open daily sunrise to sunset; closed major holidays

THE HIKE: Hikers can follow ranch paths for a look at an enormous valley oak—33-feet in circumference and estimated to be 700 years old. Gravel nature trails wind through the lushly vegetated estate, leading to a small creek with a bridge and a romantic rose garden.

94

⚘ Wilson Canyon

WILSON CANYON TRAIL
2 mile loop with 300-foot elevation gain; other short hikes possible

Oak woodlands, an alder-lined creek and commanding San Fernando Valley vistas are some of the attractions of Wilson Canyon Park. Situated just above Sylmar, the park offers some short hikes plus a connection to the trail system in adjoining Angeles National Forest.

The canyon is named for Benjamin Davis "Don Benito" Wilson, merchant, landowner, civic leader, as well as Los Angeles mayor from 1851 to 1852. Obviously, this Angeleno's name is far better known upon Mt. Wilson and its summit observatory than it is for an obscure canyon on the far fringe of the San Fernando Valley.

Wilson Canyon was purchased by the Santa Monica Mountains Conservancy and opened as a park in 1996, thus saving it from the fate of other nearby foothill canyons that have become dumpsites and suburbs. The state agency added a new park entry road and trailhead parking area.

While undeveloped, Wilson Canyon is certainly not pristine either; the work of flood control engineers is much in evidence. The U.S. Forest Service and Los Angeles County Flood Control District built Wilson Dam in the main canyon and debris dams in each of Wilson's tributary canyons.

Still, the slopes here resemble those in Mediterranean lands. This Mediterranean connection was not lost on the Los Angeles Olive Growers Association, who planted some 4,000 acres of olive trees in the area. By some estimates, Sylmar boasted the world's largest olive grove in the early years of the 20th century. Even today, remnant olive trees dot much-subdivided Sylmar.

Just below the park, and visible from the lower trails, is Olive View Hospital, damaged in the disastrous 1971 Sylmar earthquake. The long-abandoned hospital, with its stucco walls and red-tile roof, resembles a south-of-the-border resort.

The park's trail system consists of a family friendly loop plus another path that leads to a picnic area. Additional short trails lead hikers to a series of smaller canyons ending in dams.

DIRECTIONS TO TRAILHEAD: From the Foothill Freeway (210) in Sylmar, exit on Roxford Street and head north. Almost immediately, the street bends east and continues as Olive View Drive (From the Golden State Freeway (5), just north of its intersection with the San Diego Freeway (405) in Sylmar, you can also exit on Roxford Street, drive 2 miles northeast, pass under the Foothill Freeway, and join Olive View Drive.) Follow Olive View Drive past

Olive View Medical Center. The signed Wilson Canyon Park entry road is located 0.1 mile east of Bledsoe Street, just before Fenton Avenue. Follow the park road 0.6 mile to its end at the trailhead.

THE HIKE: Walk 50 yards down the asphalt road, then bear right on the signed trail. Oaks and sycamores shade the wide trail that soon penetrates Wilson Canyon. About 0.3 mile up the canyon, the path reaches a debris dam. Judging by the "USFS 1966" marking in the cement, the Forest Service is taking credit for building the dam.

The path continues a mellow ascent up-canyon. Near the head of the canyon, the trail tunnels under overhanging oaks and sycamores and makes a hairpin turn. The path travels drier slopes cloaked in chamise and other chaparral, angles west, then pops into the open for a good view of the San Fernando Valley.

The route follow a string of powerlines to a road junction. Bear left (north) and ascend 100 yards to a motley collection of eucalyptus, pepper and pine trees, and to a commanding overlook of the valley and a dozen communities.

Now head south, back downhill along the power line road. You'll descend atop the east wall of Wilson Canyon to the park access road at a point just above the old Olive View Hospital. A five-minute walk on the park road returns you to the trailhead.

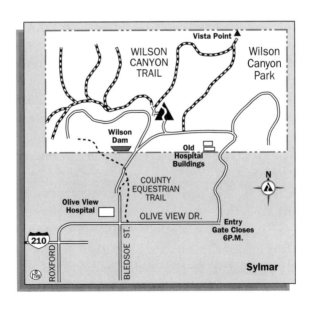

CHAPTER SIX

Santa Clarita Valley

Thanks to forward-looking conservationists, not all the valley's hilltops have been flattened by developers, not all the canyons filled with homes. There's something of a greenbelt, a collection of parks, plus the nearby Angeles National Forest around fast-growing Santa Clarita, which includes the former towns of Canyon Country, Newhall, Saugus and Valencia. From trailheads oh-so-close to the I-5 and 14 freeways, miles of trail lead to the Oak of the Golden Dream, the old oil town of Mentryville, and to many more natural scenes and historical sites.

✝ PLACERITA CANYON COUNTY PARK

PLACERITA CANYON TRAIL
From Nature Center to Walker Ranch Picnic Area
is 4 miles round trip with 300-foot elevation gain

Placerita Canyon has a gentleness that is rare in the steep, severely faulted San Gabriel Mountains. A superb nature center, plus a walk through the oak- and sycamore-shaded canyon adds up to a nice outing for the whole family.

In 1842, seven years before the '49ers rushed to Sutter's Mill, California's first gold rush occurred in Placerita Canyon. Legend has it that herdsman Francisco Lopez awoke from his nap beneath a large shady oak tree, during which he had dreamed of gold and wealth. During the more mundane routine of fixing his evening meal, he dug up some onions to spice his supper and there, clinging to the roots, were small gold nuggets. Miners from all over California, the San Fernando Placers, as they became known, poured into Placerita Canyon. The prospecting was good, though not exceptional, for several years. The spot where Lopez made his discovery is now called the Oak of the Golden Dream. A plaque marks his find.

Placerita Canyon has been the outdoor set for many a Western movie and 1950s television series, including "The Cisco Kid" and "Hopalong Cassidy." Movie companies often used the cabin built in 1920 by Frank Walker. Walker, his wife, Hortense, and their twelve children had a rough time earning a living in what was then a wilderness. The family raised cows and pigs, gathered and sold leaf-mold fertilizer, panned for gold, and hosted movie companies. The family cabin, modified by moviemakers, stands by the nature center.

Placerita Canyon's nature center has some very well-done natural history exhibits and live animal displays. Pamphlets, available at the center, help visitors enjoy park nature trails including: Ecology Trail, which interprets the canyon bottom and chaparral communities; Hillside Trail which offers a view of Placerita Canyon; Heritage Trail, which leads to the Oak of the Golden Dream.

DIRECTIONS TO TRAILHEAD: From Highway 14 (Antelope Valley Freeway) in Newhall, exit on Placerita Canyon Road and turn right (east) two miles to Placerita Canyon County Park. Park in the large lot near the Nature Center.

THE HIKE: From the parking lot, walk up-canyon, following the stream and enjoying the shade of oaks and sycamores. A 1979 fire scorched brush within a hundred feet of the nature center, but remarkably spared the oak woodland on the canyon bottom. Nature regenerates quickly in a chaparral community; some of the chamise on the slopes may be a hundred years old and veterans of dozens of fires.

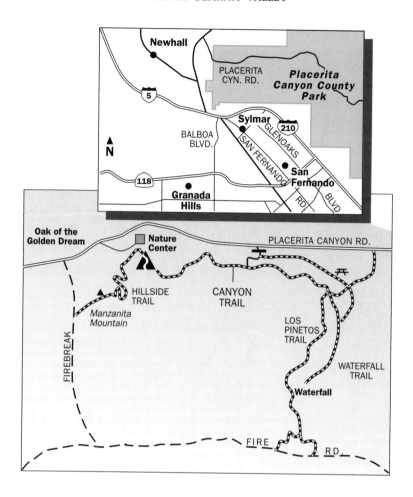

The canyon narrows and after a mile the trail splits. Take your pick: the right branch stays on the south side of the canyon while the left branch joins the north side trail. The two intersect in a half-mile, a little short of the Walker Ranch Group Campground. Here you'll find a picnic ground with tables, water and restrooms.

⚘ Los Piñetos Waterfall, Ridge

OAK PASS AND LOS PIÑETOS TRAILS

From Walker Ranch Campground to Los Piñetos Waterfall is 1.8 miles round trip with 300-foot elevation gain; loop around Los Piñetos Ridge is 7 miles with 1,600 foot gain

Two Placerita Canyon trails offer pleasant excursions into the park's backcountry. Waterfall Trail ascends along Los Piñetos Canyon's west wall, then drops into the canyon for an up-close look at a fall.

Los Piñetos Trail explores the county park's high country, entering Angeles National Forest and taking you to Los Piñetos Ridge. From the ridgetop, you can look northward over historic Placerita Canyon and Sand Canyon and southward over the San Fernando Valley sparkling below. Here on Los Piñetos Ridge, the 19th century meets the 21st century.

DIRECTIONS TO TRAILHEAD: From Highway 14 (Antelope Valley Freeway) in Newhall, exit on Placerita Canyon Road and travel (east) two miles to Placerita Canyon County Park. Continue 1.5 miles to roadside parking. Walk down Oak Pass Trail to meet Waterfall Trail.

THE HIKE: The trail to the falls (not to be confused with Los Piñetos Trail) climbs into narrow Los Piñetos Canyon. Big cone spruce, live oak and big-leaf maple shade the canyon walls. The trail crosses and recrosses the creek a few times. The waterfall, an impressive flow only after a good rain, splashes into a grotto at trail's end.

(Los Piñetos Trail) Signed Los Piñetos Trail climbs the south slopes above Placerita Canyon. It ascends first through chaparral-covered slopes, then through a sprinkling of walnut trees and an oak woodland. A few switchbacks from the summit, where firefighters have stored an emergency water supply, is Los Piñetos Spring (non-drinkable water). The trail reaches Wilson Canyon Saddle and a junction with Wilson Canyon Road and Santa Clara Divide Road.

Enjoy views of the valleys—Santa Clarita and San Fernando—then head west on Santa Clara Divide Road. Ascend a bit more, then join a fire break, or fuel break, that drops off the ridge to the south. For almost two miles the break descends steeply, finally re-entering Placerita Canyon Park just above Manzanita Mountain. A side trail leads to 2,063-foot Manzanita Mountain, which has lost much of its namesake shrub.

Near a water tank, join Hillside Trail and travel to the west end of the park's picnic area or split right and follow a path to its junction with Placerita Canyon Trail; this latter trails leads two miles east through the canyon back to the trailhead.

☦ WILLIAM S. HART COUNTY PARK

HART TRAIL
2-mile loop through William S. Hart County Park with 200-foot gain

On the Night Stage, Wild Bill Hickok, Hell's Hinges, The Narrow Trail.
These were some of the classic silent Westerns starring movie cowboy great,
William S. Hart. Hart was the personification of the strong, silent Western hero
and his films were noted for their realism and authenticity.

There is a scene near the beginning of *Tumbleweeds,* Hart's last film, in
which the cowboy–hero halts his horse atop a ridgetop. Removing his hat, he
observes the last cattle drive over land settlers will soon claim. "Boys," says Hart,
"it's the last of the West."

Tumbleweeds was also the last of the West for Hart, who retired in 1925 to
his Newhall ranch. William S. Hart County Park preserves Hart's twenty-two-
room hacienda and his ranch. Hart's home, full of Western memorabilia and
mementoes from his film days, can be viewed on a guided tour. His ranch can be
explored via a short hiking trail.

Hart Park displays the last of the
West in other ways. A small zoo with
barnyard animals recalls the Newhall
area's ranching and farming heritage.
The Saugus Train Station has been relo-
cated to the park and offers Sunday
tours of the old depot. Just outside the
park is Pioneer Oil Refinery, the first
refinery built in Southern California.

The hiker, too, can get a feel for the
last of the West, Southern California-
style, by wandering into the hills above
Hart's home. From atop the hills, hikers
can survey the Santa Clarita Valley and
see the sometimes jarring meeting of
past and present.

After Hart's retirement from act-
ing, his company, William S. Hart Pro-
ductions, filmed many westerns on his
ranch. You can get a feeling for the Old
West by hiking into the hills so beloved

William S. Hart

William S. Hart home

by Hart. Fire roads and a nature trail explore the ranch and offer easy hiking for the whole family.

DIRECTIONS TO TRAILHEAD: From the Antelope Valley Freeway in Newhall, exit on San Fernando Road and head west 1.5 miles to Newhall Avenue. Turn left on Newhall and drive into William S. Hart County Park

THE HIKE: Exit the park, walk along Newhall Avenue a short ways, then turn left on Market Street. Walk 150 yards to a senior citizen center on the left. At the edge of the center's parking lot is a Riding and Hiking Trail sign and a closed fire road.

Head up the dirt fire road, which climbs above a seasonal creek and winds into the brushy hills. The road crests at an overlook where you'll find a hitching post and some handsome cement and river rock benches.

You get good clear-day views of the Santa Clarita Valley and a glimpse of Hart's home, La Loma de Los Vientos, The Hill of the Winds. Inspired by this view, Hart wrote his autobiography, as well as some Western fiction and poetry.

From the overlook, you can descend toward a campground and the old Saugus Train Station or head down toward Hart's home. After reaching the house, hikers may join a nature trail and descend to the main part of the park.

⚕ WHITNEY CANYON

SANTA CLARA TRUCK TRAIL (aka "THE BEAST")
From Whitney Canyon to Los Pinetos Peak is 9.4 miles round trip with 2,700-foot elevation gain

Most hikers, bikers and endurance runners regard Los Pinetos Peak more as an obstacle to conquer than a thing of beauty. Neither the 3,864-foot summit, topped with twin communication towers, nor the route to it or easy on the eye.

The peak and the pathway up it appeal to our athletic, not our aesthetic, sensibilities. In order to reach the summit, one must confront Santa Clara Truck Trail, otherwise known as "The Beast," a grueling, unrelenting, unshaded ascent, so named for obvious reasons by members of a local running club.

Truly, foot-powered athletics, not aesthetics, draw the hardy to trek or pedal The Beast. Last I heard, the record ascent of The Beast was a run of just under 37 minutes.

Santa Clara Truck Trail was constructed by the U.S. Army Corps of Engineers in the early 1940s. It was improved during the 1950s Cold War era to service a Nike missile installation.

The Beast begins in Whitney Canyon Park, established in 2003 after a ten-year preservation effort by local conservationists, the City of Santa Clarita and the Santa Monica Mountains Conservancy. Brushy hills, oak woodland and a year-round stream are some of the natural highlights of the 442-acre park, which offers wildlife a corridor for passage between the San Gabriel and Santa Susana mountains. The park is also a significant portal for hikers to enter the Angeles National Forest from this side of the San Gabriel Mountains.

DIRECTIONS TO TRAILHEAD: From its junction with Interstate 5, take Highway 14 (Antelope Valley Freeway) a few miles northeast to the outskirts of Santa Clarita. Exit on San Fernando Road and head east toward the Park and Ride parking spaces. Parking is available here, particularly on the weekends, and for a fee at the end of the access road to Whitney Canyon Park.

THE HIKE: Join Santa Clara Truck Trail, which heads briefly south then turns east. The first mile of ascent passes beneath buzzing power lines and across slopes blackened in a 2004 wildfire—not exactly the most welcoming scene you'll ever see.

It could have been an even uglier scene, however. That canyon below you to the south is Elsmere, periodically proposed as a landfill site. Given local concern about such landfills, Elsmere is far more likely to become a park than a dump.

Near the halfway point, there's a clearing and, if you've had enough of The

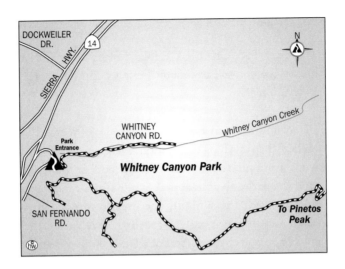

Beast, it's as good a place as any for a turnaround. At about four miles from the start, the road forks. The left fork leads to a Los Angeles County firefighters' camp and helicopter pad. Hikers bear right and soon spy the peak. Clear-day views from the summit are okay, but it's the satisfaction of having tamed The Beast that's really the true reward for this hike.

CHAPTER SEVEN

Santa Susana Mountains

Although often compared to the better-known Santa Monica
Mountains, the land of the Santa Susana Mountains is
distinctly different in both elevation and vegetation.
The Santa Susanas average more than one thousand feet
higher, and are dominated by grasslands and valley oaks,
rather than chaparral. The abundant birdlife that finds shelter
in this hospitable environment makes the area a real draw
for birders and hikers seeking a cool day on the trail.

❦ TOWSLEY CANYON

CANYON VIEW, WILEY CANYON TRAILS
2 miles round trip through Ed Davis Park

Conservationists have worked hard to create a 7,000-acre Santa Clarita Woodlands preserve within the Santa Susana Mountains. They made a good start with the preservation of part of Towsley Canyon, a tranquil retreat on the north side of the Santa Susanas, just out of sight and earshot of busy Interstate 5.

The park in the canyon is named for former Los Angeles Police Chief and state Senator Ed Davis, who authored legislation funding the purchase of Towsley Canyon in 1989, and is administered by the Mountains Recreation and Conservation Authority. Stop at Sonia Thompson Nature Center, a small facility with nature and history exhibits.

DIRECTIONS TO TRAILHEAD: From Interstate 5 in Newhall, exit on Calgrove Boulevard. Turn west, then proceed south on the Old Road 0.5 mile to the signed entrance for Ed Davis Park-Towsley Canyon and turn right. Continue another 0.5 mile to a parking lot near the nature center.

THE HIKE: Canyon View Loop Trail begins near a seasonal creek just east of the nature center. In short order, the path will take you through or near the various plant communities typical of the Santa Susana Mountains: grassland, coastal scrub and oak woodland, and you'll see evidence of a 2003 fire.

The path climbs south, then east, up a hogback ridge. Ridgetop views include the impressive canyon rock formations and the burgeoning Santa Clarita Valley. Descend from the ridge and bear left onto Wiley Canyon Trail, then turn left onto the park entrance road to return to the trailhead.

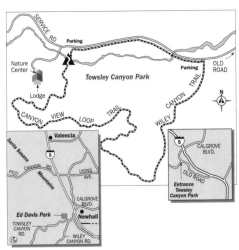

❧ EAST AND RICE CANYONS

EAST CANYON AND RICE CANYON TRAILS
From Parking Area to park boundary via East Canyon Trail is 4.4 miles round trip with 1,000-foot elevation gain; to Viewpoint via Rice Canyon Trail is 3 miles round trip with 500-foot gain

The south slopes of the Santa Susana Mountains are pretty enough: a brown, brushy backdrop above the 'burbs of the San Fernando Valley. But this southern exposure offers no clue to what lies on the other side.

The north slopes of the Santa Susana Mountains are green, woodsy and unexpectedly rugged. Pretty spectacular, I'd say. Some of these north slopes are preserved in the Santa Clarita Woodlands, a park extending along the west side of the Golden Gate Freeway (5) just north of its intersection with the Antelope Valley Freeway (14).

Thriving stands of big-cone Douglas fir on the north slopes are one highlight for the hiker. Naturalists believe the fir are a relict stand from a time (19,000 years ago or so) when the region's climate was considerably wetter and cooler than it is today.

While the Southland has warmed considerably since these trees took root, today the upper ramparts of the Santa Susana Mountains have temperatures 10 to 15 degrees cooler, and receive about twice as much rain, as the surrounding flatlands. Light snowfalls are common at elevations above 2,500 feet. The cold, rain and fog drip helps the big-cone Douglas fir prosper and also helps sustain a healthy population of valley oak.

For all the range's considerable allure, it's only half-protected. The lower and middle parts of the canyons are in public domain, while the upper portions of the canyons (where most of the big-cone Douglas fir reside) and the ridgecrest remain in private hands.

During the 1990s, the Santa Monica Mountains Conservancy, with the aid of other governmental agencies and environmental groups, painstakingly assembled a handful of canyons—Pico, Towsley, East and Rice—into the 4,000-acre Santa Clarita Woodlands Park. In order to complete the park, 3,000 more privately held acres need to be acquired, including the highest summit, 3,747-foot Oat Mountain.

After land acquisitions are made, park planners envision a "Cross Canyon Trail" that would link the range's scattered beauties. The path would be similar in concept to the spine-traversing Backbone Trail that extends across the Santa Monica Mountains.

For now, East Canyon is a trail that leads to, but not through, the big-cone Douglas fir forests. The trail, a well-graded fire road, continues into the trees and along the crest, but "No Trespassing" signs stop public passage at the current park boundary line.

Before reaching the Fir-bidden Zone, tree-loving hikers will enjoy other arboreal species, including fine specimens of coast live oak, California bay laurel, big-leaf maple, flowering ash and black walnut.

DIRECTIONS TO TRAILHEAD: From the Golden State Freeway (5), just north of its intersection with the Antelope Valley Freeway (14) in Santa Clarita, exit on Calgrove Boulevard. Turn west as Calgrove becomes the Old Road and head south 0.9 mile to parking on the west side of the road. Amenities include a native plant-landscaped picnic ground, water fountain and restroom. The trail begins just down the road from the picnic area.

When rejoining Old Road for the drive home, note that it is a divided high-way near the trailhead. Proceed with caution.

THE HIKE: From an information board, the road leads past a private corral. Mistletoe crowns the tall oaks en route. After passing an old cattle chute, a reminder of this land's ranching heritage, the path reaches a signed junction, a quarter mile or so from the start.

Branching right is Rice Canyon Trail, which offers a fine little hike for the family. The path meanders along Rice Creek and crosses it several times. Nearly a mile out, it crosses a grassy open slope up to a viewpoint. A number of extremely steep use trails climb farther up the canyon wall and might beckon the very care-

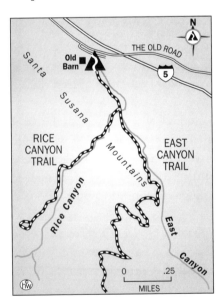

ful and very experienced hiker.

From the junction, East Canyon Trail begins to climb, first among grand old oaks and maples, then over more open slopes that deliver great views of the fir-topped ridgeline above and the Santa Clarita Valley below.

Not long after reaching the first of the Douglas firs, you encounter a locked gate and a "No Trespassing" sign. Beyond the low gate marking the park boundary, the road ascends into the fir forest and across the crest of the Santa Susanas.

❧ NEWHALL PASS

WELDON CANYON TRAIL

From Newhall Pass to Overlook is 5 miles round-trip with 700-foot
elevation; return via East Canyon and The Old Road is 8 miles round-trip.

Also called Fremont Pass and San Fernando Pass, Newhall Pass been of great historic significance to the growth of Southern California and, accompanied by freeways and a railroad line, continues to be of great importance today. Long a main
transportation route into Los Angeles, the Newhall Pass links the Santa Clarita
Valley and the San Fernando Valley.

By the geographer's definition, the Newhall Pass divides the Los Angeles
River and Santa Clara River watersheds and separates the San Gabriel Mountains
from the Santa Susana Mountains.

In 1769, explorer Gaspar de Portolá discovered the pass, later named for John
C. Frémont, who marches his troops through in 1847 on his way to Cahuenga
Pass to sign a treaty. The passageway was widened and greatly deepened in 1863
by General Edward Fitzgerald Beale. "Beale's Cut," as this dramatic slot came to
be known, was a popular locale for moviemakers of the silent film era.

For the hiker, the Newhall Pass offers a quick (though not necessarily easy)
entry into the Santa Clarita Woodlands. Weldon Canyon Mountainway, named
for a retired railroad worker of the 1930s, is a wide dirt road leading to the crest of
the Santa Susana Mountains. From the ridgeline, enjoy excellent views of East
Canyon, the Santa Clarita Valley and, yes, the Sunshine Canyon Landfill.

A word about the landfill. Weldon Canyon opened to public use in 2002 partly as a result of mitigation measures local government permitting the expansion
of the landfill.

Opt for a short out-and-back route to an overlook or a longer one to the ridgeline. Another option is to make a loop out of it with a pleasant 3-mile descent of
lovely East Canyon, then an ugly 2-mile walk along The Old Road back to the
Weldon/Newhall Pass trailhead.

DIRECTIONS TO TRAILHEAD: From Interstate 5 in Newhall, exit
on Calgrove Boulevard. Head west then south 2.5 miles on The Old Road to the
top of Newhall Pass. Turn right on a short length of Weldon Canyon Road (the I-
5 overpass) to Coltrane Avenue. Turn right and proceed 0.2 mile to the trailhead
on the left, signed Michael D. Antonovich Open Space Preserve. Parking is alongside Coltrane Avenue.

THE HIKE: Begin the steep climb on the fire road, which switchbacks
through a mixture of oak woodland and planted trees all of the same height; the

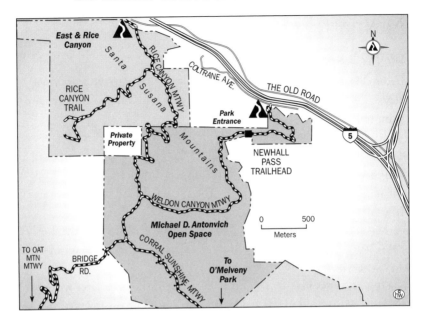

latter trees partially screen, but do not obscure the view of the great gaping hole in the earth that is the landfill.

When the path reaches the ridgeline, the ascent gentles a bit. A right-forking path leads to a shaded bench and an overlook. Take in the mountain and valley views then return to the mountainway and continue the ascent.

As Weldon Canyon Mountainway turns south, an unsigned dirt road drops north. This is northward-descending road is the way into East Canyon and an alternative loop trip back to the trailhead.

Weldon Canyon Mountainway leads south to a fork in the road and two locked gates—locked as of this writing anyway. Access will undoubtedly be improving in the years to come. As more parkland and trail easements are acquired, look for an increased number of ways to cross from one side of the Santa Susana Mountains to the other.

❦ MENTRYVILLE

PICO CANYON TRAIL

From Mentryville to Johnson Park is 1.6 miles round trip with 200-foot elevation gain; to Viewpoint is 6 miles round trip with 900-foot elevation gain; to Pico-Towsley Divide is 10 miles round trip with 1,800-foot gain.

Located in the northern reaches of Santa Clarita Woodlands Park, Pico Canyon has long been synonymous with petroleum. Pico #4 was the first commercially successful oil well in the western United States.

Master oil-driller Charles Alexander Mentry tapped black gold in Pico Canyon at a depth of 617 feet in September of 1876. By the time it was capped in 1990, Pico #4 entered the record books as the longest continually operating oil well in the world.

Success in the Pico Oil Field led to the creation of Pacific Coast Oil Company, forerunner of Standard Oil, which was later acquired by Chevron, U.S.A.. The region's wells, in partnership with and efficient refinery (California's first, located in nearby Newhall), served as a successful model for the Golden State's emerging oil industry.

Pico Canyon offers the traveler afoot three ways to go: a walk in the oak woodland, a hike high in the Santa Susana Mountains, a stroll down memory lane in the historic oil boomtown of Mentryville. The upper canyon trail branches with the right fork ascending to viewpoints on BLM land and the left fork ascending high above the Pico Canyon headwaters. A severe October 2003 wildfire blackened the park, but the canyon has benefited from considerable restoration efforts.

Town namesake Charles Alexander Mentry built an impressive looking house in 1898. Mentry's residence, along with all of the townspeople's cottages, lacked electricity, but certainly not natural gas, which was abundantly available for light and heat.

At various times more than 100 families lived in Pico Canyon. A one-room schoolhouse (which still stands) was used from 1885 to 1931.

Docent-led tours of the town of Mentryville take place from 12 P.M. to 4 P.M. on the first and third Sundays of each month.

DIRECTIONS TO TRAILHEAD: From the Golden State Freeway (5) in Valencia, exit on Lyons Road/Pico Canyon Road. Head west on Pico Canyon Road. Near its end, bear left at a Y and continue to the end of the road and a large parking area opposite the historic hamlet of Mentryville.

THE HIKE: From the historic town, follow the paved road up the canyon.

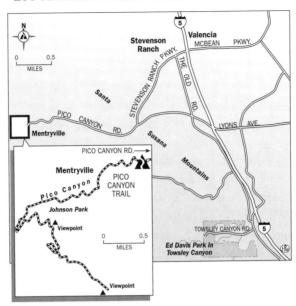

It's easier to imagine oil rigs and roustabouts than a town or townspeople in the canyon, so interpretive panels have been installed to tell the history of the canyon in its heyday. It is a bit of stretch to imagine tennis courts, croquet fields, rows of redwood cabins and Anthony Cochem's Bakery, famous throughout the region for fabulous coconut macaroons.

In contrast, Johnson Park, formerly a company picnic area, looks ready for a gathering with a barbecue and plenty of tables. Don't miss (actually, you can't miss) a replica of a late 19th-century wooden oil derrick standing at the end of Johnson Park.

Continue up-canyon to a couple of historical markers commemorating Pico #4, where the boom began back in 1876 with a thirty-barrel-a-day flow. Continue another 0.2 mile to a fork in the road.

Bear right (west) on a part asphalt-part dirt road onto BLM land that ascends buckwheat-, sage- and yucca-dotted slopes. At a minor saddle, a right-forking road leads to a viewpoint of the Santa Clarita Valley. The main trail/road works its way out onto a ledge (safe enough, but no place for anyone afraid of heights), then leads to a fairly flat vista point overlooking the valley and Pico Canyon.

A sketchy trail descends from the 2,800-foot vista point but for all practical purposes this is the end of the hike. Santa Susana Mountains activists hope one day to link Pico Canyon by trail with Towsley Canyon, some 7 miles away.

A left at the above-mentioned junction climbs 2 more miles to a 2,800-foot vista point and trail's end.

O'MELVENY PARK

BEE CANYON TRAIL
2 miles round trip

O'Melveny Park takes its name from the well-known family of Los Angeles lawyers who once owned a "gentleman's ranch" here. John O'Melveny bought the land in 1941 and called it CJ Ranch. Cattle roamed the hills, a citrus orchard was planted, and family members enjoyed spending weekends roaming the mountains.

Although areas near the ranch were oil-rich, exploration on the ranch was unsuccessful. The O'Melvenys deeded half their ranch to Los Angeles, and the city purchased the rest. The 720-acre park, which opened to the public in 1981, includes a large developed picnic area and rugged wildland laced with 10 miles of trail.

One of Southern California's many faults, the Santa Susana, tweaked the mountains of O'Melveny Park, with the happy result of helping to form Bee Canyon. The canyon is an ideal tyke hike; kids love poking around the lushly vegetated creek bottom.

The canyon—a narrow gorge, actually—has a creek that runs most of the year and a surprisingly wild ambiance. Oak and walnut trees line the base of the canyon's high sedimentary rock walls.

At the mouth of the canyon is the ranch house and barn that once belonged to the O'Melveny family. The canyon is a reminder of how much the family must have enjoyed their retreat during the 1940s at the edge of the then remote San Fernando Valley. The canyon also suggests some of the delights farther back in the Santa Susana Mountains that still need to be preserved.

DIRECTIONS TO TRAILHEAD: From the San Fernando Valley Freeway in Granada Hills, exit on Balboa Boulevard and head north to Orozco Street. Turn left and drive along the park's panhandle to parking for the picnic area.

THE HIKE: Begin at the north end of the extensive picnic grounds and follow the trail into the canyon. To the right are dramatic, sky-scraping sedimentary cliffs; to your left some shady oaks.

About 0.5 mile along the willow-crowded creek, you'll see a fire road on your left, ascending out of the canyon. You can loop back to the main part of the park on this road.

A rougher trail continues up-creek another 0.5 mile to the park boundary.

❧ MISSION POINT

MISSION POINT TRAIL
From Bee Canyon to Mission Point
is 4.5 miles round trip with 1,400-foot gain

Billowing grass and seasonal wildflowers paint a pastoral landscape on the slopes of L.A.'s second-largest city park.

In spring, a host of wildflowers—poppies, morning glory, Indian paintbrush and Mariposa lily—splash color on the hillsides. Fall wildflowers include the white trumpet-shaped jimson weed, scarlet California fuschia, and yellow goldenbrush.

Wildlife in O'Melveny Park includes deer, golden eagle, bobcat, rabbit, raccoon, and coyote. All this flora and fauna next to super-suburban San Fernando Valley!

A fire road ascends to Mission Point and explores the wild parts of the park. Bring a city map. As you climb high into the Santa Susana Mountains, you can pick out numerous natural and manmade points of interest. Views of the Southland from 2,771-foot Mission Point are often quite good.

DIRECTIONS TO TRAILHEAD: From the San Fernando Valley Freeway in Granada Hills, exit on Balboa Boulevard and head north to Orozco Street. Turn left and drive along the park's panhandle to parking for the picnic area.

A second trailhead: From Balboa Boulevard, turn west on Jolette. Follow Jolette a mile to Sesnon Boulevard. (A right turn on Sesnon will take you to the main part of O'Melveny Park.) Turn left on Sesnon, then right on Neon Way. Park at the end of Neon Way. The fire road leading to Mission Point starts here.

THE HIKE: Head west up the fire road past the park office (the former O'Melveny ranch house), rising above a walnut tree-lined canyon. You'll pass a junction with the fire road coming up from Neon Way, then join a wider road bound for Mission Point.

(From the Neon Way entrance, the fire road leads you past a seasonal brook and begins to climb high above the nearby residential area. This road soon joins the road coming up from the main part of the park.)

Evidence of the 1971 earthquake that damaged the nearby Golden State Freeway and Van Norman Dam is present in the form of fissures and slides. Seismically, the Santa Susana Mountain range is one of California's most active areas. Below, you can see the new Los Angeles Reservoir, replacement for the quake-damaged Van Norman Reservoir.

As you make your ascent, you'll notice quite a difference in vegetation

between north and south slopes. The canyon's dry north slopes are blanketed with sage and other coastal scrub. To the south, the hills are covered with grasses punctuated with occasional live oak or California walnut.

As you near the top, you'll pass a small stand of Aleppo pine, which is a tree native to Mediterranean countries. This pine is successful in Southern California's Mediterranean climate, too.

Close to the top, a couple washed-out dirt roads and bulldozer lines converge. (All roads lead toward Mission Point, but the "main road" is easier hiking.) Navigate toward four sturdy oaks, which offer a nice picnic or rest stop.

Just past the oaks, a dirt road branches left and leads to wind-blown Mission Point. A 1932 U.S. Geological Survey marker is atop the point. Two seasonal cow ponds are located on the southwest slope. Below Mission Point to the northwest are oil fields and natural gas underground storage areas.

Enjoy the view of the Santa Susana Mountains, including nearby Oat Mountain, highest peak in the range. The San Gabriel Mountains, Santa Monica Mountains, Santa Clarita Valley, and downtown Los Angeles are also part of the 360-degree panorama. Return the way you came.

PORTER RANCH

ALISO CANYON, PALISADES, SESNON AND LIMEKILN TRAILS
Through Aliso Canyon is 5 miles round trip; a loop with Sesnon, Limekiln
Canyon and Palisades Trails totals 8 miles
with a 500-foot elevation gain

Two oak- and sycamore-shaded canyons—Aliso and Limekiln—and eroded sedimentary outcroppings known as "The Palisades" are some of the highlights of a
walk through the Porter Ranch portion of the Santa Susana Mountains.

The good news for hikers is that the trail system is pretty good. Expect well-
graded paths and good signs. The bad news is that Porter Ranch is becoming one
of the largest subdivisions in Los Angles history. Political battles have taken place
over the size and scope of this gigantic undertaking.

DIRECTIONS TO TRAILHEAD: From the San Fernando Valley
Freeway (118) in Granada Hills, exit on Reseda Boulevard. Turn north to Rinaldi
Street, and head east. Turn left on Chimineas Avenue or another nearby
sidestreet and park. (There's no parking on Rinaldi.) Walk east on Rinaldi to the
bridge over Aliso Canyon. Just before the bridge, on the north side of the street, is
a dirt pathway leading down the embankment into Aliso Canyon.

If you wish to visit Limekiln Canyon first, or arrange some sort of car shuttle: Leave your car on Rinaldi just west of Tampa Avenue.

THE HIKE: Descending the embankment from Rinaldi, you soon find
yourself in quiet Aliso Canyon. The path passes a stables and meanders along the
canyon bottom among oak, sycamore and eucalyptus.

Watch for spring wildflowers—purple lupine, golden California poppies.
You'll pass junctions with a couple of side trails, but the only one to note is
Palisades Trail which climbs out of the canyon to your left.

Aliso Canyon Trail stays near the bottom of the narrow canyon for another
mile, before it climbs out of the canyon to meet the end of Sesnon Boulevard.
You'll then head west through Porter Ridge Park on Sesnon Trail, which heads
behind some houses and ends at Limekiln Canyon, near the intersection of
Sesnon Blvd. and Tampa Avenue.

Head south on bridlepath-like Limekiln Trail which soon brings you to a the
signed intersection for Palisades Trail, which climbs eastward over some sedimentary outcroppings and offers you southern views of the San Fernando Valley.
Palisades Trail crosses Reseda Boulevard, then drops you back down into Aliso
Canyon. You then retrace your steps down-canyon back to Rinaldi and your starting point.

🌸 DEVIL CANYON

DEVIL CANYON TRAIL
From Topanga Canyon Boulevard to end of public access
is 4.5 miles round trip with 400-foot elevation gain

Most of the once-wild west side of the San Fernando Valley has long been developed, but at least one heavenly place remains—with the unlikely name of Devil Canyon. It's one canyon that's an exception to the developed-to-the-max rule of the region.

This is the "cowboy side" of the valley. Many locals own horses, which they keep at home or at a number of boarding facilities in the foothills. Devil Canyon is a favorite ride of local equestrians and hikers often greet horseback riders on the trail.

So peaceful a retreat is this canyon that you wonder how it got its "Devil" name. The canyon is cool, wet, and green, in contrast to the hot, dry rim of the San Fernando Valley.

Decades before condominiums and mini-estates blossomed on the canyon walls, fire and flood ravaged the canyon, removing a road (and any possibility of vehicle travel). Nature healed itself just fine, without human intrusion. Today,

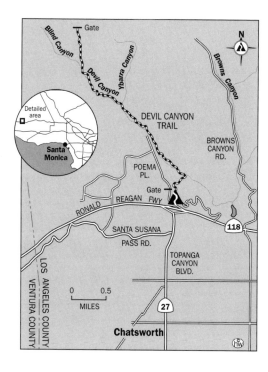

this oak-shaded canyon, through which a seasonal creek flows, is a welcoming oasis, particularly after winter rains swell Devil Canyon Creek.

DIRECTIONS TO TRAILHEAD: From the San Fernando Valley Freeway (118), exit on Topanga Canyon Boulevard. Park just north of the freeway alongside the frontage road. Construction activity and no signage add up to an ugly trailhead that's hard to locate.

THE HIKE: Begin hiking on the unsigned paved road that begins by the freeway frontage road and leads 100 yards up to a flat area rimmed with houses. Stay right as you skirt this area, then pass an abandoned auto and a unsigned footpath on the left that loops over to the housing development. The main trail dips into canyon under the shadow of the condominiums that line the west wall of the canyon, bends left and enters a more natural environment. Oaks shade the road, which de-evolves into a footpath that parallels and sometimes crosses a seasonal creek.

The canyon bottom is a lovely place, shaded by oaks, alder and sycamore. The trail narrows even more as it heads up-creek. A bit more than a mile along, just short of where Ybarra Canyon joins Devil Canyon, the path delivers you to a shady flat—an ideal picnic spot. Another mile along is trail's end at a gate, with private property beyond.

Last of the Wild West side of the Valley.

❧ SANTA SUSANA MOUNTAINS STATE PARK

STAGECOACH TRAIL
From Chatsworth Park South to Devil's Slide
is 2.5 miles round trip with 500-foot elevation gain

One of the major obstacles to stagecoach travel between Los Angeles and San Francisco was a route out of the west end of the San Fernando Valley over the Simi Hills. About 1860, a steep road was carved out of the rock face of the hills. The steepest stretch, a peril to man and beast, was known as Devil's Slide.

The slide, the old stage road and a portion of the Simi Hills are preserved in a park-in-the-making located just west of Chatsworth. In 1989, the state purchased 400 acres in the Santa Susana Pass area and added it to another 400 acres of state-owned parkland. Santa Susana Mountains State Park officially became part of the state park system in 1998. The park represents two decades of organizing and lobbying efforts by San Fernando Valley and Simi Valley environmentalists, spearheaded by the Santa Susana Mountain Park Association.

The reddish-orange sandstone outcroppings of the Simi Hills, dating from the Tertiary and Mesozoic periods 60 to 80 million years ago, form a dramatic backdrop for the park. It's easy to see why these rugged hills were a popular setting for Western movies.

A network of trails loop through the park, but the trails are unsigned and more than a little confusing. During your first visit to the park, expect to improvise a bit. Once you get the lay of the land, subsequent visits will be easier.

As you drive up Devonshire you'll notice signed Stagecoach Trail, an equestrian trail. Leave your car and pick up this trail if you wish, but it's more convenient continuing to the ample parking area in the main part of Chatsworth Park South.

DIRECTIONS TO TRAILHEAD: From the Ventura Freeway (101) in Woodland Hills, exit on Topanga Canyon Boulevard and drive 6.25 miles north to Devonshire St. Turn left and proceed 0.75 mile to Chatsworth Park South, a city-owned park with wide lawns and picnic areas, located next to the new state park. If you're coming from the Simi Valley-San Fernando Valley Freeway (118), take the Topanga Canyon Boulevard exit in Chatsworth, drive 1.5 miles to Devonshire and turn right to the park.

THE HIKE: From the parking lot, walk across the wide lawn (or take one of the dirt paths that border the lawn). With the park recreation center directly behind you, navigate toward a couple of oaks and join a gravel path that begins just below a water tower on your right.

Begin a moderate ascent. When presented with confusing choices and

Old Santa Susana Stage Road

unsigned junctions, try to keep ascending straight up the hill. Don't drift too far to the south where there's a line of electrical transmission towers, or too far to the north where the Southern Pacific railroad tracks penetrate the mountains.

A half-mile from the trailhead you'll intersect a paved road, which winds up to a small hydroelectric pumping plant. You, however, will almost immediately abandon this road at a break in a chain link fence by two telephone poles. Here you'll find the old stage road and begin to climb more earnestly toward Devil's Slide.

A century ago, the road was in much better shape. Erosion has carved wagon-wheel-sized potholes into the soft rock. The Devil's Slide is more like the Devil's Stairs these days.

Near the top of the slide is a historical marker placed by the Native Daughters of the American West commemorating "Old Santa Susana Stage-coach Road, 1859-90." This is a great place to pull up a rock, sit a spell and survey the San Fernando Valley, which spreads south and east. Just below is Chatsworth, a mixture of old ranchland and new townhouses. If you're lucky, you'll sight a freight or passenger train snaking through the Simi Hills and disappearing into the Santa Susana tunnel.

After enjoying the view, you can continue another 0.25 mile up the Stagecoach Trail and inspect the rest of Devil's Slide. Or you can retrace your steps and take one the side trails leading southeast over to the park's intriguing rock formations.

CHAPTER EIGHT

Simi Hills

It's bad news and good news for hikers who heed the call of the wild in the Simi Hills. The bad news is suburbia is advancing rapidly from the floor of the valley into the once lonely hills. The good news is enlightened park agencies and developers have grasped the popularity of hiking and are building new trails. Intriguing sandstone formations that look like Western movie backdrops are highlights of the hills. From ridgetop rock gardens, hikers get commanding views of Los Angeles and Ventura counties.

🕷 ROCKY PEAK

ROCKY PEAK, CHUMASH TRAILS
To Rocky Peak via Rocky Peak Trail is 6 miles round trip
with 1,200 foot elevation gain; to Rocky Peak via Chumash Trail
is 7 miles round trip with 1,400-foot gain

One conservation success story is the preservation of Runkle Ranch, now Rocky Peak Park. The park, which straddles the Los Angeles-Ventura county line, sets aside some much-needed parkland for fast-growing Simi Valley.

The rocks of Rocky Peak are sandstone outcroppings that geologists say were formed some 65 million years ago during the Cretaceous Period of the Mesozoic Era. Besides its namesake promontory, 4,369-acre Rocky Peak Park includes Las Llajas and Blind canyons. These canyons have two of the most pleasant seasonal streams in the mountains. After a good rain, waterfalls cascade down the canyons. Until purchased by the Santa Monica Mountains Conservancy in 1991, the Rocky Peak area was owned by entertainer Bob Hope.

Chumash Trail begins in Chumash Park on the outskirts of Simi Valley and leads 2.5 miles to a junction with Rocky Peak Trail, which leads to the peak. Park trails provide access to Blind Canyon and the rolling meadowlands of the Santa Susana Mountains to the north. This hike is a good introduction to the charms of the Santa Susanas.

DIRECTIONS TO TRAILHEAD: To reach the Rocky Peak trailhead, take the Ronald Reagan Freeway (118) through the Simi Valley and exit on Rocky

Rocky Peak area, Santa Susana Mountains

Peak Road (that's one exit west of Topanga Canyon Boulevard). The trailhead is immediately opposite the end of the freeway offramp. Caution: You can exit on Rocky Peak Road only by traveling west on Highway 118.

To Chumash trailhead: From the Ronald Reagan Freeway (118) in Simi Valley, exit on Yosemite Avenue. Head north 0.5 mile to Flanagan Drive, turn right, and drive 0.75 mile to road's end and Chumash Park.

THE HIKE: (Via Rocky Peak Trail) Begin at the locked gate of the fire road (closed to vehicles) and begin the ascent. Soon you'll get grand view (if you turn around, that is) across the freeway to the historic Santa Susana Pass, once crossed by stagecoaches.

The fire road continues up and up, with only a lone oak along the trail for shade. Rocky Peak is off to the right (east) of the trail. From the peak and related smaller peaks, you'll get vistas of the San Fernando Valley, Simi Valley, high peaks of Los Padres National Forest, Anacapa Island and the Santa Barbara Channel. Way off to the right (west) is the Ronald Reagan Presidential Library.

From Chumash Park, Chumash trailheads north from the end of Flanagan Drive: The path soon parallels a creek, makes a half-circle around a minor hill, then begins climbing in earnest high above Blind Canyon.

Some 2.5 miles of steady ascent brings you to an intersection with Rocky Peak Trail. If you turn right (south) on this trail, it's about a mile's walk to Rocky Peak. A left turn leads 2.5 miles to the park boundary and a large oak savanna.

❀ CORRIGANVILLE PARK

CORRIGANVILLE LOOP, ROCKY PEAK CONNECTOR TRAILS
Park loop is 2 miles round trip; to Rocky Peak Fire Road
is 5 miles round trip with 600 foot elevation gain

Some Hollywood historians claim this picturesque locale in the Simi Hills was the most extensively used film location outside a major studio. About a thousand Western and adventure movies were filmed at the Corriganville Movie Ranch from 1937 to 1965. Now the old movie ranch where the Lone Ranger rode, the Fugitive fled and Lassie came home is a new park that offers the hiker the chance to step back into film history.

Corriganville was founded by Raymond Bernard who changed his name to Ray "Crash Corrigan," the name of a character he played in *Undersea Kingdom*, a 1930s movie serial. Corrigan broke into the biz as a stuntman, and as a body double for "Tarzan" (Johnny Weissmuller), then starred in two Western serials. In 1938 he purchased 2,000 acres of land he was certain would be an ideal Western movie backdrop.

Among the memorable Westerns filmed in Corriganville were *Duel in the Sun, Streets of Laredo, Fort Apache* and *How the West Was Won*. Noted TV horse operas lensed here included "Gunsmoke," "Have Gun, Will Travel" and "The Cisco Kid." In 1948 Corriganville was opened to the public as a Wild West-flavored amusement park, complete with a rodeo and stagecoach rides.

Today, Corriganville Park plays a dual role as nature preserve and nostalgia. A family-friendly, twenty-stop interpretive trail explores the terrain's natural and cinematic highlights. Between stops, even more plaques and signs delve deeper into this land's movie history.

A trail and tunnel connect Corriganville with Rocky Peak and the rugged hills located on the other side of the Ronald Reagan Freeway (118).

The tunnel and trails north and south of the freeway form a "wildlife corridor" designed to allow animals to migrate across the Simi Hills without becoming road kill. The corridor appears to be working: I've seen coyotes on both sides of the freeway.

DIRECTIONS TO TRAILHEAD: From the Ronald Reagan Freeway (118) in Simi Valley, exit on Kuehner Road and drive south a mile to Smith Road. Turn left and proceed a short distance to road's end and plenty of parking in Corriganville Park.

THE HIKE: From the east end of the parking lot, follow the dirt road east past some coast live oaks and you'll soon join the park's signed nature trail. Your route parallels railroad tracks which seem to disappear up ahead into the mountains; the "disappearance" is actually a 1.5 mile long tunnel connecting Simi Valley with Chatsworth.

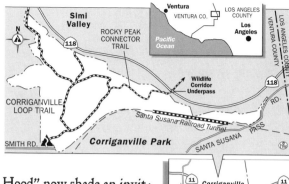

At Sherwood Forest, the oaks featured in "Robin Hood" now shade an inviting picnic ground. Here the trail splits. Those wishing to continue the nature trail's exercise in nostalgia need only follow the numbered signs.

(Hardier hikers will walk to the far end of the picnic area and a shade ramada, and join the unsigned trail leading northeast. As this path ascends it morphs into a crumbling asphalt road, then an Appian Way-like path of flat stones.)

A short but steep climb brings you to the 118 Freeway and the mouth of the tunnel leading under it. Walk through the graffiti-marred tunnel and emerge to join a footpath that briefly heads west above and parallel to the freeway, then swings northeast. What seems like a very long mile of hiking brings you to a junction with Rocky Peak Fire Road. Reward yourself by walking 100 yards south down the fire road to a bench and viewpoint of Corriganville and the Simi Valley.

From Sherwood Forest, cross a bridge over the creek that cuts through Corriganville. Note the concrete pool created by moviemakers, who filmed underwater scenes through portholes.

The path turns back west and soon passes the rocky hideouts used by many a movie bad guy. Hike the 75-yard side trail to a cave featured in episodes of "The Fugitive" television series.

The nature trail becomes just that again briefly with ecological explanations about lichen and sandstone formations. For Western movie fans, the trail saves the best for last as it visits the site of the John Ford-directed 1948 Western Fort Apache starring John Wayne and Henry Fonda.

The path skirts the scant remains of Silvertown, Corriganville's movie set town, then returns to the parking area.

SAGE RANCH PARK

SAGE RANCH LOOP TRAIL
2.5-mile loop with 200-foot elevation gain

Intriguing sandstone formations and backdrops that are literally right out of a Western movie are two highlights of a hike in Sage Ranch Park. The park, perched high in the Simi Hills on the Los Angeles-Ventura county line, offers magnificent rural and metropolitan views from its 2,000-foot high ridges.

Mostly what you notice at Sage Ranch is an odd tapestry of native, exotic and cultivated flora. Native plants are well represented within the oak woodland ecosystem, and by such chaparral community members as chamise, ceanothus, coffeeberry and California buckwheat. Invaders include castor bean, Australian salt bush and assorted thistles. Abandoned orange and avocado groves are the third component of the ranch's diverse plant life.

One might reasonably conclude that Sage Ranch was named for the presence of native sage species (white, black, purple and pitcher), but this was not the case. The ranch namesake is actually Orrin Sage, who began a cattle operation in these then-remote Simi Hills just after World War II.

What was once the Wild West of Los Angeles County and the equally wild

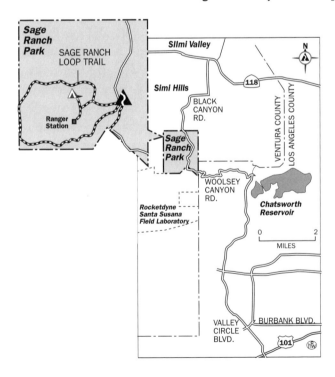

126

east of Ventura County got fenced in by freeways. Bordering Sage Ranch to the south is the Rocketdyne Santa Susana Field Laboratory, established in 1958. Rocket engine testing can be a noisy business, so the company chose the site, then called Paradise Valley, because of its isolation. The company and its successor, Rockwell International, have tested systems for the Apollo, Delta, Jupiter and Atlas projects, as well as for the Space Shuttle. Engine testing continues today.

Rocketdyne's lab was the site of an early, glitch-prone nuclear reactor. The reactor was shut down long ago, but not before causing some low level contamination of some of the nuclear research buildings. This accident, plus engine-cleaning toxic chemicals that seeped into the groundwater, created a dilemma for the lab's neighbor, Orrin Sage: In the 1980s, when he wished to sell his ranch, he couldn't prove his ranch wasn't contaminated and thus couldn't market it. The Mountains Recreation Conservation Authority tested soil, water and air quality and found no contamination whatsoever. The agency purchased the ranch for parkland in 1990. (Controversy over the aerospace firm's toxic clean-up efforts on its own property has lingered.)

Sage Ranch Loop Trail offers excellent views. I prefer a counter-clockwise hike of the ranch, but the loop is a fine one anyway you hike it.

DIRECTIONS TO TRAILHEAD: From the Ventura Freeway (101) in Woodland Hills, exit on Valley Circle Boulevard and drive north 6 miles to Woolsey Canyon Road. Turn left (west) and proceed 2.7 miles to Sage Ranch Park. The park entrance is on the left, a short distance past the Rockwell International Santa Susana Field Laboratory, where Woolsey Canyon Road bends north and continues as Black Canyon Road.

THE HIKE: From the parking area, walk up the paved park road past a hillside cloaked in an eclectic mixture of scrub oak, eucalyptus, orange and avocado trees. Alas the years, along with freezing temperatures, several drought years and Ventura County's restrictions on agricultural water use, have not been kind to the orange and avocado trees.

You'll soon arrive at the "Campground Overflow Parking" lot and join the signed loop trail. The path winds briefly among oaks and drops into a cluster of sandstone boulders. Enjoy inspiring views north of the Simi Valley and the distant peaks back of Ojai. The trail curves south, drops into a boulder-filled bowl, crosses it, then passes sandstone outcroppings that look like giant skulls. A gentle ascent brings you by a far corner of the Santa Susana Field Lab's parking lot. The path climbs past some brush-engulfed avocado trees back to the parking area.

✿ MEDEA CREEK

NATURE, MEDEA CREEK TRAILS
Nature Trail Loop through park is 1.5 miles round trip; from Oak Canyon
Community Park to trail's end is 3.2 miles round trip

Medea Creek has as many moods and manifestations as the sorceress Medea of
Greek mythology. From its headwaters on the shoulder of Simi Peak, the creek
descends the Conejo Ridge among grand old oaks with a nature trail at its side.
Medea Creek continues its epic journey through a suburban greenbelt before coming to a near fatal end in a flood control channel behind a shopping center.

Medea's life story is that of many Southland streams: Mountain-born, suburban tamed, urban-annihilated.

The Medea Creek environs was owned for a time by Fibber McGee, a celebri-
ty during the early days of radio. Oak Park, a kind of modern-day Pleasantville,
was developed in the 1980s and 1990s, and portions of the creek were placed in the
care of the Rancho Simi Recreation and Park District.

Oak Canyon Community Park, which features picnic areas, playgrounds and
a nature trail, embraces the upper reaches of Medea Creek. A long narrow greenway—Medea Creek Park—straddles a lower segment of the creek as it flows
through Oak Park.

The nature trail is a twenty-stop tour keyed to interpretive signs. It begins in
the developed part of the park, then gets more pastoral as it journeys streamside
among the oaks. Medea Creek Trail, which extends along its namesake waterway
south of the community park, adds a bit more walking.

DIRECTIONS TO TRAILHEAD: From Highway 101 in Agoura, exit on
Kanan Road and drive north 3 miles to Hollytree Drive. Turn right then left into
Oak Canyon Community Park. Follow the park access road past a small lot locat-
ed near duck pond to the main parking area located a bit farther up the road.

If you want to jump right onto the Medea Creek trailheading south, turn
south off of Kanan Road onto Oak Hills Drive. In a half block, turn left onto
Calle Rio Vista. The trailhead is at the end of this little cul-de-sac.

THE HIKE: Begin your counter-clockwise jaunt on the interpretive trail by
leaving the picnic area and following the sidewalk from station to station. The
sidewalk gives way to a dirt pathway and passes a cement dam.

The trail changes direction and heads downstream along the willow-lined
creek. As the path nears Kanan Road you'll pass a little lagoon and an ersatz
waterfall. From the lagoon, you can make your way to Kanan Road, cross it, and
walk the short distance down Oak Hills Drive and Calle Rio Vista to the begin-

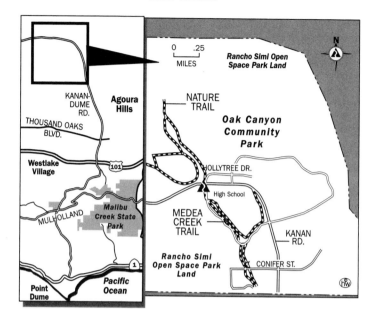

ning of Medea Creek Trail. Those wishing to complete the nature trail will fol-low a paved pathway back to the trailhead.

Medea Creek Trail skirts the ball fields behind the local high school. The path branches into two trails, both of which meander along with the creek. (This path also doubles as an exercise trail called the Advanced Challenge Course with stations that offer the opportunity to climb ropes and twist the physique into all manner of contortions.)

After a half-mile of mellow walking, you'll cross Medea Creek Lane and soon come to an unsigned trail junction. The left fork bends sharply northeast and leads back to Kanan Road near the Oak Park library. Stay right, continuing south. You'll cross Conifer Street and spot a footbridge over Medea Creek.

From the bridge, Medea Creek Trail enters a grassy greenbelt. Stay on the left (east) side of the creek as you continue another 0.5 along the greenway between Oak Park residences and the oak-lined creek. The trail ends 0.2 mile after crossing Laro Drive behind a row of shops in the Agoura Hills City Mall.

❀ CHEESEBORO CANYON

CHEESEBORO CANYON TRAIL
From NPS Parking Lot to Sulfur Springs is 6 miles round trip
with 100-foot elevation gain; to Sheep Corral is 9.5 miles round trip with
200-foot elevation gain

It's the old California of the ranchos: Oak-studded potreros, rolling foothills that glow amber in the dry months, emerald green in springtime. It's easy to imagine vaqueros rounding up tough Mexican range cattle.

For years this last vestige of old California faced an uncertain future, but thanks to the efforts of conservationists it was saved from golf course and suburban development.

From the days of the ranchos to 1985, Cheeseboro Canyon was heavily grazed by cattle. Grazing altered canyon ecology by displacing native flora and allowing opportunistic plants such as mustard and thistle to invade. As you walk through the canyon, you'll see signs indicating research areas. The National Park Service is attempting to re-colonize native flora and eradicate nonnatives.

DIRECTIONS TO TRAILHEAD: From the Ventura Freeway (101) in Agoura, exit on Chesebro Road. Loop inland very briefly on Palo Comado Canyon Road, then turn right on Chesebro Road, which leads to the National Park Service's gravel entrance road and parking lot.

THE HIKE: Note your return route, Modello Trail, snaking north up the wall of the canyon, but follow the fire road east into Cheeseboro Canyon. The fire road soon swings north and dips into the canyon. You'll pass a signed intersection with Canyon Overlook Trail, a less-than-thrilling side trail that leads to a knoll overlooking the Lost Hills landfill.

After this junction, the main canyon trail, now known as Sulfur Springs Trail, winds through valley oak-dotted grassland and coast live oak-lined canyon. Watch for mule deer browsing in the meadows and a multitude of squirrels scurrying amongst the oaks.

The old road crisscrosses an (usually) all-but-dry streambed. A bit more than 3 miles from the trailhead, your nose will tell you that you've arrived at Sulfur Springs. You can turn around here or continue another 1.75 miles up a narrowing trail and narrowing canyon to an old sheep corral.

You can continue a bit farther on the trail to a junction with Palo Comado Canyon Trail and head south on this path back to the trailhead. Ranch Center Trail, a 1.1 mile long path, connects Palo Comado and Cheeseboro canyons, as does the 1.5 mile Palo Comado Connector Trail. The latter path leads to a junction 0.7

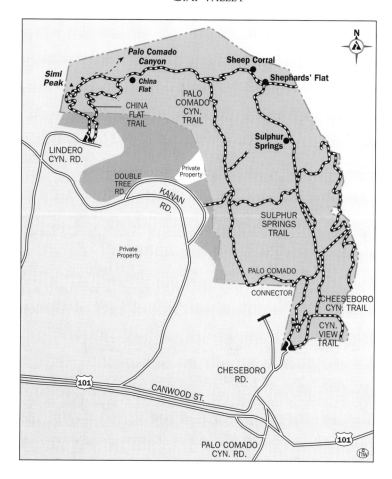

mile from the trailhead. Modelo Trail ascends a ridgetop for a good view of Cheeseboro Canyon and one of the finest remaining oak woodlands in Southern California.

❀ SIMI PEAK

CHINA FLAT TRAIL (see map on page 131)
5 mile loop with 1,000-foot elevation gain

China Flat Trail is an excellent (but not easy) introduction to the Simi Hills. It leads to China Flat, perched on the wild west side of the National Park Service's Cheeseboro Canyon Site. The trail's return loop contours high over the shoulder of 2,403-foot Simi Peak, highest summit in the Simi Hills.

Ambitious hikers will enjoy China Flat Trail as a backdoor entry along the ridgecrest to Cheeseboro and Palo Comado canyons, part of the Santa Monica Mountains National Recreation Area. Expect a 10- or 12-mile hike (or more), as well as a measure of solitude on this lightly traveled route.

China Flat Trail is a bit of a misnomer; the trail is anything but flat. And China Flat itself, while of more level relief than surrounding Simi peaks, will never be confused with one of those truly flat Flats found in other mountain ranges.

Still, China Flat Trail is a most enjoyable loop, requiring only a one-block neighborhood stroll to connect trail's end with the trailhead.

DIRECTIONS TO TRAILHEAD: From the Ventura Freeway (101) in Westlake Village, exit on Lindero Canyon Road and head north 4 miles. A few blocks from the trailhead, Lindero Canyon Road bends east. Look for the signed trailhead on the left (north) side of the road between King James Court and Wembly Avenue. Park on Lindero Canyon Road.

THE HIKE: Follow the trail north up a short, steep hill. Here a connector trail rising from King James Court meets the path. Continue on the main (China Flat) trail as it ascends past a sandstone formation. After climbing some more, the path gentles a bit and contours east to an unsigned junction. Keep to the left (north) and begin a stiff climb toward the ridgeline.

Finally the trail gains the ridge and you encounter another unsigned junction. Bear left and continue an ascent along the ridge to a saddle and yet another trail junction. (Ambitious trekkers bound for Cheeseboro Canyon will take the right fork.)

This hike uses the left fork and begins a moderate descent. Views from the shoulder of Simi Peak include Westlake Village, Agoura Hills and other communities clustered on the Ventura-Los Angeles County line, as well as the peaks of the Santa Monica Mountains.

The trail ends at a gate on King James Court. Follow this short street one block down to Lindero Canyon Road and your vehicle.

❧ MT. McCoy

MT. MCCOY TRAIL
To Mt. McCoy summit is 2.6 miles round trip
with 600-foot elevation gain; to Reagan Library is 4 miles round trip

Two hundred years ago a cross atop this Simi Valley peak was a landmark to the friars and other travelers who trudged the dusty trail from mission to mission. A cross still stands atop this peak, now named Mt. McCoy; it remains a beacon to travelers and ready reference point for valley residents. But the twelve-foot-high concrete cross has been the object of controversy in recent years, provoking much discussion about the location of religious symbols. Finally, in 2004, the small parcel on which the cross stands was sold to the Simi Valley Historical Society.

Thanks to recent efforts by the Rancho Simi Trail Blazers, the cross and 1,325-foot mountaintop are now accessible by a very well constructed new footpath. From Mt. McCoy's summit ridge, hikers can then join an old dirt road that leads to Presidential Drive that, in turn, leads a short distance to the entrance of the Ronald Reagan Presidential Library and Museum.

The museum's 18,000 square feet of exhibits highlight Reagan's years as a Hollywood actor, as California governor and as president (1981-1989). Displays range from a full scale replica of the White House Oval Office to an authentic cruise missile to odd objets d'art fashioned from jelly beans. Visitors can board Air Force One, the plane that served as the "Flying White House" for President Reagan and six other U.S. presidents.

For an intriguing half-day adventure, hike over Mt. McCoy through Reagan Country to the presidential library, tour the museum and have lunch at the museum café, then march back.

In those bygone days, the landmark peak was known as Verde Hill—part of the surrounding Verde (Green) Ranch. The peak was later re-named for 1880s' realtor Harvey McCoy, a major player, along with the Simi Land & Development Company, in the early development of Simi Valley.

The new Mt. McCoy Trail with its carefully engineered switchbacks replaces a straight-up-the-hill path that appeared to be made by use, not design. Reward for the now-moderate ascent to the summit are clear-day vistas of Mt. Baldy and the San Gabriel Mountains, the Santa Monica Mountains, the Ojai backcountry, the Channel Islands and the wide blue Pacific.

DIRECTIONS TO TRAILHEAD: From westbound Highway 118, in the city of Simi Valley, exit on Madera Road south and go one mile south to Royal Avenue. Turn right, then make an immediate right on Acapulco followed by an immediate left on Washburn Street. Drive a block to the trailhead on the left. Park carefully and courteously along this residential street.

Alternatively, from the Ventura Freeway (101) in Thousand Oaks you could drive north on Highway 23 and exit on Olsen Road. Head east on Olsen, which soon becomes Madera Road and bends north. Turn left (west) on Royal Avenue, then follow the above directions.

THE HIKE: The path heads southwest, skirting the base of Mt. McCoy. Off to your right, you'll spot the old retired trail, which makes a switchback-less, straight-line assault on the summit.

Shadeless Mt. McCoy Trail twice passes tantalizingly close to (but does not enter) an oak grove. Near the top, the trailbuilder's fine art is displayed: well-done switchbacks over the volcanic rock topping Mt. McCoy.

Make your way to the cross and admire the mountain and valley views. Reagan Library-bound hikers will double-back along the summit ridge and join the dirt road heading south, then bending west. The view south takes in a couple of reservoirs and golf courses as well as Conejo Ridge, crowned by 2,403-foot Simi Peak.

The dirt road ends at Presidential Drive. Ascend the drive 0.3 mile to the Reagan Library.

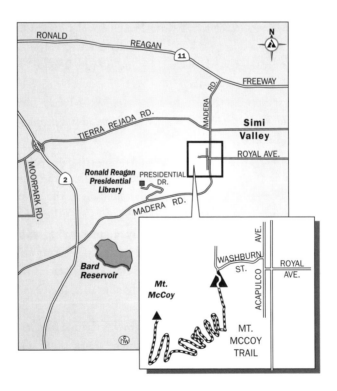

CHAPTER NINE

San Gabriel Valley

What was once an orange-growing empire is now thoroughly suburbanized, but the area's natural history has been preserved in botanic gardens, hilltop retreats and river-side parks. The hiking trails through the chaparral-covered slopes of the hills surrounding the San Gabriel Valley offer fine opportunities to explore the area and take in panoramic views of the valley below. Historically considered a destination for those seeking a healthful environment, the San Gabriel Valley, with its trails anyway, continues to beckon the hiker seeking improved health and a little adventure along the way.

❧ PASADENA'S ARROYO SECO

ARROYO SECO TRAIL
From Arroyo Seco Park to the Rose Bowl is 3 miles round trip

In Pasadena, between the end of the freeway and the beginning of the Angeles National Forest, the arroyo takes on a third dimension, what land-use planners, in the peculiar jargon of their trade, refer to as "the urban-rural interface." Here the arroyo has been domesticated, but not destroyed. And here the walker will find a little leg-stretcher of a hike that recalls the Pasadena of a century ago.

Since before the turn of the 20th century, the arroyo has been a pleasurable destination for nature-loving Pasadena residents. Old photos show a verdant canyon, with trails meandering along wooded banks. For most of the last one hundred years or so, engineers, not ecologists, have controlled nature in the arroyo; still, some tranquil places remain.

During the last decade of the 19th century and the first decade of the 20th, the banks of the Arroyo Seco hosted a way of life historians now call Arroyo Culture. Artists, writers, wealthy eccentrics and assorted nonconformists settled in this suburb, so uniquely positioned between the wilderness and fast-growing Los Angeles. Arroyo residents gloried in Native American and Mexican cultures. They filled their homes with Native American blankets and pottery, stained glass and colored tile. Two of the many writers whose careers were influenced by their contact with Arroyo Culture included Mary Austin and Robinson Jeffers.

Over the years, the arroyo hasn't always been so "seco"; in fact during some winters, quite a torrent rushed down the arroyo. Devil's Gate Dam and Reservoir were built to capture the arroyo's runoff and a cement channel built to direct its flow. Today, as a result of all these flood control measures, the trail along the Arroyo Seco is no wilderness adventure, but it does afford a a pleasant walk into Pasadena's past.

DIRECTIONS TO TRAILHEAD: From the Pasadena Freeway in South Pasadena, exit on Marmion Way/Avenue 64. Bear left and follow the signs to York Avenue. Turn right on York and then almost immediately turn left on San Rafael Avenue. Drive 0.75 mile to Arroyo Seco Park, where there's plenty of parking. Best bet for hikers is the small lot near the softball field. Arroyo Seco Trail departs from San Pasqual Stables, just up the avenue on the left side of the road. Don't park in the stables' lot.

THE HIKE: The trail, signed "Horseback Riding Trail," begins at the north end of the stable grounds. A 50-yard walk brings you to a small bridge over the arroyo flood control channel. Here you may choose which side of the arroyo you'd like to walk upon; equestrian trails parallel both sides of the channel for about a mile.

Arroyo Seco Trail passes native oak, alder and sycamore, as well as arboreal imports from faraway lands—eucalyptus, palm and pepper trees. Pasadenans have been cultivating gardens at the arroyo's edge for about a century, and some mighty strange flora has escaped from these gardens and sprouted on the canyon walls and bottom: bougainvillea, bird of paradise, and dozens of other exotic plants.

High above you, atop the arroyo walls, are some fine old homes—Bavarian, Craftsman, Victorian, Tudor and Anyone's Guess in style—and all but hidden by the lush vegetation.

As you approach an archery range, note the huge castle-like structure high on the arroyo's east bank. This is the Vista del Arroyo Hotel, finished in 1936 and now a federal government office building.

The trail takes you beneath a trio of bridges arching over the Arroyo Seco. Unlike the arroyo flood control channel, the bridges are an aesthetic triumph. Pleasing to the eye—but upsetting to the spirit—is the Colorado Boulevard Bridge, known in the 1930s as "Suicide Bridge." Many wealthy Pasadenans were hard hit by the 1929 stock market crash and decided to leave this world by leaping off the bridge.

Somewhat ironically, the most natural part of the arroyo that you'll encounter along this trail is found beneath the Colorado Boulevard and Ventura Freeway bridges. Eastside and westside arroyo trails join together near a spillway and finally depart from the straight line course of the cement flood control channel. The path follows a little creek, which hints at what the arroyo might have looked like before its ecology was forever altered by engineers.

Arroyo Seco Trail emerges from the greenery near the corner of Arroyo Boulevard and Seco Street. The Rose Bowl is dead-ahead. Walk along Arroyo Boulevard a short distance to Brookside Park, where you can picnic in the shadow of the Rose Bowl.

A signed "Horseback Riding Trail" continues north another mile, first passing through the Rose Bowl parking lot, then continuing alongside West Drive past Brookside Golf Course. Skip this boring path, eat your lunch at Brookside Park and return the same way.

❧ LOS ANGELES ARBORETUM & BOTANIC GARDEN

ARBORETUM TRAIL
1 mile or so round trip

The former estate of E.J. "Lucky" Baldwin is now home to 30,000 plants. Los Angeles Arboretum & Botanic Garden includes Tropical Greenhouse, the Garden for All Seasons, and specialty gardens featuring plants from around the world. Colorful peacocks strut the gardens; a collection of ducks populate the 4-acre lake. A 50-foot waterfall forms a beautiful backdrop for a collection of ferns and water-loving species.

Businessman and developer Baldwin purchased the old Rancho Santa Anita in 1875 and constructed a striking Queen Anne-style home on his property over-looking a natural lagoon. While the arboretum gets plenty of visitors, many more head for that other Baldwin-inspired creation across the street—the Santa Anita racetrack.

If the arboretum scene looks familiar, it's because you've seen it on the screen: old Tarzan flicks, the "Fantasy Island" television series, and much more. With Katharine Hepburn along, Humphrey Bogart pulled the "African Queen" through the arboretum jungle.

Strictly in terms of exercise, the road circling the arboretum offers the walker the best workout. But to really see the flora, get off the road onto the garden paths. Paths wind past some of America's tallest palm trees, streams, and a water-fall to greenhouses for bromeliads, orchids, begonias and tropical plants. Particularly fun is a stroll through the Jungle Garden.

For a good clear-day view of Mt. Wilson, follow the path up Tallac Knoll, and in the process you will encounter a stand of the rare Pasadena oak.

Amidst the colorful flora, the walker will likely encounter the arboretum's dominant fauna—peacocks, descendants of a couple of peafowl brought from India by Lucky Baldwin at the beginning of the twentieth century.

DIRECTIONS TO TRAILHEAD: From the San Bernardino Freeway (10) in El Monte, exit on Baldwin Avenue and drive north to the entrance of the Los Angeles Arboretum & Botanic Garden on the west side of the street. From the Foothill Freeway (210) in Arcadia, exit on Baldwin Avenue and go south a short distance to the arboretum entrance.

❧ WHITTIER NARROWS NATURE CENTER

AQUATECOS LAKE TRAIL
1 mile round trip

Birds, lots of them, have long attracted birders to Whittier Narrows. At last count, more than 250 species had been recorded in the area between the San Gabriel and Rio Hondo Rivers. Diverse habitats—lakes and rivers, sandbars and mudflats, riparian vegetation and open fields—account for the high number of species.

Abundant bird life was one of the reasons the National Audubon Society established its Southern California headquarters in Whittier Narrows during the 1930s, with the name "San Gabriel River Wildlife Refuge."

A wild river, vines that climbed high into the trees, and jungle-like vegetation attracted moviemakers to Whittier Narrows. The Narrows doubled for deepest darkest Africa in the Tarzan movies starring Johnny Weissmuller.

Over the years Whittier Narrows survived fire and floods, but nearly perished, as a wildlife sanctuary anyway, when the Audubon Society was displaced by the Army Corps of Engineers, who built berms, dams and concrete channels.

Today's 200-acre Whittier Narrows Nature Center is but a fraction of the much larger Whittier Narrows Recreation Area, which is a developed area that includes Legg Lake and all manner of fields and facilities.

While thousands of motorists on the San Gabriel Freeway (605) whiz through Whittier Narrows, undoubtedly very few of them think about the river itself.

But you can explore the ecology—what's left of it, anyway—of the San Gabriel River via a path that loops around the Whittier Narrows Nature Center. To get more out of the walk, pick up a leaflet at the nature center. Stop by the small nature museum, which exhibits native flora and fauna.

DIRECTIONS TO TRAILHEAD: From the Pomona Freeway in South El Monte, exit on Peck Road. Pick up Durfee Avenue, south of the freeway overpass, and enter Whittier Narrows Recreation Area. Turn left into the parking lot for Whittier Narrows Nature Center

THE HIKE: The path, paved at first, explores riparian vegetation—willows, sycamores and elderberry—then reaches bulrush- and cattail-lined Lake Aquatecos, a pond that attracts many birds.

Hikers more in the mood for exercise than education will join nearby San Gabriel River Trail or Rio Hondo River Trail.

❧ BOSQUE DEL RIO HONDO NATURAL AREA

CAMINO AL RIO
2 miles round trip

Back in the 1930s and for a couple of decades thereafter, going to the beach had an altogether different meaning than it does nowadays. San Gabriel Valley families flocked not to the popular Pacific shores but down by the river—to a sand strand along the Rio Hondo locals called Marrano Beach.

Then, a day along the river was like a day at the beach anywhere—sunning, swimming, picnicking. But such activities at Marrano Beach had a distinctly Spanish accent, often including a pot of menudo (tripe soup) bubbling on the campfire and guitar-accompanied songs from south of the border.

Progress dimmed, then doomed the Rio Hondo's attraction as a recreation site. By the 1960s, an upwardly mobile population drove new freeways to ocean beaches.

Oil wells were drilled on the riverbanks and factories discharged waste into the water. Invasive, nonnative plants choked off access to the Rio Hondo, making its "deep-river" Spanish name a grand misnomer. The river de-evolved into a sluggish watercourse, straightened and lined by concrete banks.

Finally, though, after more than 30 years of riparian abuse, there's some good news to report about the Rio Hondo. Thanks to the skilled park-making abilities of the Santa Monica Mountains Conservancy and the Mountains Recreation and Conservation Authority, as well as lots of community involvement and about a million bucks in park bond money, an amazing landscape transformation has taken place on a stretch of river sandwiched between Whittier and Montebello.

Bamboo and thickets of foreign flora were yanked from the banks and replaced by native sycamore and cottonwood trees. Now the river attracts such wildlife as hawks and blue herons, carp and mosquito fish. The popular name Marrano Beach (Spanish for "dirty" or "pig") is no longer appropriate.

For the walker, Bosque del Rio Hondo Natural Area offers picnicking, access to some secluded beaches, and a fine starting point for an up-river exploration.

DIRECTIONS TO TRAILHEAD: From the Pomona Freeway (60) in South El Monte, exit on Rosemead Boulevard and drive south 0.7 mile to San Gabriel Boulevard. Turn right, then make another right into the parking area for Bosque del Rio Hondo Natural Area.

THE HIKE: Leave behind the park's Mission Revival-style entry gate and restrooms and walk toward the river. The path soon forks; the leftward path joins the bikepath while the rightward one (Camino al Rio) leads to the river.

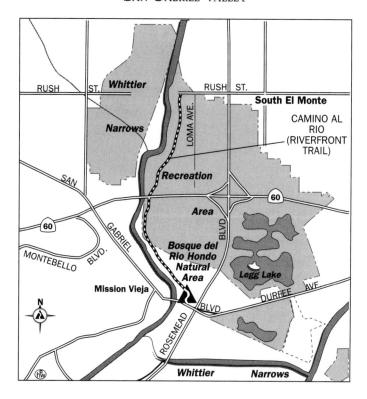

Once at the Rio Hondo, you can either follow the bikeway/walkway above the river or some sketchy, intermittent dirt paths closer to the water. You'll pass a couple of oil wells, as well as unrestored segments of the Rio Hondo that are silty, sluggish, shopping cart repositories. On a happier note, enjoy clear-day views to the northeast of Mt. Baldy, towering above the San Gabriel Valley.

About 0.8 mile from the trailhead, the path travels under the Pomona Freeway. Part company with the bikepath, which bends east, and join a wide sandy pathway that leads north through Whittier Narrows Recreation Area. The trail, which parallels the Rio Hondo, soon approaches a model airplane flying area, which can be annoyingly loud on a busy weekend.

Trail's end is the northern boundary of the recreation area at Rush Street.

❧ WALNUT CREEK REGIONAL COUNTY PARK

WALNUT CREEK TRAIL
6.5 miles round trip with a 500-foot elevation gain

On the map, Walnut Creek County Park appears as a green worm wriggling through a suburbanized corner of the San Jose Hills. On the ground, the long, narrow park seems even more removed from its civic surroundings than indicated on the map.

Walnut Creek is really a creek. No cement channel to contain it. It runs even during drought years. You might even get your feet wet crossing it. Sure, it eventually meets the fate of all county waterways and becomes incarcerated by various flood control works, but for more than two miles, through Walnut Creek County Park, the creek runs free.

The 4-mile creekside trail can be enjoyed in a couple of different ways. You can walk it one way with a car shuttle, or as a 4-mile out and back, or cross San Dimas Avenue and add a 6-mile loop of Frank G. Bonelli Regional County Park.

DIRECTIONS TO TRAILHEAD: Exit the Foothill Freeway (210) on San Dimas Avenue. Head south a short ways, passing under the freeway overpass and park on the Avenue's shoulder on your right. Signed Walnut Creek Trail begins here.

THE HIKE: From San Dimas Avenue, leave the noisome freeway behind and descend into the tranquil canyon. The narrow canyon isolates you from the busy world beyond. You'll pass a nmber of side trails, most of which meander along the other side of the creek.

You'll meander under the shade of coastal live oak and the California black walnut, which the canyon its name. Depending on the year's rainfall, there's often not much trail to hike once you reach a point about 2.5 miles from the trailhead. the Puente Street bridge or, a bit farther, Covina Hills Road, make good turn-around points.

BONELLI REGIONAL PARK

BONELLI PARK TRAIL
6-mile loop of Frank G. Bonelli Park

Considering that two of the park's borders are the Foothill and San Bernardino Freeways, Bonelli offers more peace and solitude than one might expect. Fourteen miles of trail cross the park's chaparral-covered hills and lead through quiet canyons shaded by oak and walnut groves.

The Los Angeles Flood Control District built Puddingstone Dam in the San Jose Hills near San Dimas. Completed in 1928 for the purpose of capturing and storing rainwater and storm runoff, the dam created a 250-acre lake, which soon attracted swimmers and fishermen, and has remained a popular destination ever since.

As the population of the San Gabriel Valley mushroomed during the 1950s and 1960s, the State Department of Parks and Recreation began purchasing land around the reservoir. Puddingstone Reservoir State Park as it was known, remained a little-developed, low-key place until 1970, when the property was transferred to Los Angeles County.

Today, the park features the aquatic amusement park Raging Waters, a golf course, giant RV campground and more. The 2,000-acre park, the county's second-largest, has long been the center of controversy between those who want to further develop the park and those who would prefer that the park's hills and canyons remain wild.

Plantations of pepper, eucalyptus, cedar and pine have been planted in the park. Wildlife includes squirrels, cottontail rabbits, blacktail rabbits, raccoons and deer. About 130 bird species have been counted.

Trails and trail junctions are rarely signed, but the paths don't stray too far from park roads and landmarks, so you won't get lost. Your best bet for hiking Bonelli is to pick up a park map from headquarters and improvise your own route.

DIRECTIONS TO TRAILHEAD: Exit the Foothill Freeway (210) on Via Verde Road. Park in the CalTrans lot just west of the freeway. There is a vehicle parking fee; no charge to walk in.

THE HIKE: From the CalTrans parking lot, cross (with caution) to the south side of Via Verde Road and follow the sidewalk over the freeway overpass into the park. Look right (south) for the path signed "Equestrian Trail." The trail enters the bougainvillea-draped mouth of the underpass beneath Via Verde. Ever-adaptive mud swallows have affixed their nests to the ceiling of the underpass.

Emerging from the underpass, you'll follow the horse trail into a quieter world. Crossing slopes covered with ceanothus, thistle and prickly pear cactus, the

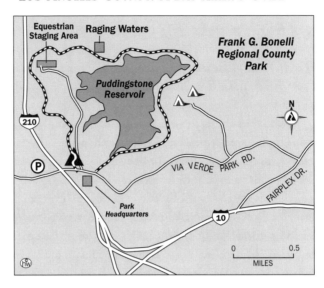

trail soon offers its first view of Puddingstone Reservoir. Depending on the day's ozone level, the San Gabriel Mountains rise majestically or murkily before you. In spring, the hills are green and brightened with mustard and California poppies, but most of the year, they're bare and brown.

The trail descends into a shallow, walnut-shaded canyon, and crosses a (usual-ly dry) creek. Nearing the park's equestrian center, the path emerges from the greenery and reaches a fork located by a thicket of blackberry bushes. The left fork ascends a hillock and dead-ends at an overlook high above Raging Waters. On clear days, this overlook offers a panorama from Mt. Baldy to San Bernardino. You'll take the right fork, proceed along a fence line, then switchback up a jimson weed- and monkeyflower-dotted slope to Boater Picnic Area. The trail descends an oak- and pine-shaded draw, passes a fig tree, then joins a fire road that leads near the Raging Waters amusement park.

Crossing Puddingstone Road, near the entrance to Raging Waters, you'll pick up the signed Equestrian Trail, which soon deposits you at a boat-launching area on the north side of the reservoir. Now your improvisation begins in earnest.

Join the paved walkway and head east along the north shore of the reservoir. When the walkway gives out, pick up the unmarked dirt trail that continues east then south along the moist, willow-choked lakeshore. Perched on the hill above you is the park's campground. You'll join a paved bike path and pass several picnic areas.

After passing through well-named Picnic Valley walk up Eucalyptus Park Road to its junction with Via Verde Park Road. At this point you're just about opposite park headquarters. A right turn and a short walk along Via Verde will return you to the starting point.

❧ Marshall Canyon Park

MARSHALL CANYON TRAIL
7-mile loop through Marshall Canyon with 800-foot elevation gain; shorter walks possible

For several years this semi-wild area above San Dimas and Claremont has been something of a secret—frequented by very few hikers. County park planners say Marshall Canyon will remain as "open space"—something to be thankful for in the fast-growing eastern edge of the metropolis.

Marshall Canyon and its neighbor, Live Oak Canyon, are shaded with oak, alder and sycamore. From atop the canyon walls, walkers gain great clear-day views of the mountains to the north and San Gabriel Valley to the south. Depending on time and inclination, the walker can fashion a number of loop trips ranging from 2 to 8 miles.

DIRECTIONS TO TRAILHEAD: Follow the Foothill Freeway (210) to its end, continuing east on Highway 30 and still farther east on Foothill Boulevard. Turn left, north on Wheeler Avenue, ascend to Golden Hill Road and turn right. You'll see signs for Marshall Canyon Golf Course. Just before the road turns right toward Live Oak Reservoir, turn left into a dirt parking lot.

THE HIKE: The trail begins at the east end of the lot and soon begins descending into the Marshall Canyon. During winter, the snow-covered San Gabriel Mountains framed by oaks are a picturesque sight.

Just before a creek crossing, the trail splits. Marshall Canyon is to the left, Live Oak Canyon to the right. (The trails intersect again, so you may choose either.) Marshall Canyon Trail crosses the creek a couple times, then rises out of the canyon as a dirt road.

Rather than traveling a northeast course through the canyon, it's enjoyable to wind along in a half-circle toward a prominent water tower and partake of the fine ridgetop views. Atop the ridgeline, the trail roller-coasters along. Turn left on signed Miller Road, then descend into Live Oak Canyon. At a three-way junction, continue a hundred yards along the main fire road to a picnic area. Enjoy this oak-shaded retreat, then double back and look sharply right for the footpath descending into Live Oak Canyon.

The canyon's oaks are accompanied by sycamores, walnuts, cottonwoods, mosses and ferns. It's a most delightful 0.5 mile descent to the canyon bottom. Continue your descent to an unsigned junction. The right fork follows Marshall Canyon back to the trailhead. Bear left and meander along with Live Oak Canyon 1.5 miles back to the trailhead.

❧ RANCHO SANTA ANA BOTANIC GARDEN

WOODLAND AND RIPARIAN TRAILS
1 mile or so round trip

On the right day, in the right light, this botanic garden offers a scene from a 1920s postcard: wildflower-bedecked fields in the foreground, snow-capped Mt. Baldy in the background.

Located in the foothills of the San Gabriel Valley, this botanical research and educational institution features a 40-acre collection of native California plants. Trails lead to desert, coastal, woodland and riparian plant communities.

Native California flora (more than 1,500 species) is the emphasis at Ranch Santa Ana Botanic Garden. Particularly prominent are a multitude of manzanita and a ceanothus (California lilac) collection that's attracted nationwide attention.

Although the garden welcomes hikers, its main orientation is toward science. Affiliated with the Claremont Colleges, it has a modern botany lab and a huge herbarium. The garden has developed, nurtured and introduced to nurseries many varieties of plants that have in turn greatly influenced Southern California landscaping.

The walker will enjoy stepping down the garden paths, which explore several representative plant communities. Highlights include a collection of more than two dozen California conifers, the Coastal Garden, and the Desert Garden which displays California cactus species plus related succulents and desert shrubs.

DIRECTIONS TO TRAILHEAD: Rancho Santa Ana Botanic Garden is located on College Avenue, north of Foothill Boulevard and east of Indian Hill Boulevard in Claremont. From the San Bernardino Freeway (10) exit on Indian Hill Boulevard, travel 2 miles north to Foothill Boulevard, turn right, and proceed 3 blocks east to College Avenue.

CHAPTER TEN

Puente Hills

Bounded by the City of Industry on the north,
Hacienda Heights on the east, Whittier on the south
and west, the Puente Hills provides creatures with
habitat and an uninterrupted travel corridor. The hills,
which rise from 400 to 1,400 feet in elevation,
offer San Gabriel Valley residents a natural backdrop,
and hikers many miles of trail to roam.
The hills have two unusual claims to fame:
Rose Hills is the single largest memorial park in the world.
Puente Hills Landfill is the largest in the U.S.;
"tipping fees" collected have funded considerable
parkland acquisition in the hills.

❀ HELLMAN WILDERNESS PARK

HELLMAN, TANK AND SIDE TRAILS (see map page 149)
2.5 mile loop with 400-foot elevation gain; to Sycamore Canyon entrance is 5.5 miles round trip with 400-foot elevation gain

Sure wish Hellman Park was around when I spent my freshman year at Whittier College way back when. Instead of jogging through the streets for exercise, I would have gone trail-running through the park and on more extended adventures up and down the Whittier Hills.

Bordered on two sides by Rose Hills Memorial Park and on the other two sides by the far fringes of Whittier, this 200-acre park is perched above the college in the Whittier Hills, the westernmost region of the Puente Hills. Hellman's attractions include great clear-day views earned by the aerobic workout required to climb from the trailhead to the ridgeline overlooking Sycamore Canyon. The views can include the San Gabriel Valley, downtown Los Angeles, the Pacific and Catalina Island.

DIRECTIONS TO TRAILHEAD: If you're familiar with Whittier and Whittier College, head up Greenleaf Avenue to the entrance of Hellman on your right.

Otherwise, from the 605 Freeway on the northern outskirts of Whittier, exit on Rose Hill Road and head east a half-mile to Workman Mill Road. Turn right. Note the entrance to Sycamore Canyon Park on your left as you pass by and continue to Beverly Boulevard. Turn left on Beverly and follow it first south then west to Greenleaf Avenue. Turn left on Greenleaf and travel 1.5 miles to the entrance of Hellman Park on your right.

THE HIKE: Stay left and walk along the left side of the covered reservoir. The trail turns toward the back side of the reservoir and looks like it's coming to an end, but no . . . it resumes as a dirt track heading north up the canyon bottom. Soon the path abruptly ascends in a northeasterly direction by means of steep switchbacks, some accompanied by pipe handrails.

The trail reaches the canyon wall and continues climbing up a brush-and prickly pear cactus-dotted ridge. Look right (southeast) and you'll see your return route—the trail on the other side of the canyon.

At the top of the ridge you'll intersect unsigned Tank Fire Road and head right. (Left on this ridgetop road takes you toward Sycamore Canyon Park.) Take in the grand view to the north of Rose Hills Memorial Park, particularly the Fo Guang Shan Buddhist Columbarium, the largest Buddhist pagoda in the U.S. Clear-day views of the San Gabriel Valley to the south can be spectacular. After a half-mile or so, you'll reach an unsigned junction with Side Fire Road, a footpath that descends the canyon wall amongst chaparral and sage flora back to the trailhead.

❀ HACIENDA HILLS

AHWINGA, NATIVE OAK, SCHABARUM TRAILS
5-mile loop with 700-foot elevation gain

For more than 25 years, the Seventh Avenue Trailhead, as it was known, provided access (and little else) to the Puente Hills trail system. In 2005, vast improvements were made, and this key entryway renamed the Hacienda Hills Trailhead.

Trailhead improvements include better parking, restrooms, native plant landscaping, interpretive panels, wrought iron entry gates that are works of art, and improved trail signage. Some fine hiking trails were constructed to link with the pre-existing dirt service roads built by ranchers and oil companies.

Hacienda Hills Trailhead is the gateway to a 225-acre reserve set aside as a mitigation measure after an approved expansion of the nearby mega-landfill. The considerable conservation successes that have occurred in the Puente Hills have been funded by the Puente Hills Landfill Native Habitat Preservation Authority, which collects "tipping fees" from the Puente Hills Landfill, the largest landfill in the U.S. Created in 1994, this agency has purchased Powder Canyon, Sycamore Canyon and other key parcels in the hills.

A loop trail from the Hacienda Hills Trailhead offers the hiker a great introduction to the Puente Hills. Excellent views reward the hiker for the exertion required to reach the crest of the hills.

En route, you'll view typical flora, with coastal sage scrub thriving on south-facing slopes, and oak woodland in the arroyos. This diversity of habitats, woodland and scrubland, attract abundant birds, both resident and migratory. Squirrels and rabbits are commonly sighted as are coyotes and mule deer.

Millions of years ago, seismic activity thrust these hills upward from the

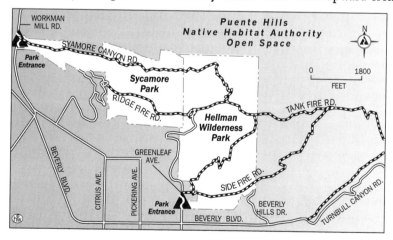

valley floor. Long eroded by wind and water, the hills now stand 400 to 1,400 feet in elevation.

As you hike the rugged hills, you'll understand why the precipitous, unstable slopes discouraged several generations of home-builders.

DIRECTIONS TO TRAILHEAD: From the Pomona Freeway (60) in Hacienda Heights, exit on Seventh Avenue and head south four blocks to the avenue's end at Orange Grove Avenue. Park in the small lot by the signed trailhead.

THE HIKE: Meander into the park on signed Ahwinga Trail alongside a bioswale, an environment you can learn about via strategically posted interpretive signs. The path diverts onto asphalt road for a short distance then switchbacks up the canyon wall, soon offering grand views of the San Gabriel Valley.

After you crest a minor ridge you'll reach a horse tie and an unsigned junction. Join right forking Native Oak Trail which descends into a lovely woodland, and descends some more nearly back to Orange Avenue and the edge of suburbia.

Next the serious climb starts, where the hiker experiences both the beauty of the hills on the one hand and the enormity of the Puente Hills Landfill on the other.

Close to the crest, you'll pass the unsigned junction with steep Puma Trail and soon thereafter reach a junction with unsigned Schabarum Trail.

Clear-day views from the ridgetop include the San Gabriel Valley to the north and the coastal plain to the south. Looking east, you'll see the range extending to the Orange County line, where the Puente Hills transition into the Chino Hills.

Schabarum Trail follows a fence line to a meeting with Ahwinga Trail, which you'll take on a pleasant mile of downhill hiking back to the junction with Native Oak Trail. From the junction, retrace your steps back to the trailhead.

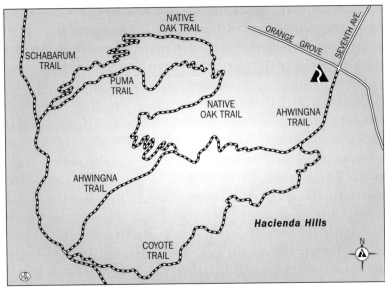

❂ PUENTE HILLS

PUENTE HILLS SKYLINE TRAIL

From Seventh Avenue to Overlook is 5 miles round trip with 800-foot
elevation gain; to Rio Hondo College is 5 miles round trip with 800-foot
gain; to Schabarum Park is 12 miles one-way with 1,000-foot gain

The Puente Hills divide the Los Angeles Basin into a northern one-third and a
southern two-thirds. North is the San Gabriel Valley, an alluvium-filled basin.
South of the hills is a coastal plain, a flatland tilted gently toward the Pacific.

Puente Hills Skyline Trail, under the jurisdiction of the Los Angeles County
Parks Department, extends through the canyons and over the mustard-covered
crests of the hills. This tramp through the Puente Hills offers both short and
lengthy samples of the Skyline Trail. All the options offer fine clear-day views of
the metropolis from scenic overlooks.

DIRECTIONS TO TRAILHEAD: Exit the Pomona Freeway (60) on
Seventh Avenue and drive four blocks south to its end at Orange Avenue. Park
near the traffic barrier. (To reach Schabarum Regional Park, end point for one of
this day hike's options, exit the Pomona Freeway on Azusa Avenue. Proceed
south and turn left on Colima, then right into the park.)

THE HIKE: Ramble up Seventh Avenue Trail, a dirt road beyond the traffic barrier. Pass some private horse corrals and ascend briefly on a paved road to a
San Gabriel Water Company facility. Here a dirt trail picks up and you begin
ascending a mile though a small forest of thistle and mustard. You reach a long
plateau and are treated to views of the San Gabriel Valley. Atop the plateau, you
intersect the Puente Hills Skyline Trail.

Bear right on the Puente Hills Skyline Trail, following a fence along the
plateau's perimeter. The land belongs to Rose Hills Memorial Park, but the county has easements for its trail system. The cemetery is located just on the other side
of the hill.

After hiking the length of the mustard-smothered plateau, you'll reach an
unmarked junction. Bear left here and ascend the hill. From the overlook, where a
missile facility once stood, you can see Whittier to the south, San Gabriel Valley
to the north. On clear winter days, you'll spot the Pacific and Catalina on one side,
and snow-capped Mt. Baldy and the San Gabriel Mountains on the other.

Return the same way, loop back by another trail back to Seventh Avenue
Trail, or continue on to Rio Hondo College.

To reach Rio Hondo College: From the overlook, the trail stays briefly with a
crumbling road, passes another picnic area, then veers off from the road at an

unsigned junction. You look down at the gardens of Rose Hills Memorial Park. Civilization grows more evident as you descend toward Workman Mill Road. The trail leads to North Drive at Rio Hondo College.

For the full Puente Hills experience, Schabarum Park-bound hikers will bear left on the Skyline Trail. A thicket of prickly pear cactus lines the trail. A right turn at an unmarked junction keeps you on the trail, which descends through sage and monkeyflowers into Turnbull Canyon. After a short ascent, the trail reaches and crosses Turnbull Canyon Road. More climbing brings you to an overlook for fine views of downtown Los Angeles, the Westside and the Pacific.

The trail angles toward the suburb of Hacienda Heights, and actually passes right behind some homes (with swimming pools that look inviting on a hot day), before dropping down to Colima Road. Follow the pedestrian-equestrian underpass underneath Colima. The trail then ascends to Hacienda Boulevard, where the hiker makes use of another pedestrian-equestrian underpass.

The Skyline Trail is anything-but for the next half-mile as it turns southeast and follows a culvert alongside Hacienda Boulevard. This trail ends at Leucadia Road, where the hiker joins a fire road and begins ascending above La Habra Heights. Stay right on the fire road at a junction and pass a locked gate. The trail ascends through a eucalyptus grove and passes another of the many microwave towers in the Puente Hills. Civilization—in the form of Puente Hills Mall and the Pomona Freeway—appears close-in to the north. The trail descends a last mile to the wide lawns and picnic areas of Schabarum Park.

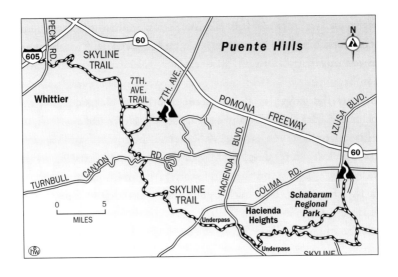

❁ SCHABARUM REGIONAL PARK

SCHABARUM TRAIL

5 mile round trip loop of park with 700-foot elevation gain

County Supervisor (from 1972-1990) Pete Schabarum is remembered by Schabarum Avenue in Irwindale and Schabarum Senior Center in South El Monte. More surprisingly, to conservationists, are Schabarum Regional Park and Schabarum Trail.

Park-lovers were not at the top of his list; he once said of environmentalists: "A lot of them are living out there, in nice rural areas, and they don't want to be disturbed. I don't blame them. Why should they give a damn about the guy next door, sitting on acres of undeveloped property that's doing nothing for him? They don't care what's fair. But I do."

For a decade and a half, Otterbein was the name of this regional park; in 1989 it was renamed for Schabarum. At the park office is a Presidential library-like display of Schabarum's political career, complete with trophies, newspaper clippings and photos and plaques.

Schabarum Park is a mile-long band of green full of happy picnickers. Schabarum Trail explores the brush-covered slopes—the wilder part of the park.

DIRECTIONS TO TRAILHEAD: From the Pomona Freeway in Hacienda Heights, exit on Azusa Avenue. Head south a short ways to Colima and turn left to the entrance to the park on your right. The signed trail begins behind some restrooms near the park entrance.

THE HIKE: The trail tacks this way and that as it ascends a steep hillside. Almost a mile out, you reach a junction and Schabarum Trail splits. (The left branch goes to a corral and horse rental facility). Take the right branch, which climbs steeply for a long mile toward the brushy hilltops.

When you meet Skyline Trail, turn left (east) climbing a little bit more of a hillock, then beginning your descent back to the park. When you reach the park equestrian center, you can return to the trailhead either via a bridle path that parallels the park road, or by way of an asphalt path that bisects the park's long picnic grounds.

✵ POWDER CANYON

POWDER CANYON TRAIL
From Old Fullerton Road to Schabarum Park is 3 miles round trip with 300-foot elevation gain

Powder Canyon, 517 acres managed as a Habitat Authority Wilderness Reserve, beckons the hiker with attractive walnut groves and oak woodland. The canyon is relatively undisturbed habitat in the middle of the Puente Hills; in fact, the canyon is part of what's called the Puente Hills Significant Ecological Area, one of the last remaining natural areas in the hilly region of eastern L.A. County and one of the few with a relatively undisturbed, self-contained watershed. One of the larger canyons in the hills, Powder Canyon boasts particularly large complexes of oak woodland and oak riparian forest.

The canyon's trail system links with Schabarum Trail (Skyline Trail).

DIRECTIONS TO TRAILHEAD: Three entrances to the reserve are situated along Old Fullerton Road from Harbor Boulevard to East Road. Large green "Habitat Authority Wilderness Reserve" signs are posted at these entrances, which have very limited parking nearby. I prefer the easternmost trailhead located a short distance from Harbor Boulevard,

Powder Canyon can also be accessed from two more locales: Leucandia Drive off of Hacienda Boulevard and from the horse stables located in Schabarum Park.

THE HIKE: Trails lead through the main canyon and several tributaries, as well as onto the canyon walls. The paths cross brushy slopes, dip into oak-lined ravines and ascend to ridgetop views of the San Gabriel Valley.

For a longer hike, continue west on a dirt road (part of the Skyline Trail). This winding path, which locals appreciate for its springtime wildflower displays, leads to a trailhead at the end of Leucandia Road.

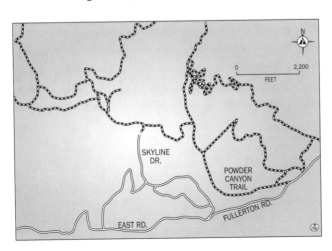

CHAPTER ELEVEN

San Gabriel Mountains

Sixty miles long, twenty miles wide, the San Gabriels
bless Los Angeles by keeping out hot desert winds and
curse it by keeping in the smog. Most of the mountains
and some 800 miles of trail are included in the
Angeles National Forest, one of the most heavily used
national forests in America. Hikers are drawn
to 10,064-foot L.A. County high point Mt. Baldy,
lovely foothill arroyos and forests of pine and incense cedar.
For more than a century, ever since the dawn of the first
Great Hiking Era, the front range and high country
of the San Gabriels have delighted Southland residents
seeking quiet retreats and tranquil trails.

🦅 LITTLE TUJUNGA CANYON

OAK SPRING TRAIL

From Gold Creek Road to Oak Spring is 3.5 miles round trip with 1,000 foot gain; to Yerba Buena Ridge Road is 6 miles round trip with 1,800-foot gain

We hikers—not to mention freeway commuters—know the Los Angeles River as a cement-lined flood control channel. It's surely not a thing of beauty.

Ah, but the river's source is another story; it hasn't been tamed or touched by engineers, nor engulfed by the metropolis. Oak Spring is a river source and a great place to relax.

Oak Spring Trail follows Gold Creek, a tributary of Little Tujunga Creek. True to its name, Gold Creek yielded some fair-sized nuggets. The gold is long-gone and these days the land belongs to Angeles National Forest and a few private ranchers.

Another lure of this trail is the views of city and forest from Yerba Buena Ridge. Vistas to the south take in the San Fernando Valley while those to the north include the one-time Paradise Movie Ranch where many a Western was filmed.

You can begin or conclude the hike by using the Doc Larsen Trail, which leads east from the Forest Service Tujunga work center to an intersection with Oak Spring Trail. Just up Oak Spring Trail from this intersection is Fascination Spring, another oak-shaded retreat.

DIRECTIONS TO TRAILHEAD: From the Foothill Freeway (210) in Pacoima, exit on Osborne Street. Head north on Osborne, which soon becomes Little Tujunga Canyon Road and travel 4 miles to Gold Creek Road. Turn right and wind a short mile to signed Oak Spring trailhead on your right. Park in the oak-fringed lot by the trailhead.

THE HIKE: The path crosses Gold Creek and immediately begins its ascent, soon leaving shady Gold Creek Canyon and heading into the high chaparral. Top one minor ridge, then another, and enjoy good clear-day views of the San Fernando Valley as well as the handsome foothills to the north.

The trail then descends to Oak Spring. The spring is a modest enough source for the Los Angeles River, but the shady surroundings are a delight. Linger at this tranquil spot before deciding whether to head back the way you came or climb Yerba Buena Ridge for the fine view.

TRAIL CANYON

TRAIL CANYON TRAIL
To Trail Canyon Falls is 3 miles round trip with a 700-foot elevation gain
to Trail Canyon Falls; to Tom Lucas Camp is 8 miles round trip
with a 2,000-foot gain

Trail Canyon Trail isn't quite as redundant as it sounds. The "Trail" in Trail
Canyon refers not to a footpath but to the "trail" left by tiny flakes of gold found
in the gravel of the canyon's creekbed. Turn of the 20th-century placer miners
worked the creek, but the "trail" didn't lead to any riches.

The real wealth of Trail Canyon is in its scenery: steep canyon walls that con-
ceal a bubbling creek and a surprising waterfall. During dry months and drought
years, the creek is a pokey watercourse, but swollen by rain and runoff it becomes
lively, even raging. The path to the falls and to the trail camp crosses the creek
numerous times; be careful at times of high water.

Beyond the falls, the trail leads to shady Tom Lucas Camp, named for a grizzly bear hunter and early forest ranger.

DIRECTIONS TO TRAILHEAD: From the Foothill Freeway (210) in
Sunland, exit on Sunland Boulevard. Head east on Sunland, which soon merges
with Foothill Boulevard. Continue to Mt. Gleason Avenue, turn north (left) and
drive to its end at a T at Big Tujunga Canyon Road. Turn right and proceed 5
miles to a dirt road on the left, where a sign indicates parking for Trail Canyon.
The road ascends 0.25 mile then forks; descend 0.25 mile to the right to an oak-
shaded parking area.

THE HIKE: The trail, a closed fire road, passes some private cabins and
arrives at the creek. The road ends and the footpath begins 0.75 mile from the
trailhead at a creek crossing.

Trail Canyon Trail heads up-creek in the shade of sycamores, oak and alder.
After a half-mile, the path switchbacks up the canyon's chaparral-covered west
wall. After a couple of bends in the trail, look for Trail Canyon Falls below.

The side trail to the falls is a precipitous path, made by use, not design; proceed at your own risk. An alternative route to the falls is to simply bushwhack up
Trail Canyon from the point back where the trail leaves the canyon. The latter
route is safer, except at times of high water.

Past the side trail to the falls, Trail Canyon Trail drops back into the canyon,
crossing and recrossing the creek for 2.5 miles to Tom Lucas Trail Camp. This
oak- and alder-shaded camp is perched on the edge of a meadow watered by the
headwaters of Trail Canyon Creek. The meadowland is known as Big Cienega.

❧ BIG TUJUNGA CANYON

GRIZZLY FLAT TRAIL
From Big Tujunga Creek to Grizzly Flat is 5 miles round trip
with 900-foot elevation gain

These days you won't find any grizzlies atop Grizzly Flat, just a few hikers enjoying a pine-shaded retreat above one of L.A.'s more renowned canyons–Big
Tujunga.

During the 19th century, a large population of grizzlies roamed the San
Gabriel Mountains. The bears frightened early miners and settlers, and in later
years, had many a run-in with sportsmen and forest rangers. Big Tujunga Canyon
was particularly attractive habitat to the big bears; in fact, the last wild grizzly in
Southern California was killed in the lower reaches of the canyon in 1916.

Grizzly Flat Trail explores Tujunga Canyon, then rises into the storied hills
where notorious highwayman Tiburcio Vasquez eluded a posse in 1874. Vasquez,
after robbing a San Gabriel Valley rancher, rode over the top of the San Gabriels,
descended north along a then-unnamed creek to Big Tujunga Canyon, and made
good his escape. The unnamed creek, which cuts through the eastern edge of
Grizzly Flat, has since been known as Vasquez Creek.

Big Tujunga Canyon–or "Big T" as it's sometimes nicknamed–has certainly
felt the hand of man. Its creek has been dammed and diverted by the Los Angeles
County Flood Control District. The purpose of these flood control efforts is to
control the runoff of Big Tujunga Creek and prevent it from rushing into the
eastern lowlands of the San Fernando Valley.

Damming a wild, but seasonal, mountain stream such as Big Tujunga solves
one problem but creates another: when rains swell the creek, millions of cubic
yards of sand and gravel are carried downstream and clog up flood control structures. Obviously, to be effective, a flood control reservoir should not be filled with
rock debris. So the debris must be hauled away. But where?

The urban mountaineer may ponder a not altogether facetious question: If
Los Angeles and its flood control projects keep growing and we keep carting away
rock debris, will we one day haul our mountains entirely away?

Grizzly Flat Trail departs from Stonyvale Picnic Area, one of the less-visited
locales in the front range of the San Gabriel Mountains. The trail, while not difficult, does require four crossings of Big Tujunga Creek, and should be avoided
after heavy rains and during times of high water.

DIRECTIONS TO TRAILHEAD: From the Foothill Freeway (210) in
Sunland, exit on Sunland Boulevard and head west to Foothill, continuing west

Front-range canyons are a hiker's delight.

to Mt. Gleason Avenue. Turn left and drive 1.5 miles to a stop sign. Turn right, proceed 6 miles to Vogel Flat Road, and turn right again. The road drops to a stop sign. To the right is a Forest Service fire station. Turn left and park by Stonyvale Picnic Area.

THE HIKE: The trail begins at a vehicle barrier at the east end of Stonyvale Picnic Area. Almost immediately you cross Big Tujunga Creek. Small trail markers keep you on the path, which crosses a boulder field and fords the creek three more times.

A bit more than a mile from the trailhead, Big Tujunga creek and canyon bend northeast, but the trail heads right, south. Soon you'll begin ascending up oak- and chaparral-covered slopes. After a mile, you'll dip to a seasonal fern-lined creek, then ascend briefly to grassy Grizzly Flat. The Forest Service planted pines here in 1959, shortly after a fire scorched the slopes above Big Tujunga.

From Grizzly Flat you can make your way northeast a few hundred yards to spruce-shaded Vasquez Creek. Picnic here or at Grizzly Flat and return the same way.

❧ MT. LUKENS

STONE CANYON TRAIL
From Vogel Flats to Mt. Lukens is 8 miles round trip
with 3,200-foot elevation gain

Mt. Lukens, a gray whale of a mountain beached on the eastern boundary of Los Angeles, is the highest peak within the city limits. A hike up this mile-high mountain offers a great aerobic workout and terrific clear-day views of the metropolis.

Theodore P. Lukens, for whom the mountain is named, was a Pasadena civic and business leader, and an early supporter of the first scientific reforestation effort in California. A self-taught botanist, Lukens believed that burnt-over mountainsides could be successfully replanted. During 1899 alone, Lukens and fellow mountaineers planted some 65,000 seeds in the mountains above Pasadena.

After the death of Lukens in 1918, a 5,074-foot peak was named to honor the one-time Angeles National Forest Supervisor and Southern California's "Father of Forestry." Stone Canyon Trail is by far the nicest way to ascend Mt. Lukens. (Other routes are via long wearisome fire roads.) The trail climbs very steeply from Big Tujunga Canyon over the north slope of Lukens to the peak. (Another way to climb Mt. Lukens is via Haines Canyon Road. Consult the Deukmejian Wilderness Park trail description.)

Carry plenty of water on this trail; none is available en route. It's fun to unfold a city map on the summit to help you identify natural and man-made points of interest.

One warning: In order to reach the beginning of the Stone Canyon Trail, you must cross the creek flowing through Big Tujunga Canyon. During times of high water, this creek crossing can be difficult and dangerous—even impossible. Use your very best judgement when approaching this creek.

DIRECTIONS TO TRAILHEAD: From Foothill Boulevard in Sunland, turn north on Mt. Gleason Avenue and drive 1.5 miles to Big Tujunga Canyon Road. Turn right and proceed 6 miles to Doske Road and make another right. Descend to Stonyvale Road, then left and drive 0.5 mile to a parking area at road's end.

THE HIKE: After carefully crossing the creek, begin the vigorous ascent, which first parallels Stone Canyon, then switchbacks to the east above it. Pausing now and then to catch your breath, enjoy the view of Big Tujunga Canyon.

The trail leads through chamise, ceanothus and high chaparral. Fires have scorched the slopes of Mt. Lukens. Stone Canyon Trail could use a few more shady conifers and a little less brush. Theodore Lukens and his band of tree planters would today be most welcome on the mountain's north slopes!

About 3.5 miles from the trailhead, you'll intersect an old fire road and bear left toward the summit. Atop the peak is a forest of radio antennae.

Old maps called the summit "Sister Elsie" before the peak was renamed for Lukens. As the story goes, Sister Elsie Peak honored a beloved Roman Catholic nun who was in charge of an orphanage for Native American children located in the La Crescenta area.

Enjoy the sweeping panorama of the Santa Monica and Verdugo mountains, Santa Monica Bay and the Palos Verdes Peninsula, and the huge city spreading from the San Gabriel Mountains to the sea.

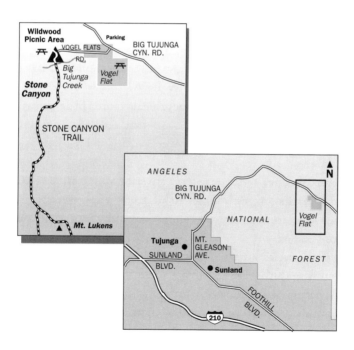

🐝 DEUKMEJIAN WILDERNESS PARK

DUNSMORE CANYON, LE MESNAGER LOOP TRAILS
2 miles round trip semi-loop with 400-foot elevation gain

RIM OF THE VALLEY TRAIL
From Le Mesnager Barn to Haines Canyon Road is 3.2 miles round trip with 1,200-foot elevation gain; to Mt. Lukens summit is 9 miles round trip with 3,000-foot gain

Even the former governor's most ardent supporters concede that naming a wilderness after George Deukmejian was, to say the least, surprising. Ecology was most certainly not the centerpiece of Deukmejian's two terms as governor of California. Naming a prison or a highway after the governor would be more in-synch with the ex-governor's political philosophy, some citizens opine.

The city of Glendale purchased the property in 1989 with monies from park bond funds and from the Santa Monica Mountains Conservancy. The conservation group SWAP (Small Wilderness Area Preservation) was particularly effective in saving the canyons from subdivision and helping to secure the necessary park funds.

Deukmejian Wilderness Park preserves 704 acres in the foothills of the San Gabriel Mountains just above Glendale-La Crescenta. Two steep canyons—Dunsmore and Cook—make up the bulk of the park, which adjoins Angeles National Forest.

In 1898 French immigrant George La Mesnager, vitner and businessman, acquired the property. He planted a vineyard and built a little winery in Dunsmore Canyon. The grapes grown in the canyon were used in the making of fortified brandies. In Los Angeles, the brandies were bottled and marketed under the "Old Heritage" label.

The barn, used for the storage and shipment of grapes, still stands today. It's historical significance arises from its architecture (a rare two-story rock structure with arched roof trusses) and its connection with Southern California's early wine-making industry.

Most of the park consists of chaparral-cloaked hillsides and a seasonal stream lined with oak and alder. On the higher slopes grow scattered big cone spruce.

Bird-watchers will find many native and migrant species: the California towhee, rufous-sided towhee, Berwick's wren, yellow-rumped warbler and that most ubiquitous of chaparral dwellers, the wrentit.

The park's trail system consists of a couple miles of dirt roads (closed to vehicles). One rocky road leads a long mile up Dunsmore Canyon and deadends. Another road circles a hill and offers good San Fernando Valley views. The park's

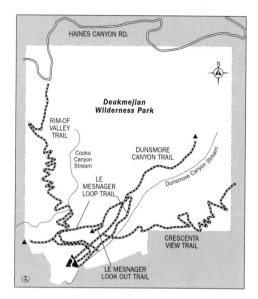

trail system now connects with trails and fire roads in the adjacent Angeles National Forest.

DIRECTIONS TO TRAILHEAD: From the Foothill Freeway (210) in Glendale, exit on Pennsylvania Avenue, and head a half-mile north to Foothill Boulevard. Turn left and travel 1.25 miles to Dunsmore Avenue, turn right and drive a short mile to the avenue's end at Deukmejian Wilderness Park and enter its good-sized parking lot.

THE HIKE: From the stables, walk up-canyon on unsigned Dunsmore Canyon Trail, which is the main park road. The dam and flood control works you see below are mentioned in John McPhee's book, *The Control of Nature.* Anyone who wants to know more about Los Angeles ecology and how engineers have battled the forces of nature in the front range of the San Gabriel Mountains will find McPhee's book fascinating.

The route up Dunsmore Canyon stays above the creekbed and dead-ends at a woodsy perch above the seasonal creek. If you want to proceed from here, the route is trail-less. You can bushwhack and boulder-hop up either of two ravines.

As you return down-canyon, join Le Mesnager Loop Trail, which leads to a good viewpoint of the San Fernando Valley. The trail then skirts Cook Canyon, reaches another overlook by some eucalyptus, and descends back to the trailhead.

For a more ambitious trek, join signed Rim-of-the-Valley Trail. The path dips into Cook Canyon, switchbacks out of it, and reaches a ridgeline. Follow the very steep ridge to Haines Canyon Road.

To reach the top of Mt. Lukens (5,074 feet) continue about another 3 miles, gaining 1,500 feet in elevation. The summit is north of the road and east of the radio towers.

🦅 MT. GLEASON

PACIFIC CREST TRAIL

To Mt. Gleason is 5.5 miles round trip with 1,000 foot elevation gain

At 6,502 feet in elevation, Mt. Gleason stands above lesser summits on the west-ern end of the San Gabriel Mountains. A delightful, well-maintained length of the Pacific Crest Trail crosses the long, forested shoulder of the mountain and an old road leads to Gleason's summit.

On the way to the top of Gleason, the hiker gains vistas of the surrounding Angeles National Forest high country, as well as a view down at shimmering heat waves rolling across the Mojave Desert and the outskirts of Palmdale. You'll enjoy this path because it travels in the welcome shade of many trees: live oak, big-cone spruce, incense cedar and Jeffrey pine.

In 1869, this mountain's pine-spiked shoulders caught the attention of George Gleason, superintendent of the profitable Eureka Mine, located down in Soledad Canyon. Gleason figured the mountain would be an ideal source of timber, neces-sary to brace the mine's tunnels. Gleason and his fellow gold miners dug a rough road up the mountain and built a sawmill near the summit.

Before many boards were hauled down the mountain, gold was discovered north of the summit—by George Gleason himself, some historical accounts sug-gest. The newly built logging road soon became a mining road for prospectors rushing up to the Mt. Gleason Mining District, as it became known. Mt. Gleason's mines never lived up to their rich expectations, though mining contin-ued sporadically for another 50 years.

Mt. Gleason was home to one of California's last grizzly bears, a huge, fierce creature known as Monarch by the shepherds, miners and hunters who lived in the area during the 1880s. In 1889, a cub reporter, assigned by the *San Francisco Examiner* to capture a grizzly alive and tell a sensational story, teamed with some savvy local hunters to capture Monarch. Trapped in a canyon, the crafty bruin was transported to the San Francisco Zoo, where he lived until his death in 1911.

DIRECTIONS TO TRAILHEAD: From the Foothill Freeway (210) in La Canada, drive up Angles Crest Highway (2) 9 miles to Clear Creek Junction. Bear left on Angeles Forest Highway (N3) and proceed some 14 miles north to signed Mt. Gleason Road. Turn left and drive 6 miles west to a signed fork on the road. (No, you don't want to go right to "Prison Camp #16"!) Go left to "Public Camps" and descend 0.5 mile to a saddle and an unsigned turnout on the right side of the road. Park here.

THE HIKE: Find the trail by walking to a locked yellow gate and a sketchy

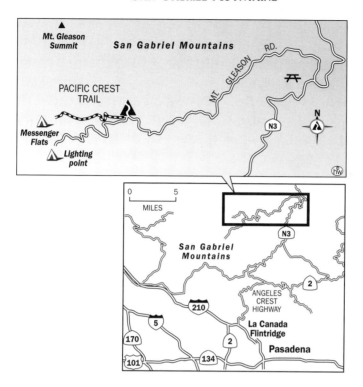

dirt road descending 100 feet to the footpath. Go left (west) on signed Pacific Crest Trail. The path ascends moderately under oaks and mixed conifers. Look for grand desert views about a mile up the PCT. At higher elevation, you'll travel in the company of stately Jeffrey pine.

After a bit more than two miles of hiking, the PCT makes a hairpin switch-back and gains Mt. Gleason's west ridge. Soon thereafter, PCT intersects a dirt road leading south toward the summit. (Before you join the summit road, contin-ue very briefly on the PCT to the lip of the ridge and enjoy far-reaching moun-tain and desert views.)

March up and down several ridgetop hillocks on the dirt road, which transi-tions to a crumbling asphalt road atop Gleason. The top is not a distinct promon-tory but a long ridge. The road traverses the summit ridge and leads to a junction with Mt. Gleason Road.

ARROYO SECO

ARROYO SECO TRAIL (GABRIELINO NATIONAL RECREATION TRAIL)

From Windsor Avenue to Teddy's Outpost is 3 miles round trip; to Gould Mesa Campground is 4 miles round trip; to Paul Little Picnic Area is 6.5 miles round trip with a 400-foot elevation gain; to Oakwilde Trail Camp is 10 miles round trip with a 900-foot gain

During the early decades of this century, Arroyo Seco was an extremely popular place for a weekend outing. About halfway up the wild section of the canyon stood Camp Oak Wilde, a rustic resort constructed in 1911. Hikers and horsemen stayed a night or two or used the hostelry as a rest stop on the way up to Mt. Wilson. During the 1920s, a road was constructed and automobilists traveled the arroyo to Camp Oak Wilde.

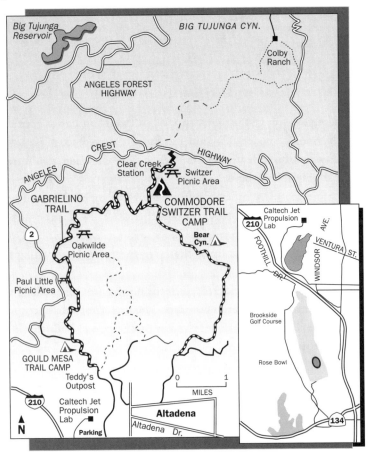

Southern California's "flood of the century" wiped out Oak Wilde in 1938. The awesome torrent also washed away the road and many vacation cabins. A few stone steps and foundations, ivy-covered walls and bridges give today's hiker hints of a time gone by.

Besides the Southern California history lesson, oak-, sycamore- and bay-filled Arroyo Seco has much to offer. The modern-day traveler can walk the old 1920s auto road and newer Forest Service trails to quiet picnic areas. Because the path up the Arroyo Seco is officially part of the Gabrielino National Recreation Trail, it's usually kept in very good condition.

This is a great morning walk. On hot afternoons, however, you might want to exercise elsewhere; smog fills the Arroyo Seco.

DIRECTIONS TO TRAILHEAD: From the Foothill Freeway (210) in Pasadena, take the Arroyo Boulevard/Windsor Avenue exit. Head north on Arroyo, which almost immediately becomes Windsor, and travel 0.75 mile. Just before Windsor's intersection with Ventura Street, turn into the parking lot on your left. From the small lot you can look down into the bottom of the Arroyo Seco and see the Jet Propulsion Laboratory.

THE HIKE: As you walk up Windsor you'll spot two roads. The leftward road descends to JPL. You head right on a narrow asphalt road, closed to vehicle traffic. You'll pass some fenced-off areas and facilities belonging to the Pasadena Water Department and a junction with Lower Brown Mountain Road. A short mile from the trailhead are some Forest Service residences.

The road, dirt now, penetrates the arroyo and enters a more sylvan scene, shaded by oaks and sycamores. Often you can't help but chuckle at the "No Fishing" signs posted next to the creekbed; most of the time the arroyo is quite "seco" and if there are any fish around, they must've walked here.

Teddy's Outpost Picnic Area is your first destination. In 1915, Theodore Syvertson had a tiny roadside hostelry at this site. A half-mile beyond Teddy's is large Gould Mesa Campground, with plenty of picnic tables. Next stop, a short distance past the campground, is a small picnic area called Nino. A mile beyond Gould Mesa Campground is Paul Little Picnic Area.

Now you leave the bottom of the arroyo and climb moderately to steeply up the east wall of the canyon. After curving along high on the wall, the trail then drops back to the canyon floor, where oak-shaded Oakwilde Trail Camp offers a tranquil rest stop. A few stone foundations remind the hiker that Arroyo Seco was once Pasadena's most popular place for a weekend outing.

ᨉ UPPER ARROYO SECO

GABRIELINO NATIONAL RECREATION TRAIL
From Switzer Picnic Area to Switzer Falls is 4 miles round trip with 600-foot elevation loss; to Bear Canyon is 8 miles round trip with 1,000-foot gain; to Oakwilde is 9 miles round trip with 1,400-foot loss

Arroyo Seco is undoubtedly the best-known canyon in Southern California. It's the site of the Rose Bowl and has the dubious distinction of hosting California's first freeway, the Pasadena. But the ten miles of canyon dominated by the freeway bear little resemblance to the ten miles of wild and rugged arroyo spilling from the shoulder of Mt. Wilson.

And the arroyo is rugged. A quiet stream—lined with colonnades of alder, live oak and mountain lilac clinging to the narrow sides of the gorge—cascades over boulders of big gray granite. A walk through the wildest part of Arroyo Seco that visits Switzer Falls and a couple of peaceful trail camps.

Perry Switzer, a carpenter who regained his health in the invigorating San Gabriels, built a trail up the Arroyo Seco and decided to build a trail resort. He put up some rough log cabins, despite arguments that "no one would want to pay for a bed up among the grizzlies, mountain lions and bobcats." He earned the nickname "Commodore" because of his skill in navigating his squadron of burros as they forded the Arroyo Seco. His hospitality made Switzer's the most popular trail camp in the San Gabriels.

The resort passed into the hands of Lloyd Austin, who added a tennis court, chapel and dance floor. A sign across from the resort greeted visitors: "Leave your cars and animals this side of the stream." Switzer-land was popular with hikers well into the 1930s, until Angeles Crest Highway rendered the camp "obsolete."

During the Great Hiking Era, a hiker could venture up the Arroyo Seco and within an hour lose all signs of civilization. Amazingly, you still can today. This hike takes you past the site of Switzer's retreat and visits Switzer Falls. Further exploration of the Arroyo Seco country is possible by taking optional trails.

(See previous hike description of the Lower Arroyo Seco.)

DIRECTIONS TO TRAILHEAD: Take Angeles Crest Highway (2) north from La Canada for 10 miles. A short way past the junction of Angeles Crest and Angeles Forest (N3) Highways, you'll see the Angeles National Forest Clear Creek Information Station on your right. Inquire here about trails or road conditions.

A half-mile past the information station, park in the Forest Service lot on the right side of the highway. Walk down the paved road 0.25 mile to Switzer Picnic Area. The trail begins across the bridge at the lower end of the picnic grounds.

THE HIKE: Cross the bridge and follow the trail into the canyon. The pathway meanders with the stream under oak, alder and spruce. You'll cross and recross the stream several times and do some easy boulder-hopping. Plan to get wet. In some places, stream-crossing is quite difficult in the spring. In a mile, you'll reach Commodore Switzer Trail Camp. Perched on a bench just above the falls, it's an inviting place complete with picnic tables. The creek trail below the camp dead-ends above the falls.

From the camp, cross the stream and follow the trail on the west slope. You'll soon get a nice view of the falls. A signed junction soon appears. To the right (southwest) is the main trail down to Oakwilde and Pasadena. Bear left here and hike down into the gorge of the Arroyo Seco below the falls. When you reach the creek, turn upstream 0.25 mile to the falls. Heed the warning signs and don't try to climb the falls; it's very dangerous.

Return the same way.

To Bear Canyon Trail Camp: Continue down the Arroyo gorge. After 0.75 mile, the trail reaches Bear Canyon and heads east up the canyon, crossing and re-crossing the creek. Along the way are many nice pools. In spring, the water is cold from snowmelt and little sun reaches the canyon floor. The trail, shaded by big cone spruce, closely parallels the creek.

When you look at an Angeles Forest map, you'll discover that Bear Canyon is surrounded on all sides by highways, dams and development. It doesn't make sense that the canyon is so quiet, so pristine, but it is. As you boulder-hop from bank to bank, the only sound you'll hear is that of water cascading over granite and clear pools. Give thanks that there is at least one spot in the front range of the San Gabriels that is untouched wilderness, and continue to Bear Canyon Camp, two miles up the canyon.

To Oakwilde: From the signed junction above Commodore Switzer Trail Camp, continue right on the Gabrielino National Recreation Trail. The trail leaves the main Arroyo Seco canyon, crossed a chaparral ridge, then drops into Long Canyon. It then descends to Arroyo Seco creek bottom and follows the creek an easy mile to Oakwilde Trail Camp.

"Oak Wylde," as it was known during the Great Hiking Era, was a jumping-off place for trips farther up the Arroyo Seco. Pack burro trains connected Oak Wylde with the stage station in Pasadena. The trail camp is located among the crumbling stone foundation of a resort. Alder and oak shade a pleasant camp-ground and picnic area.

Return the same way, or continue down the Arroyo Seco. (See Lower Arroyo Seco trail description.)

❧ MILLARD CANYON, DAWN MINE

MILLARD CANYON TRAIL
From Sunset Ridge to Millard Canyon Falls is 1 mile round trip;
to Dawn Mine is 5 miles round trip with 800-foot elevation gain

Hidden from the metropolis by Sunset Ridge, lush Millard Canyon is one of the more secluded spots in the front range of the San Gabriels. A cold stream tumbling over handsome boulders, a trail meandering beneath a canopy of alder, oak and sycamore, a waterfall and a historic mine, are some of Millard's attractions.

Millard Canyon is best known as the site of the Dawn Mine which, unfortunately for its investors, produced more stories than gold. The mine was worked off and on from 1895, when gold was first discovered, until the 1950s. Enough gold was mined to keep ever-optimistic prospectors certain that they would soon strike a rich ore-bearing vein, but the big bonzana was never found.

You can explore Millard Canyon by two different routes, which lack an official name, but are often referred to as Millard Canyon Trail. An easy half-mile path meanders along the canyon floor to 50-foot Millard Falls. This is a walk suitable for the whole family.

More experienced hikers will enjoy the challenge of following an abandoned trail through Millard Canyon to the site of the Dawn Mine. Enough of the old trail remains to keep you on track, but it's slow going with many stream crossings en route.

DIRECTIONS TO TRAILHEAD: From the Foothill Freeway (210) in Pasadena, exit on Lake Avenue. Drive north four miles, at which point Lake veers left and becomes Loma Alta Drive. Continue a mile to Chaney Trail and turn right. Proceed another mile to a junction atop Sunset Ridge. If you're hiking to Dawn Mine, bear right at this junction and park outside the gate blocking Sunset Ridge Fire Road. If you're bound for Millard Canyon Falls, stay left at the junction and descend to a parking lot at the bottom of the canyon.

THE HIKE: To Millard Canyon Falls: From the parking area at the bottom of Millard Canyon, walk a hundred yards up a fire road to Millard Canyon Campground. Walk through the campground and pick up the signed trail leading to the falls. The trail heads east along the woodsy canyon bottom, crosses the stream a couple times, and arrives at the base of the waterfall. Don't try to climb up, over, or around the falls; people have been injured attempting this foolhardy ascent.

To Dawn Mine: From the Sunset Ridge parking area, head up the fire road. Enjoy the clear-day ridgetop views of the metropolis. You'll soon pass a junction on your left with a trail leading down to Millard Canyon Campground.

A short 0.25 mile from the trailhead, you'll spot signed Sunset Ridge Trail, which you'll join and begin descending into Millard Canyon. A few minutes of walking down the well-graded path will reward you with a view of Millard Canyon Falls.

Near the canyon bottom, you'll meet a trail junction. Sunset Ridge Trail continues along the canyon wall, but you bear left and descend to the

Picnic at Millard Canyon Falls, ca. 1890s

canyon floor. As you begin hiking up-canyon, turn around and note the trail that brought you down to the canyon; it's easy to miss on your return trip.

As you pick your way stream-side amongst the boulders and fallen trees on the canyon floor, you'll follow vestiges of the old trail. Typically, you'll follow a fifty- or hundred-yard stretch of trail, boulder-hop for a bit, cross the stream, then pick up another length of trail. The canyon floor is strewn with lengths of rusting pipe and assorted mining machinery. Several pools, cascades, and flat rocks suggest a stream-side picnic.

After hiking a bit more than a mile up-canyon, you'll find that Millard Canyon turns north. From this turn, it's a bit less than a mile to the Dawn Mine site. Don't go into the mine shaft. Darkness and deep holes filled with water make it very dangerous.

Return the same way, and remember to keep a sharp lookout for the trail that leads out of the canyon back to the trailhead.

ECHO MOUNTAIN

SAM MERRILL TRAIL
From Cobb Estate to Echo Mountain is 5 miles round trip
with 1,400-foot elevation gain

Professor Thaddeus Sobieski Coulincourt Lowe's Echo Mountain Resort area can
be visited not only by retracing the tracks of his "Railway to the Clouds" (See
Mt. Lowe Railway hike), but also by way of a fine urban edge trail that ascends
from the outskirts of Altadena.

This historic hike visits the ruins of the one-time "White City" atop Echo
Mountain. From the steps of the old Echo Mountain House are great clear-day
views of the megalopolis. Energetic hikers can join trails leading to Inspiration
Point and Idlehour campground.

Pasadena and Altadena citizens have been proud to share their fascination
with the front range of the San Gabriels. This pride has extended to the trails
ascending from these municipalities into the mountains.

Local citizens, under the auspices of the Forest Conservation Club, built a
trail from the outskirts of Altadena to Echo Mountain during the 1930s. During
the next decade, retired Los Angeles Superior Court clerk Samuel Merrill over-
hauled and maintained the path. When Merrill died in 1948, the trail was named
for him.

Sam Merrill Trail begins at the former Cobb Estate, now a part of Angeles
National Forest. A plaque placed by the Altadena Historical Society dedicates the
estate ground as "a quiet place for people and wildlife forever."

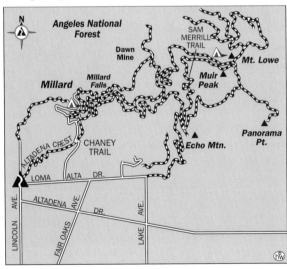

Mt. Lowe Railway on Echo Mountain

DIRECTIONS TO TRAILHEAD: From the Foothill Freeway (210) in Pasadena, exit on Lake Avenue and travel north 3.5 miles to its end at Loma Alta Drive. Park along Lake Avenue.

THE HIKE: From the great iron gate of the old Cobb Estate, follow the trail along the chain-link fence. The path dips into Las Flores Canyon, crosses a seasonal creek in the canyon bottom, then begins to climb. As you begin your earnest, but well-graded ascent, enjoy good, over-the-shoulder views of the San Gabriel Valley and downtown Los Angeles. Two long, steep and mostly shadeless miles of travel brings you to a signed junction. Bear right and walk 100 yards along the bed of the old Mt. Lowe Railway to the Echo Mountain ruins. Just before the ruins is a drinking fountain, very welcome if it's a hot day.

Up top, you'll spot the railway's huge bull wheel, now embedded in cement, and just below is a pile of concrete rubble, all that remains of the railway depot.

Energetic hikers can join signed trails that lead to Mt. Lowe Camp and to Inspiration Point and Idlehour Campground.

The steps and foundation of the Echo Mountain House are great places to take a break and enjoy the view straight down precipitous Rubio Canyon, the route of Lowe's railway. A bit down the mountain to the east stood another hotel—the Chalet—but nothing remains of it.

Echo Mountain takes its name from the echo that supposedly bounces around the semicircle of mountain walls. I've never managed to get very good feedback; perhaps even echoes fade with time.

❦ Rubio Canyon

RUBIO CANYON TRAIL
From Rubio Vista to the falls is about 2 miles round trip with a 200-foot elevation gain.

Nature always has the last word.

Maybe that's the lesson to be learned from the on-and-off-and-on-again waterfalls of Rubio Canyon in the San Gabriel Mountains.

The falls, beloved by Southland hikers for more than a century, were snuffed out in 1998 when Rubio Cañon Land & Water Association workers, attempting to re-route pipe damaged by the 1994 Northridge Earthquake, accidentally triggered a massive rockslide. Tons of rock rubble buried a half-dozen heavenly cascades: Moss Grotto, Ribbon Rock, Grand Chasm, Lodged Boulder, Roaring Rift and Thalehaha.

Hikers were furious, as were local conservationists who, for decades, had questioned why the canyon's sanctity was violated by miles of pipe when the water company's small number of customers could be served by wells and other sources at the base of the mountains. The tiny water company said no way it could afford to clean up the mess. Lawsuits and legal claims were readied. Finally the U.S. Forest Service agreed to build a road into the canyon and haul out the rock debris. The water company, concerned about getting stuck with a $3 million invoice for the Rubio Canyon rock removal, appealed the Forest Service's decision.

But before the Forest Service began trucking out the rocks, before the water company's appeal was heard in court, along came the rain. Lots of it. By some estimates as much as 10 inches monsooned upon this part of the San Gabriel Mountains. The great deluge of October 2004 washed away what the Forest Service intended to haul away and the historic waterfalls returned as quickly as they had vanished.

The Pacific Electric Railway "Red Cars" delivered passengers from locations around the Southland to Rubio Canyon, where a pavilion and hotel were located. After taking refreshments, they boarded the "airships" of the great cable incline, which carried them 3,000 feet (gaining 1,300 feet) straight up to the Echo Mountain Resort Area. In the early years of the railway, guests congregated at the stylish Rubio Pavilion, which was connected to the canyon by way of a system of wooden walkways and stair-steps. These boardwalk trails helped hikers easily reach the lovely waterfalls. Alas for Rubio Pavilion, a devastating thunderstorm (beginning a hundred-year long tradition of such storms) dislodged huge boulders, which then crashed into and demolished the Pavilion. Thereafter Rubio Canyon became a mere utilitarian transfer center for the Mt. Lowe Railway.

I had long wanted to share the delights of Rubio Canyon with my readers but could not, in good conscience, write-up this hike and publish it in one of my guide-books based on what seemed like the slim chance that the Forest Service or private sector would one day restore the waterfalls. When I got word that the spigot had been turned back on, so to speak, I was delighted. Skilled hikers can navigate to higher falls beyond the first ones, but for now, enjoy the pleasure of a short hike into historic Rubio Canyon.

DIRECTIONS TO TRAILHEAD: From the Foothill Freeway (210) in Pasadena, exit on Lake Avenue and head north 3 miles. Make the first right after Altadena Drive on Palm Street, which angles north as Maiden Lane. When you junction Rubio Canyon Road, follow it north to Rubio Crest, turn left, then make a right on Rubio Vista and follow it one block to intersect Pleasant Ridge Drive. Park courteously on the residential streets near the junction of Rubio Vista and Pleasant Ridge Drive. You'll spot the trailhead, posted with warning signs, at the beginning of a pathway that extends alongside a house on the east side of Rubio Vista.

THE HIKE: Departing the Altadena residential area, the narrow foothpath travels the brushy slopes on the lip of Rubio Canyon. As you make a very modest climb, you can look back and get impressive vistas of the San Gabriel Valley and downtown L.A.

About a half-mile out, the trail narrows to almost nothing and we hikers have to crowd up against a pipeline for a short stretch. The path bends and the careful observer can see bits of the cement foundation where Rubio Pavilion once extended across the canyon. Soon after this major bend, the path descends to the boulder-strewn bottom of Rubio Canyon. Next pick your way up-canyon among the rocks and rivulets.

You'll hear the waterfall before you see it. Trail's end, for most everybody but experienced climbers, is at the resurrected double-tiered waterfall. The lower fall is Ribbon Rock; the upper fall is Moss Grotto. Of course, Moss Grotto will be misnomer until the moss and other greenery grow again around the newly uncovered falls. Right after the falls were uncovered it was a very elemental scene—just two rock chutes and falling water.

Beyond Rubio is Grand Chasm. It is relatively easy to reach by cutting up the draw to the left of Moss Grotto/Ribbon Rock about 50 yards and turning left up a use trail, which will take you to the area bounded by the top of Moss Grotto and Grand Chasm Falls.

If you continue up the draw another 50 yards, you get to a bay tree, you cut left again and proceed to Thalehaha Overlook, where you look down on Thalehaha and Roaring Rift Falls. The highest falls, Leontine, is also the largest in the San Gabriel Mountains. Only experienced, nervy hikers skilled at cross country travel to it. Canyon supporters aim to build a trail to the base of the falls.

🦅 MT. LOWE

MT. LOWE RAILWAY TRAIL

From Sunset Ridge to Mt. Lowe Trail Camp is 10 miles round trip
with 2,700-foot gain; to Inspiration Point is 11 miles round trip

Professor Thaddeus Lowe, Civil War balloonist, man of fame and fortune, was
the quintessential California dreamer. His dream was to build a railway into—and
a resort complex atop—the San Gabriel Mountains high above Pasadena. In the
1890s, his dream became a reality.

During the height of its popularity, millions took Professor Lowe's "Railway to
the Clouds" to fine hotels and spectacular views of Southern California. Until it was
abandoned in the 1930s, it was the Southland's most popular tourist attraction.

From Pasadena, visitors rode a trolley up Rubio Canyon, where a pavilion and
hotel were located. After taking refreshments, they boarded the "airships" of the
great cable incline, which carried them 3,000 feet (gaining 1,300 feet) straight up to
the Echo Mountain Resort Area. "Breathtaking" and "hair-raising" were the
most frequent descriptions of this thrilling ride. Atop Echo Mountain was the
White City, with a hotel, observatory, and a magnificent searchlight purchased
from the Chicago World's Fair. When the searchlight swept the mountaintop,
the white buildings of the resort were visible from all over Los Angeles. From
Echo Mountain, tourists could board a trolley and ride another few miles to Mt.
Lowe Tavern at the end of the line.

This historic walk follows the old railway bed, visits the ruins of the White
City and Mt. Lowe Tavern, and concludes with some fine views of Los Angeles
from Inspiration Point. The old railway bed with its gentle seven percent grade
makes for easy walking. An interpretive brochure is (sometimes) available from
Angeles National Forest headquarters in Arcadia. Begin this hike as described
below or from Echo Mountain (see my account of this trail).

DIRECTIONS TO TRAILHEAD: Exit the Foothill Freeway (210) at
Lake Avenue and follow it north to its end. Turn left on Loma Alta Drive. Go
one mile to Chaney Trail Road and turn right. At a Y in the road, take the right
fork to the Sunset Ridge parking area. The trailhead is located at the locked gate,
which bars vehicles from Sunset Ridge Fire Road.

THE HIKE: The trail begins just past the locked gate. Follow the paved
Sunset Ridge Fire Road. You may follow the fire road two miles to the junction
with Echo Mountain Trail, but a more attractive alternative is described below.

Follow the road 0.25 mile to the signed Sunset Ridge Trail on your left. Join
this trail, which parallels the fire road, and leads into peaceful Millard Canyon.

Alpine section of the Mt. Lowe Railway

Near the canyon bottom, the trail forks at a signed junction. Bear right and ascend back up to Sunset Ridge Fire Road. Follow the fire road about 75 yards, and on your right you'll spot the signed junction with Echo Mountain Trail.

To Echo Mountain: Bear right on Echo Mountain Trail, which leads one-half mile over the old railway bed to Echo Mountain. Echo Mountain takes its name from an echo that bounces around the semicircle of mountain walls.

On Echo Mountain are the foundations of Echo Mountain House and the chalet. The most prominent ruin is the large iron bull wheel that pulled the cars up the steep incline from Rubio Canyon. A fire swept Echo Mountain in 1900, leveling all of the White City except the observatory. Picnic tables suggest a lunch stop among the ruins. Leave behind the ruins of the White City, return to Sunset Ridge Fire Road and bear right.

The paved road soon becomes dirt and an interpretive sign at "Cape of Good Hope" lets you know you've joined the Mt. Lowe Railway tour. Continue along the railway bed, passing the attractions that impressed an earlier generation of travelers: Granite Gate, Horseshoe Curve, and the site of the Great Circular Bridge.

Near the top, you'll come to the site of Mt. Lowe Tavern, which burned in 1936. Almost all signs of the tavern are gone, but this peaceful spot under oaks and big cone spruce still extends its hospitality. In its place is Mt. Lowe Trail Camp, which welcomes hikers with shade, water, restrooms and picnic tables.

Before heading down, follow the fire road east and then south for 0.5 mile to Inspiration Point. Where the fire road makes a hairpin left to Mt. Wilson, go right. At Inspiration Point, you can gaze through several telescope-like sighting tubes aimed at Santa Monica, Hollywood and the Rose Bowl. After locating a sight that inspires you, return the same way.

❧ EATON CANYON

EATON CANYON TRAIL
From the Nature Center to Eaton Falls is 3 miles round trip with 200-foot gain

Late one August afternoon in 1877, John Muir set out from Pasadena to begin his exploration of the San Gabriel Mountains. The great naturalist was very impressed with Eaton Falls, as he wrote in his book, *The Mountains of California:* "It is a charming little thing, with a low, sweet voice, singing like a bird, as it pours from a notch in a short ledge, some thirty-five or forty feet into a round mirror-pool."

He spent the night camped with a blindly optimistic, half-Irish, half-Spanish water prospector, who was convinced that his digging would soon result in a wealth of water. Muir was dubious of this cash flow, and the next morning bade his acquaintance farewell and began tramping up the canyon. After enjoying Eaton Falls, Muir followed bear trails, sometimes on all fours, up the chaparral-smothered ridges of the mountains.

It was not the water-seeker Muir met, but Judge Benjamin Eaton, who channeled and piped the canyon's waters to nearby ranches. The judge's neighbors laughed when he planted grapevines, but the vines were quite successful and commanded a high price. Soon many other San Gabriel Valley farmers planted vineyards.

Much of the canyon named for Judge Eaton is now part of Eaton Canyon

Eaton Canyon Falls was a favorite destination of hikers a hundred years ago.

County Park. A nature center has exhibits which emphasize Southern California flora and fauna. Nature trails explore a variety of native plant communities—chaparral, coastal sage, and oak-sycamore woodland.

Eaton Canyon County Park is a busy place on weekends. Family nature walks are conducted by docent naturalists; the park also has birdwalks, natural history classes and children's programs.

The walk up Eaton Canyon to the falls is an easy one, suitable for the whole family. Eaton Canyon Trail leads through a wide wash along the east side of the canyon to a junction with Mt. Wilson Toll Road. In fact, Eaton Canyon Trail was once a toll road itself; fees were collected from 1890 to 1911. The hiker seeking strenuous exercise can join Mt. Wilson Road for a steep, eight-mile ascent of Mt. Wilson.

DIRECTIONS TO TRAILHEAD: From the Foothill Freeway (210) in Pasadena, exit on Altadena Drive. Proceed north 1.75 miles to the signed entrance of Eaton Canyon County Park. Turn right into the park and leave your car in the large lot near the nature center.

THE HIKE: From the parking lot, hike through the attractive grounds of the nature center. Cross the creek, then meander beneath the boughs of large oak trees and pass a junction with a connector trail that leads to the Mt. Wilson Toll Road. Check on conditions before hiking.

To the east, you'll spy the plateau overlooking Eaton Canyon. A hundred years ago this land belonged to the wealthy capitalist and pioneer forester and builder of Venice Beach, Abbott Kinney, and his Kinneloa Ranch. Kinney loved this area and was a bit miffed when a nearby peak was named Mt. Harvard for the university that built an observatory atop the mountain, rather than for him.

The trail leads along the wide arroyo. Eaton Canyon was widened considerably by a 1969 flood that washed away canyon walls. This flood, and the many floods before and since, have spread alluvium, or water-transported sand and rock, across the canyon floor. It takes a hearty group of drought-resistant plants to survive in this soil and Southern California's sometimes not-so-benign Mediterranean climate. Notice the steepness of the canyon's walls. Early Spanish settlers called the canyon "El Precipio."

A mile's travel from the nature center brings you to the Mt. Wilson Toll Road bridge. A right turn on the toll road will take you on a long, steep ascent to the top of Mt. Wilson. A left turn on Mt. Wilson Toll Road will bring you a very short distance to the unsigned junction with Altadena Crest Trail. This rather dull trail travels two miles above the reservoirs and backyards of residential Altadena. Walking 0.5 mile on Altadena Crest Trail to a vista point will reward you with great clear-day views of the Los Angeles Basin.

To reach Eaton Falls, continue straight up Eaton Canyon wash. You'll rock-hop across the creek several times as you walk to trail's end at the falls.

⚜ IDLEHOUR

IDLEHOUR TRAIL
11 miles one way with 4,100-foot elevation loss

Lofty ridges, dramatic canyons and a trail camp cradled in the peaceful woods are a few of the many attractions visited by Idlehour Trail, which offers the hiker a grand tour of the Front Range of the San Gabriel Mountains. For all but the most die-hard hikers, this is a one-way tour, an 11-mile descent from Eaton Saddle at the crest of the range to Eaton Canyon County Park on the outskirts of Altadena.

Bold and beautiful, Eaton is among the most rugged of the range's metropolis-facing canyons. From the head of the canyon under the white visages of San Gabriel Peak and Mt. Markham, a creek cascades all the way down a V-shaped gorge to spill over Eaton Falls near the mouth of the canyon. The great naturalist John Muir called this country "rigidly inaccessible" after an 1877 exploration.

Later a trail was built, but it was no walk in the park. Early hikers stepped gingerly up and down Eaton Canyon via a narrow trail across the wall of the gorge high above the canyon bottom. These days, the well-engineered Mt. Wilson Toll Road offers hikers a safe way around the precipitous lower canyon while the fine Idlehour Trail traverses the canyon's more mellow upper reaches.

During the Southland's Great Hiking Era (1895-1935), hikers ascended Front Range footpaths to Camp Idle Hour, a modest trail resort. The resort (1915 to 1929) was a favorite of hikers who loved its idyllic location in the peaceful shade of oak, bay and spruce.

These days Idlehour Trail Camp, located at about the exact mid-point of this ramble, invites hikers to idle away an hour or so in the same tranquil setting that pleased an earlier generation of travelers.

If car shuttle arrangements for the one-way adventure crimp your plans, the 11-mile round trip hike from Eaton Canyon Park to Idlehour Trail Camp is a worthy substitute.

(Hiker's heads-up: While you might see hikers and cyclists traveling the Mt. Wilson Toll Road between Eaton Canyon and Henninger Flats, a portion of the road is officially closed due to landslides.)

DIRECTIONS TO TRAILHEAD: To Eaton Canyon Park, hike's end point: From the Foothill Freeway (210) in Pasadena, exit on Altadena Drive. Proceed north 1.75 miles to the signed entrance of Eaton Canyon County Park. Turn right into the park and leave your car in the large lot near the nature center.

To start of hike: From the Foothill Freeway (210) in La Canada Flintridge, take the Angeles Crest Highway (2) 14 miles north and east to Mt. Wilson Road. Turn right (south) and drive 2.4 miles to unsigned Eaton Saddle and a parking area.

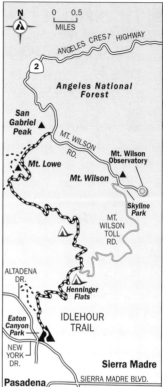

THE HIKE: Head west up Mt. Lowe Fire Road. You'll pass through a tunnel and a half-mile's hike from Eaton Saddle delivers you to Markham Saddle and a junction with two trails.

The fire road continues southwest, the right-forking trail climbs toward San Gabriel Peak, but you angle left onto Mt. Lowe Trail. Continue 0.75 mile and keep proceeding straight when a western branch of Mt. Lowe Trail intersects your route from the right. After another mile of walking, you'll meet a fire road and head south. Pass by another fire road that leads to Mt. Lowe Trail Camp and very soon reach the signed start of Idlehour Trail, some 2.5 miles from the trailhead.

The trail drops through stands of spruce and oak, climbs a short distance over a brushy divide, then resumes its descent into Eaton Canyon, about 4.75 miles from the beginning of this hike.

Idlehour Trail explores Eaton's sylvan beauty under great oaks and maples near the sprightly creek and delivers you to Idlehour Trail Camp with its picnic tables perched on an oak-shaded flat. From the camp, the trail heads 1.5 miles over a ridge to meet Mt. Wilson Toll Road. After a bit more than a mile's descent, you'll pass Henninger Flats, home to great stands of conifers and the Los Angeles County Experimental Nursery. Southern California's finest tree plantation welcomes hikers with shade, water, and campgrounds.

From the flats, 1.75 miles of descent brings you to signed Eaton Canyon Trail. Take the trail left and switchback 0.5 mile down to meet a wider Eaton Canyon Trail that follows Eaton Canyon wash. Head left and hike a last 0.5 mile to Eaton Canyon County Park and its nature center.

❧ HENNINGER FLATS

MT. WILSON TOLL ROAD
From Altadena to Henninger Flats
is 6 miles round trip with 1,400-foot elevation gain

Consider the conifers.

A wind-bowed limber pine clinging to a rocky summit. A sweet-smelling grove of incense cedar. The deep shade and primeval gloom of a spruce forest.

Where do trees come from?

I know, I know. "Only God can make a tree."

Keep your Joyce Kilmer. Hold the metaphysical questions. Our inquiry here is limited to what happens in the aftermath of a fire or flood, when great numbers of trees lie dead or dying.

Fortunately for California's cone-bearing tree population—and tree lovers—there is a place where trees, more than 120,000 a year, are grown to replace those lost to the capriciousness of nature and the carelessness of humans. The place is Henninger Flats, home of the Los Angeles County Experimental Nursery.

Perched halfway between Altadena and Mt. Wilson, Henninger Flats is the site of Southern California's finest tree plantation. On the flats you'll be able to view trees in all shapes and sizes, from seedlings to mature stands. It's a small museum with reforestation exhibits.

Seedling sprouts.

After careers as a gold miner, Indian fighter and first Sheriff of Santa Clara County, Captain William Henninger came to Los Angeles to retire in the early 1880s. While doing a little prospecting, Henninger discovered the little mesa that one day would bear his name. He constructed a trail over which he could lead his burros.

Atop the flats he built a cabin, planted fruit trees, raised hay and corn. His solitude ended in 1890 when the Mt. Wilson Toll Road was constructed for the purpose of carrying the great telescope up to the new observatory. Captain Henninger's Flats soon became a water and rest stop for hikers, riders and fishermen who trooped into the mountains.

After Henninger's death in 1895, the flats were used by the U.S. Forest Service as a tree nursery. Foresters emphasized the nurturing of fire- and drought-resistant varieties of conifers. Many thousands of seedlings were transplanted to fire- and flood-ravaged slopes all over the Southland. Since 1928, Los Angeles County foresters have continued the good work at Henninger Flats.

The Pasadena and Mt. Wilson Toll Road Company in 1891 fashioned a trail to the summit of Mt. Wilson. Fees were 50 cents per rider, 25 cents per hiker. A 12-foot wide road followed two decades later. During the 1920s, the road was the scene of an annual auto race, similar to the Pike's Peak hillclimb. In 1936 the Angeles Crest Highway opened and rendered the toll road obsolete. Since then the toll road has been closed to public traffic and maintained as a fire road.

A moderate outing of just under 6 miles, on good fire road, the trail up to Henninger Flats is suitable for the whole family. The flats offer a large picnic area and fine clear-day city views.

At this writing, a 2005 landslide covered a portion of the old road and prompted authorities to close it. A trail bypass has been constructed but the road remains officially closed. Call the Eaton Canyon Nature Center for the latest trail conditions.

DIRECTIONS TO TRAILHEAD: From the Foothill Freeway (210) in Pasadena, exit on Altadena Drive. Proceed north 1.75 miles to the signed entrance of Eaton Canyon County Park. Turn right into the park and leave your car in the large lot near the nature center.

THE HIKE: From the parking lot, hike through the attractive grounds of the Nature Center. Cross the creek, then meander beneath the boughs of large oak trees to a junction with the signed connector trail leading to the Mt. Wilson Toll Road. Ascend this steep, long footpath to the toll road and turn right. The road begins a series of switchbacks up chaparral-covered slopes. Occasional painted pipes mark your progress.

Henninger Flats welcomes the hiker with water, shade, and two camp-grounds where you may enjoy a lunch stop. Growing on the flats are some of the more common cone-bearing trees of the California mountains including knob-cone, Coulter, sugar, digger and Jeffrey pine, as well as such exotics as Japanese black pine and Himalayan white pine.

After your tree tour, return the same way.

Ultra-energetic hikers will continue up the old toll road to Mt. Wilson; the journey from Altadena to the summit is 9 miles one-way with an elevation gain of 4,500 feet.

❧ MT. WILSON

MT. WILSON TRAIL

From Sierra Madre to Orchard Camp is 9 miles round trip
with a 2,000-foot elevation gain; to Mt. Wilson
is 15 miles round trip with a 4,500-foot gain

The tale of the Old Mt. Wilson Trail begins with Benjamin Davis Wilson, who gazed up at the commanding peak located high above his San Gabriel Valley vineyard and figured those abundant stands of pine and cedar on the mountain's shoulders would be an ideal source of timber. He built the first trail to "Wilson's Peak" in 1864.

As the communities located at the base of the San Gabriel Mountains grew in population during the 1880s, the townspeople began hiking up Mt. Wilson for weekend recreation. Eager to keep the hiking customer refreshed and satisfied, local entrepreneurs constructed trail resorts on the mountain.

The trail struggled with a rival thoroughfare when the Mt. Wilson Toll Road Company opened a wide, well-graded route in 1891 for a charge of 25 cents per hiker. But by the dawn of the 20th century, the old trail made a big-time comeback when a hiking fervor known as the Great Hiking Era swept the Southland.

In 1905 the Pacific Electric Railway extended its trolley service to Sierra Madre, reaching within a quarter mile of the trail head. Hikers came in droves on the weekend to tramp the path; others took the easy way by renting a mule or burro. Some 40,000 travelers passed through the trail's mid-point, Orchard Camp, in 1911.

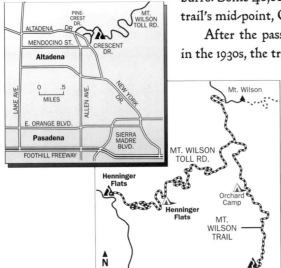

After the passing of the Great Hiking Era in the 1930s, the trail was all but abandoned until the late 1950s when rebuilding efforts began. Sierra Madre citizens, aided by Boy Scout troops, rebuilt the trail all the way up canyon to its junction with the old Mt. Wilson Toll Road.

Sierra Madre citizens also prevented county flood control engineers from bulldozing and check-damming Little Santa Anita Canyon. The aroused citizenry established Sierra Madre Historical Wilderness Area to preserve the canyon.

This hike takes you up Little Santa Anita Canyon, visits Orchard Camp, and climbs to the top of Mt. Wilson. It's a classic climb, one of the nicest all-day hikes in the Southland.

DIRECTIONS TO TRAILHEAD: From the Foothill Freeway (210) in Arcadia, exit on Baldwin Avenue and head north. Turn right on Miramonte Avenue near the junction of Mt. Wilson Trail Road, which is on your left. The trail begins 150 yards up this road and is marked by a large wooden sign. After passing some homes, the trail shortly intersects the main trail.

THE HIKE: After trudging 1.5 miles up Santa Anita Canyon you reach a junction with a side trail, which leads to the nearby canyon bottom. Here you can lean against an old oak, cool your heels in the rushing water, relax and watch the river flow.

Continue hiking on the ridge trail as it climbs higher and higher above the canyon floor onto sunny, exposed slopes. A hot 3 miles of walking brings you to Decker Spring and another 0.5 mile to Orchard Camp, a shady glen dotted with oak and spruce trees. When Wilson was building his trail, a construction camp called Halfway House was built here. Later homesteaders tried their hand planting apple and cherry trees—hence the name Orchard Camp.

During the Great Hiking Era, a succession of entrepreneurs utilized Orchard Camp as a trail resort and welcomed thousands of hikers. Hikers traveling through the canyon in the 1920s reported seeing "The Nature Man of Mt. Wilson," a tall bronzed hermit who looked like he stepped out of the pages of the Old Testament. The nature man carried a stone axe and worked on the trail for his keep. Some say he's still around, protecting the canyon—though he no longer springs out of the brush and greets every hiker who passes.

Orchard Camp is a nice place to picnic. You might want to call it a day here and return the same way.

The trail continues through thick chaparral up Santa Anita Canyon to its head. It contours on the shelf-like trail, heads east on a firebreak and crosses over a steep manzanita-covered ridge. At the intersection with Winter Creek Trail, turn left (west) and ascend steeply to Mt. Wilson Toll Road, 2 miles from Orchard Camp.

Turn right on the Toll Road and follow it a mile as it ascends through well-spaced spruce to Mt. Wilson Road, just outside Skyline Park.

❧ BIG SANTA ANITA CANYON

GABRIELINO NATIONAL RECREATION TRAIL
From Chantry Flat to Sturtevant Falls is 3.5 miles round trip with 500-foot gain; to Spruce Grove Camp is 8 miles round trip with 1,400-foot gain; to Mt. Wilson is 8 miles one-way with 4,000-foot gain

Cascades, a waterfall and giant woodwardia ferns are a few of the many delights of historic Big Santa Anita Canyon. The bucolic canyon has been popular with Southern California hikers for a hundred years.

William Sturtevant, known to his friends as "Sturde," pioneered many miles of San Gabriel Mountains trails. He traveled from California to Colorado in the early 1880s with forty burros. A packer par excellence, he soon found his services to be in great demand in the San Gabriels.

Sturtevant hewed out a trail over the ridge from Winter Creek to the top of the canyon and in 1898 opened Sturtevant Camp. The rustic resort consisted of a dining hall, tents, and a store and was a popular trail resort well into the 1930s.

In Santa Anita Canyon today some eighty-odd cabins are serviced by a burro train from Chantry Flats, named for another early packer, Charlie Chantry. One of the more colorful sights in the local mountains—and a look backward into a bygone era—is a glimpse at the pack animals plodding up the trail to Sturtevant Camp, now a Methodist Church retreat.

Sturtevant's trail is now a section of the 28-mile long Gabrielino National Recreation Trail. The trail to Sturtevant Falls is very popular on weekends—but not as popular as it was on Fourth of July weekend 1919 when 5,000 people tramped into the canyon and signed the trail register! The ambitious hiker may continue past the falls to Spruce Grove Camp and even as far as the top of Mt. Wilson.

DIRECTIONS TO TRAILHEAD: From the Foothill Freeway (210) in Arcadia, exit on Santa Anita Avenue and drive six miles north to its end at Chantry Flat. (Unfortunately, this road is often closed for repair.) The trail begins across the road from the parking area. A tiny store at the edge of the parking lot sells maps and refreshments.

THE HIKE: Descend on the paved fire road, part of the Gabrielino Trail, into Big Santa Anita Canyon. At the bottom of the canyon you'll cross a footbridge near the confluence of Big Santa Anita and Winter Creeks. Here a small sign commemorates Roberts Camp, a resort camp founded in 1912. Owner Otto Lyn Roberts and other canyon boosters really "sold" the charms of the canyon to Southern Californians in need of a quiet weekend. As you follow the path up-canyon along the oak-and alder-shaded creek, you'll soon determine that the canyon "sells" itself.

The only blemish on the pristine scene is a series of check-dams constructed of giant cement "Lincoln logs," by the Los Angeles County Flood Control District and the Forest Service in the early 1960s. In their zeal to tame Big Santa Anita Creek, engineers apparently forgot that fast-moving water is supposed to erode canyon bottoms; floods are what originally sculpted this beautiful canyon. Today, thanks to the check-dams, the creek flows in well-organized fashion, lingering in tranquil pools, then spilling over the dams in fifteen-foot cascades. Over the years, moss, ferns, alders and other creekside flora have softened the appearance of the dams and they now fit much better into the lovely surroundings.

The trail passes some private cabins and reaches a three-way trail junction. To visit Sturtevant Falls, continue straight ahead. You'll cross Big Santa Anita Creek,

Big Santa Anita Canyon: The type of retreat we all long to find—and it's just a mile's hike from the parking lot.

then re-cross where the creek veers leftward. Pick your way along the boulder-strewn creek bank a final hundred yards to the falls. The falls drops in a silver stream fifty feet to a natural rock bowl. (Caution: Climbing the wet rocks near the falls can be extremely hazardous to your health. Stay off.)

Return the same way, or hike onward and upward to Spruce Grove Trail Camp. Two signed trails lead toward Spruce Grove. The leftward one zigzags high up on the canyon wall while the other passes above the falls. The left trail is easier hiking while the right trail heads through the heart of the canyon and is prettier. Either trail is good walking and they rejoin in a mile.

After the trails rejoin, you'll continue along the spruce-shaded path to Cascade Picnic Area. You can call it a day here or ascend another mile to Spruce Grove Trail Camp. Both locales have plenty of tables and shade.

Still feeling frisky? Hikers in top condition will charge up the trail to Mt. Wilson—an 8-mile (one way) journey from Chantry Flat. Continue on the trail up-canyon a short distance, cross the creek and you'll find a trail junction. A left brings you to historic Sturtevant Camp, now owned by the Methodist Church. The trail to Mt. Wilson soon departs Big Santa Anita Canyon and travels many a switchback through the thick forest to Mt. Wilson Skyline Park.

WINTER CREEK

WINTER CREEK TRAIL
From Chantry Flat to Hoegees Camp is 6 miles round trip with 300-foot elevation gain; return via Mt. Zion Trail, Gabrielino Trails is 9 miles round trip with 1,500-foot gain

Before the dawn of the 20th century, packer/entrepreneur William Sturtevant set up a trail camp in one of the woodsy canyons on the south-facing slope of Mt. Wilson. This peaceful creekside refuge from city life was called Sturtevant's Winter Camp. In later years the name Winter was given to the creek whose headwaters arise from the shoulder of Mt. Wilson and tumble southeasterly into Big Santa Anita Canyon.

In 1908, Arie Hoegee and his family built a resort here that soon became a popular destination for Mt. Wilson-bound hikers; it remained so until it was battered by the great flood of 1938. A trail camp named for the Hoegees now stands on the site of the old resort and offers the modern-day hiker a tranquil picnic site or rest stop.

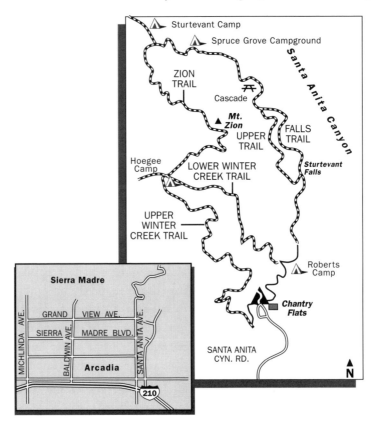

A hike along Winter Creek is a fine way to greet the arrival of winter. One of a half-dozen trails accessible from the popular Chantry Flat trailhead located just above Altadena in the Angeles National Forest, Winter Creek Trail offers a pleasant family hike in the front range of the San Gabriel Mountains.

DIRECTIONS TO TRAILHEAD: From the Foothill Freeway (210) in Arcadia, exit on Santa Anita Avenue and drive six miles north to its end at Chantry Flat. (Unfortunately, this road is often closed for repair.) The trail begins across the road from the parking area. A tiny store at the edge of the parking lot sells maps and refreshments.

THE HIKE: Descend 0.75 mile on the paved fire road, part of the signed Gabrielino Trail, into Big Santa Anita Canyon. At the bottom of the canyon, you'll cross a footbridge near the confluence of Big Santa Anita and Winter Creeks.

After crossing the bridge, look leftward for the signed Lower Winter Creek Trail. Following the bubbling creek, the trail tunnels beneath the boughs of oak and alder, willow and bay. The only blemish on the pristine scene is a series of check dams constructed of giant cement "Lincoln logs" by the Los Angeles County Flood Control District and Forest Service in the early 1960s. Fortunately, moss, ferns and other creekside flora have softened the appearance of the dams over the years and they now fit much better into the lovely surroundings.

You'll pass some cabins, built early in the 20th century and reached only by trail. Ever since, the needs of the cabin owners have been supplied by pack train.

When you see man and beast moving through the forest, it's easy to imagine that you've stepped a century back in time, back into Southern California's Great Hiking and Trail Resort Era.

After crossing Winter Creek, you'll arrive at Hoegees Camp. A dozen or so tables beneath the big cone spruce offer fine picnicking. Almost all signs of the original Hoegees Camp are gone, with the exception of flourishing patches of ivy. (In later years, Hoegees was renamed Camp Ivy.)

Walk through the campground until you spot a tiny tombstone-shaped trail sign. Cross Winter Creek here and bear left on the trail. In a short while you'll pass a junction with Mt. Zion Trail, a steep trail that climbs over the mountain to Sturtevant Camp and Big Santa Anita Canyon.

After recrossing the creek, you'll pass a junction with a trail leading to Mt. Wilson and join the Upper Winter Creek Trail. This trail contours around a ridge onto open chaparral-covered slopes. This stretch of trail offers fine clear-day views of Sierra Madre and Arcadia. The trail joins a fire road just above Chantry Flat and you follow this road through the picnic area back to the parking lot where you left your car.

🦅 HERMIT FALLS

GABRIELINO, FIRST WATER TRAILS
From Chantry Flat to Hermit Falls is 3 miles round trip with 400-foot elevation gain

Hermit Falls, in contrast to well-known Sturtevant Falls, is relatively unknown and infrequently visited. You could spend a wonderful day exploring Big Santa Canyon and visiting 30-foot Hermit Falls and 50-foot Sturtevant Falls.

Now for a hiker's truth-in-advertising disclosure about Hermit Falls. The view of the lovely cascade is restricted by the fact that the path delivers you to its rim not its base; thus full-frontal viewing and photography are not possible. In waterfall-watching parlance, this is called "an impeded view."

Once I was in Boston and lucky enough (I thought) to buy a ticket to watch our beloved Lakers play the Celtics at Boston Garden. The ticket was cheap, too, because the arena seller mumbled something about "impeded view." Talk about impeded—there was a concrete pillar in front of my seat! I couldn't see a thing.

Well, the view of Hermit Falls is by no means as impeded as my non-view of the Garden's basketball court. Just walk (carefully, please) to the lip of the falls and watch it spill out of a handsome rock notch.

The other disclosure is a sad one to report. Certain cretins periodically desecrate the boulders around the canyon's waterfalls with graffiti, though volunteers act quickly to erase it.

DIRECTIONS TO TRAILHEAD: From the Foothill Freeway (210) in Arcadia, exit on Santa Anita Avenue and drive 6 miles north to its end at Chantry Flat. (Unfortunately, this road is often closed for repair.) The signed trail (a paved road) begins across the road from the first parking area.

THE HIKE: Descend on the paved fire road, part of the 28-mile long Gabrielino National Recreation Trail. Just 0.2 mile or so from the parking lot, look for a signed junction on the right with First Water Trail.

Join this path as it switchbacks down to the bottom of Big Santa Anita Canyon. About 0.75 mile from Chantry Flat, the path passes some modest cabins and crosses the creek to a signed split in First Water Trail. Roberts' Camp and Sturtevant Falls lie up-canyon to the north. The path to Hermit Falls heads down-canyon. Saunter 0.75 mile among the tall trees, sword ferns and maidenhair ferns to the top of Hermit Falls.

When you retrace your steps on First Water Trail, consider continuing up-canyon to Sturtevant Falls. A visit to this classic waterfall and the return to the trailhead will add about 4 miles to your hike.

❧ BAILEY CANYON

BAILEY CANYON TRAIL

From Bailey Canyon Wilderness Park to falls is 1.2 miles round trip with 300-foot elevation gain; to Jones Peak summit is 6.6 miles round trip with a 2,275-foot gain; return via Mt. Wilson Trail is 8 miles round trip with 2,500-foot gain

When the light is right and the air is clean, the purple mountains beckon with the sweet smell of sage and many a winding trail. One of these inviting trails leads up Bailey Canyon from the town of Sierra Madre. The attraction is the view: clear-day vistas of the San Gabriel Valley are your reward for scaling many a steep switchback. If you want to get a feel for the area's geography, take a map along a San Gabriel Valley map.

Most of what you see of the San Gabriel Valley from Bailey Canyon Trail is commercial and residential. However, there are two significant splotches of green almost due south of the canyon: the Los Angeles County Arboretum and the Santa Anita Golf Course. Between the green is Santa Anita racetrack.

In 1875, this canyon on the outskirts of Sierra Madre was homesteaded by R.J. Bailey, who left little behind but his name. Over the years the property was divided. The Sierra Madre Municipal Water Company acquired part of the canyon, as did the Passionist Fathers, who built a monastery. The Carter family owned the lower part of the canyon and in 1965 donated land to the city of Sierra Madre for Bailey Canyon Park. For quite some time, the path leading up Bailey Canyon was known as the Carter Trail.

The trail has for several decades been something of an orphan. Angeles National Forest officials have paid scant attention to the path. Boy Scouts and conservation groups have pitched in with periodic maintenance, but the trail has had a long history of neglect.

Bailey Canyon Trail begins just one mile west of one of the Southland's most famous footpaths—the Mt. Wilson Trail. A longtime dream of front-range hikers was realized when a connector trail was built to link Bailey Canyon Trail with the trail to Mt. Wilson.

The trailhead is located at the city of Sierra Madre's Bailey Canyon Wilderness Park, which offers picnic areas and interpretive displays, as well as an easy family outing on two nature trails—Live Oak and Canyon View.

Little known and little chronicled, Jones Peak offers terrific clear-day views from its 3,375-foot summit. Vistas include Mt. Wilson to the north, Mt. San Jacinto to the east, the Pacific and Catalina Island to the south.

DIRECTIONS TO TRAILHEAD: From the Foothill Freeway (210) in Arcadia, take the Rosemead Blvd./Michillinda exit and head north on Michillinda. Continue a bit more than a mile to Grand View Avenue, turn right and proceed a few blocks to Grove Street. Follow Grove to its end at Bailey Canyon Wilderness Park, where you'll find ample parking.

THE HIKE: From the west end of the parking lot, head out on to the trail. You'll pass an ancient pedestrian gate with an old turnstile and head north on the paved service road, which transitions to a trail.

A quarter-mile from the trailhead, look for Live Oak Nature Trail meandering off to the right; the interpretive path offers a short and easy loop around numbered posts. After another 0.1 mile, the trail splits, with the left fork (Canyon View Nature Trail) leading to a seasonal waterfall.

Bailey Canyon Trail begins a no-nonsense climb and, after a couple of switchbacks, it's good-bye shade, hello steep ascent. Below you, adding a touch of European style, is the Passionist Fathers Retreat, a monastery.

Many a switchback takes you up the steep, brushy, east wall of the canyon and then north, higher and higher into the San Gabriel Mountains. The shadeless and relentless ascent leads to a saddle on the north side of Jones Peak. Head south (right) up the steep summit trail to the top of the peak.

For a longer, looping return trip, return to the saddle and head straight up the ridgeline a quarter mile to a signed junction. Continue straight on what is known as the Crossover Trail, a route that descends steeply east a mile into Little Santa Anita Canyon to meet Mt. Wilson Trail. Upon junctioning the famed footpath, you'll turn right (east) and hike 3.2 miles down-canyon to the Mt. Wilson trailhead.

Now you have a mile to walk on surface streets to return to Bailey Canyon Park. Hike a half-block west on Miramonte and turn right on Carter Avenue, which soon bends left (west) and follows the avenue 0.75 mile to Grove Street. Bear right and head back to the Bailey Canyon parking lot.

❁ MONROVIA CANYON PARK

WATERFALL TRAIL
1.5 miles round trip with 200-foot elevation gain

Shaded by live oak and sycamore, Monrovia Canyon is delightful retreat, complete with a little waterfall and a nature museum.

Monrovia Canyon Park preserves its namesake canyon as well as one other: Sawpit Canyon. At the junction of these two canyons was once a sawpit. Two sawyers, one standing at ground level, the other in a pit, operated the huge hand-saws of old.

Sawing logs might put the canyons on the map, but it was water that attracted civic attention in the 1880s. William P. Monroe's new city of Monrovia wanted the water and built a reservoir. L.H. Emerson wanted it, too, and a court battle ensued. City Hall won. Eventually, the name Monrovia was applied to a canyon, a peak and a park. Emerson had only a flat named after him.

For more than a hundred years Monrovia Canyon has been a popular picnicking area for San Gabriel Valley residents. Early Monrovians built a road to the park, which they dedicated in 1913.

A pleasant goal of a 0.75 mile stroll is a two-tiered waterfall, which cascades into a oak- and spruce-shaded grotto in the midst of Monrovia Canyon. Hikers can extend their adventure a bit by joining the park's nature trail. (A pamphlet is available at the nature museum.)

DIRECTIONS TO TRAILHEAD: From the Foothill Freeway (210) in Monrovia, exit on Myrtle Avenue and proceed two miles north. Turn right on Scenic Drive, jogging right, then left, and turning north on Scenic as if becomes Canyon Boulevard and continues another mile to the entrance of Monrovia Canyon Park. The park is open short hours: 12 P.M.-5 P.M. weekdays, 9 A.M.-5 P.M. weekends, and there's a small entrance fee. Signed Waterfall Trail begins opposite the Mal Parker Mesa Picnic Area near the park's small nature museum.

THE HIKE: Before you descend into the canyon, look behind you at the distinct V-shaped gorge, which frames a pie-shaped view of Monrovia and the San Gabriel Valley.

Waterfall Trail descends to the canyon bottom where you'll see the park's trail heading down-canyon. But you head up-canyon on the shady, creekside trail, which passes a series of check-dams.

The cascade of the little falls, mingled with the murmur of the creek, is restful music to the ears.

❋ SAWPIT CANYON

OVERTURFF TRAIL
From Monrovia Canyon Park entrance to Deer Park Lodge site
is 6 miles round trip with 1,000-foot elevation gain

In 1993, a honey of a trail was constructed through Sawpit Canyon above Monrovia. It has become a favorite in the San Gabriel Mountains. The path leads through Sawpit Canyon, owned by the city of Monrovia, which coordinated trail-building efforts.

DIRECTIONS TO TRAILHEAD: From the Foothill Freeway (210) in Monrovia, exit on Myrtle Avenue and proceed two miles north. Turn right on Scenic Drive, jogging right, then left, and turning north as Scenic becomes Canyon Boulevard. Continue another mile to the Monrovia Canyon Park entrance. Leave your car near the signed trailhead or farther up the road in the main part of the park.

THE HIKE: Walk up Sawpit Canyon Road toward the face of Sawpit Dam, erected by the Los Angeles County Flood Control District in 1929. The road (paved at first) soon turns to dirt as you ascend steadily along the wall of Sawpit Canyon. On your left, behind a chain-link fence, is Tallman H. Trask Boy Scout Camp (closed to the public).

After a mile's climb, at a bend in the road, look left for two stone pillars and a

Deer Park Lodge in the old days.

Overturff Trail

sign for Overturff Trail. The path descends briefly to Sawpit Creek and crosses it, then switchbacks uphill to Razorback—a sharp, narrow divide between Sycamore and Sawpit canyons. As you cautiously cross Razorback, enjoy the great views down into the canyon.

The trail resumes climbing the brush-covered hills toward The Gap, a man-made divide. What from a distance appears to some pagan object of worship turns out to be a pipe sticking out of The Gap. The pipe, which dates from the 19th century when it was part of the Monrovia waterworks system, was a vacuum break, designed to prevent a vacuum lock in the lines.

Past The Gap, the path is a pleasant, creekside jaunt beneath a leafy canopy of oaks and bay laurel. Overturff Trail drops into Twin Springs Canyon, where a creek has sculpted what appears to be a natural bridge.

You'll soon pass a junction with a right-forking trail leading to Strawberry Canyon Road. Continue straight on the steep trail, cross a tributary of Sawpit Creek, and you'll bear left on a spur trail to the Deer Park Lodge site. Near the foundation ruins of the lodge is an old corral, with fence posts fashioned from water pipes—an ingenious use of material at hand.

For a change of pace, you could descend back to the trailhead via Sawpit Fire Road, a faster (albeit less scenic) way to go.

❂ MT. BLISS

VAN TASSEL TRAIL
From Valley View Park to Overlook is 1 mile round trip with 200-foot gain; to Mt. Bliss is 8 miles round trip with 3,000-foot gain

The route to Bliss uses both Van Tassel Fire Road and Van Tassel Trail. The fire road—and others in the front range of the San Gabriels—came into existence after the monstrous fire of September 1924, the worst fire in the history of the mountains. The fire began in San Gabriel Canyon and rapidly spread westward. Despite the best efforts of fire fighters, the blaze burned for three weeks and for a time threatened the town of Monrovia.

As then Angeles National Forest Superintendent Rush Charleton put it: "The greatest difficulty in fighting the fires was the lack of roads over which to transport supplies to the men." Determined to prevent the occurence of another fire of this size, the Forest Service began building roads and firebreaks throughout the San Gabriels. One of these roads was the Van Tassel Fire Road.

Today the Van Tassel Fire Road is patrolled by both the Los Angeles County Fire Department and the Angeles National Forest. Only official vehicles are allowed, but hikers and mountain bicyclists are welcome to travel the road.

Van Tassel Trail, a footpath that leads from Valley View Park on the outskirts of Duarte a short ways to an intersection with Van Tassel Road, also came into existence

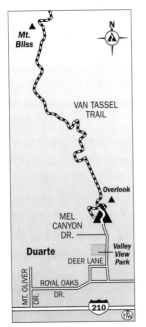

thanks to the efforts of fire fighters. Captain Ross Marshall of the Los Angeles County Fire Department supervised a hardworking CDC (California Division of Corrections) crew from Camp 19. Crew members cut brush and dug trail—skills employed when fighting a fire. Their trail efforts earned the men time off their sentences.

The ascent of Mt. Bliss constitutes what hikers call a "conditioning hike," that is to say a real aerobic workout. The incline is quite steep, the cardiovascular system gets revved up, and clear-day views from the summit of this peak are the reward for the effort.

DIRECTIONS TO TRAILHEAD: From the Foothill Freeway (210) in Duarte, exit on Mt. Olive Drive and head north to Royal Oaks Drive. Turn right and continue to Greenbank where you'll turn left, then Deer Lane, where you'll turn right, then Mel Canyon Drive where you'll turn left and park near Valley View Park.

On the trail to Mt. Bliss

THE HIKE: From the end of Mel Canyon Drive, follow the unsigned foot-path up the brushy slope. The view down at first isn't too inspiring. You'll see the 605 and 210 freeways, as well as the huge gravel pits of Irwindale, including the "Raider Crater" the stadium site once proposed as a new home for the then-Los Angeles Raiders (remember them?). The view east, where a quarry has chewed up mountainsides, isn't too inspiring either.

The trail briefly joins a road, and continues ascending to a fire department helipad, which does offer a pretty good view. On clear day, you'll have the San Gabriel Valley, downtown Los Angeles, and Santa Monica Bay at your feet.

Continue on the trail, a short ways past the helipad to an unsigned junction, where the trail joins Van Tassel Fire Road. You'll hike around a locked gate, and begin some steep switchbacks. The dirt road climbs to a ridgeline and takes you past some big cone spruce, which frame great views of the higher snow-covered San Gabriel peaks. Enjoy the panorama from 3,720-foot Mt. Bliss, catch your breath, and return the same way.

❀ FISH CANYON FALLS

FISH CANYON TRAIL
From Encanto Road to Fish Canyon Falls
is 9 miles round trip with 1,200-foot elevation gain

You've heard "fish stories" before—tales of secret spots, anglers' heavens and the big one that got away. This is a story about Fish Canyon and its enchanting but elusive waterfall, whose story has become as legendary a tale among Southland hikers as any fish story concocted by local fishermen.

For earlier generations of hikers, Fish Canyon and its handsome 80-foot waterfall enjoyed a reputation as one of the most attractive destinations in the foothills of the San Gabriel Mountains. The five-mile round trip hike to the falls was considered a most pleasant front-country saunter.

The good times ended in 1956 when the Azusa Rock Company began quarry operations in the mouth of Fish Canyon. This was in the era of dig-first-ask-questions-later, and the company was not required to explain—much less mitigate—the adverse environmental impacts caused by moving and removing millions of tons of rock.

To their chagrin, hikers of the 1950s found they had even less legal protection than the earth. The quarry company fenced off the canyon mouth and stationed guards to turn hikers away from Fish Canyon Trail.

After more than 30 years of hikers' protests and guerrilla hiking (sneaking past Azusa Rock Company gendarmes), the company condescended to construct a bypass trail around its diggings in 1988. Trouble was, this path was a bloody awful, precipitous route over rocky, unstable slopes.

Now there's another way to go. The city of Duarte, with the hard-working young people of the Los Angeles Conservation Corps, completed a new trail into Fish Canyon. The path, a three-mile long bypass of the quarry operation, climbs steeply up the west wall of Fish Canyon, then drops precipitously to the canyon bottom at a point just a few hundred yards above the Vulcan Materials Company diggings.

Given the five-decade-long struggle to gain access to Fish Canyon it might seem the height of ingratitude to complain about the layout and design of the new trail, which follows far too steep a course for the average hiker.

What was an easy family hike is now a strenuous outing best left to experienced hikers and those training for a trek in Nepal. The first half of this hike is nothing less than horrible. Once you get past the quarry, though, the balance of the hike is quite pleasant.

The allure of Fish Canyon Falls will motivate some hikers to undertake this semi-masochistic adventure. Some hikers are convinced that it's the most beautiful waterfall in the San Gabriels.

It is a beauty. Cascades fall in stair-step fashion into a rock amphitheater. Fish Canyon's rock walls amplify the roar of the falls.

Check with the Duarte Parks Department about something called Duarte Family Wilderness Day held in the spring, which includes a shuttle through the quarry and a mercifully mellow 4-mile round trip hike to the falls. Also monitor the access situation for other opportunities for shuttling across the mining company's holdings.

DIRECTIONS TO TRAILHEAD: From the Foothill Freeway (210) in Duarte, exit on Mt. Olive Drive. Head north to the first signal and turn right on Huntington Drive (Old Route 66). Proceed a half-mile mile to Encanto Parkway and turn left. Continue 1.5 miles to the signed Fish Canyon Trailhead and parking on the left side of the road.

THE HIKE: Begin the ascent of the west wall of Fish Canyon. The path climbs aggressively over chaparral-clad slopes and soon offers views of the mouth of the canyon, whose quarry operations have left it looking like a battlefield. Adding to the war-torn effect is the echo of gunfire emanating from the adjacent San Gabriel Valley Gun Club.

Higher elevations bring more inspiring views: peaceful reservoirs, a good deal of the San Gabriel Valley, the snow-capped San Gabriel range. The path climbs to meet a dirt road, where you bear left and pass an old rusty water tank. A very steep climb leads over the crest of a ridge, and then the path begins a rapid, knee-jarring, mile or so descent.

The new Fish Canyon Trail joins the old one at an unsigned junction at the bottom of the canyon. Turn left (north) and savor what is now a delightful saunter along the west slope above Fish Creek. The trail passes stone walls and ruins of cabins that once lined the creek. A 1958 fire and a big flood the following year wiped out most of these cabins.

The trail switchbacks a bit higher up the canyon slope before descending back to the creek. After crossing the creek, the mellow path leads along the east side of the creek to a sharp bend in the canyon walls and a sudden meeting with Fish Canyon Falls. Rest a long time at the falls before tackling the return trip.

❧ SANTA ANITA RIDGE

SAN OLENE FIRE ROAD
From Chantry Flat to viewpoint
is 7.5 miles round trip with 1,300-foot elevation gain

Count me among the legions of hikers who've long ignored the San Olene Fire Road. Maybe it's the name (not very inspiring) or its location—beautiful Big Santa Anita Canyon and the famed Gabrielino Trail that leads to Mt. Wilson.

In comparison, what can San Olene Fire Road possibly offer?

In a word, a view. "From Santa Anita Ridge, you can see almost everything you can see from the top of Mt. Wilson," claims Glen Owens, founder of the Big Santa Anita Historical Society.

The Channel Islands, Catalina Island, Santa Monica Bay, Mt. San Jacinto, Saddleback Peak in Orange County and Palomar Mountain in San Diego are part of the clear-day view from the ridge, adds Owens, who hikes or mountain bikes the San Olene Fire Road once a week every week of the year. From Chantry Flat, the fire road ascends at a moderate, but unrelenting 6 percent grade all the way to the viewpoint.

DIRECTIONS TO TRAILHEAD:
From the Foothill Freeway (210) in Arcadia, exit on Santa Anita Avenue and drive six miles north to its end at Chantry Flat. (Unfortunately, this road is often closed for repair.) From the large parking lot, locate the paved, signed fire road at the edge of the picnic area.

THE HIKE: From Chantry Flat Picnic Area, follow the paved fire road. You'll soon pass a junction with right-branching Winter Creek Trail and three-quarter mile from the trailhead reach a Forest Service heliport—officially the Chantry Flat Air-Attack Station.

Here the pavement ends and a dirt road continues, ascending chaparral-covered slopes dotted with monkeyflowers. Look for small groves of bay and maple, as well as a handsome stand of young madrone about two miles from the trailhead.

San Olene Fire Road finally levels out at the 3.5 mile mark, where you'll spot (can't miss, really) a futuristic looking microwave relay tower on the left and a big water tank on the right. For the very best view of the vast metropolis, as well as distant mountains, walk a few hundred yards south down Santa Anita Ridge.

SAN GABRIEL RIVER'S WEST FORK

WEST FORK NATIONAL SCENIC TRAIL
From Highway 39 to Glenn Camp
is 14 miles round trip, but (much) shorter trips are possible

Downriver, the San Gabriel (along with its sister streams the Santa Ana and the Los Angeles) is best-known for depositing the alluvium that now covers the surface of the Los Angeles Basin. Upriver, the San Gabriel has two major forks, each with a claim to fame. East Fork is known for its gold, West Fork for its trout.

For more than a century, Southern California anglers have been hooking trout in the San Gabriel River. The Pasadena Bait Club was the most prominent of early West Fork fishing camps catering to men looking for camaraderie, rustic accommodations and good fishing.

The 1890s were a particularly grand time to cast a line. While most anglers caught no more than the limit—50 (!) fish—others were greedy and some even used dynamite to "fish" for trout. California Governor Henry H. Markham was hardly an example of the conservation-minded sportsman; he landed 98 fish in six hours of fishing the West Fork. Finally, the California Department of Fish and Game stepped in to enforce limits and replenish the West Fork with fingerlings and trout brought in from Lake Tahoe.

West Fork, its course determined by one of Southern California's significant faults, the San Gabriel, is even today one of the Southland's best fishing rivers. Most of the West Fork has been set aside as a wild trout preserve. Fishing is of the "catch and release" variety. Barbless hooks must be used and the daily limit is zero. Fishing for keeps is permitted along a portion of the West Fork—the first 1.5 mile stretch of river reached by trail from Highway 39.

West Fork, as trout habitat, is still recovering from the desilting of Cogswell Dam, which lies upriver. Some years ago, during less enlightened times, Cogswell Dam was cleaned out and tons of silt dumped into West Fork, thus wiping out most of the fish.

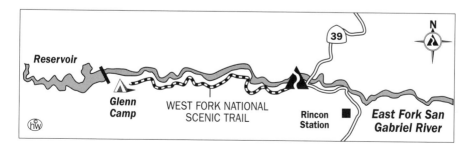

The river can be reached from a couple different directions, but most fishermen, as well as hikers and bicyclists, join the West Fork Scenic Trail which departs from Highway 39. The trail is actually an asphalt road that was built at the same time as Cogswell Dam.

West Fork Trail meanders seven miles with the river to shady Glenn Camp. (The road continues another 1.5 miles past Glenn Camp to Cogswell Reservoir, which is closed to the public, and connects with forest service fire roads heading west.) You can walk the whole way to Glenn Camp or pick a picnic or fishing spot anywhere you choose.

DIRECTIONS TO TRAILHEAD: From the Foothill Freeway (210) in Azusa, exit on Azusa Avenue (Highway 39) and head north. Fourteen miles later, and 0.5 mile past the Forest Service's San Gabriel Canyon Off-Highway Vehicle Area and Rincon Station, look for a parking lot and locked gate on your left. Signed West Fork National Scenic Trail is the asphalt road descending into the canyon.

THE HIKE: Head past the locked gate and down the road into the canyon. On the weekends, you'll have plenty of company along the first mile of trail. Most of these canyon visitors will be toting coolers, lawn chairs and fishing poles.

After a mile you'll intersect the Bear Creek Trail that leads north into the San Gabriel Wilderness. Pioneers had many an encounter with a grizzly along this creek, which is how this tributary of the San Gabriel River got its name. After another 0.5 mile's travel, you'll recross the river and enter the designated wild trout preserve.

The road, which climbs very slowly, but steadily, upriver leads past many, tranquil, oak- and sycamore-shaded pools.

Seven miles from the trailhead is Glenn Camp, set on a shady flat right by the river. It's a peaceful place with tables that invite a picnic.

CRYSTAL LAKE

PINYON RIDGE, CEDAR CANYON, SOLDIER CREEK, TOTOTNGNA NATURE, LAKE TRAILS

Pinyon Ridge (1 mile loop), Cedar Canyon (0.5 mile), Soldier Creek (0.75 mile), Tototngna Nature Trail (0.75 mile loop), Lake Trail (2 miles round trip)

Just below the crest of the Angeles Crest is a well-watered, cedar and pine-forested basin. This basin has no outlet and thus gathers rainwater and snowmelt from the San Gabriel Mountains above. A happy result of this geographical happenstance is Crystal Lake, the only natural lake in the San Gabriel Mountains.

During the 19th century, the lake was known as Sycamore Lake; that is, until Pasadenan Judge Benjamin Eaton visited in 1887 and proclaimed: "The water is clear as a crystal and the party found it good to drink." The name Crystal Lake has remained ever since; the pristine quality, however, has not.

Crystal Lake came under the protection of the U.S. Forest Service, first under the old San Gabriel Timberland Reserve, later under the Angeles National Forest. During the early years of this century, it was a popular beat-the-heat get-away for residents of the San Gabriel Valley. It was also a favorite summer vacation spot for Occidental College students, who built cabins near the lake.

During the 1930s, Los Angeles County took over Crystal Lake and operated it as a county park, complete with swimming, camping and recreation facilities. World War II, with its gas rationing and driving restrictions drastically reduced visitation, compelling the county to hand the lake back to the Forest Service.

Workin' on the trail–Islip Ridge

Today, the Forest Service, along with dedicated volunteers, have made Crystal Lake Recreation Area an attractive destination, complete with nature trails, a pleasant campground and a visitor information center.

Crystal Lake itself, however, often disappoints visitors. Periodic droughts have reduced the lake's size, overuse has dirtied the lakeshore. The lake suffers from heat pollution, human pollution and heavy algae growth. The devastating 2002 Curve fire closed the area for several years and required a massive cleanup and restoration effort.

The Forest Service is trying to help the little lake. The agency has installed an aeration system to provide the lake with more oxygen, and to mix surface and bottom waters in order to reduce water temperatures.

No swimming is allowed in the lake, but the lake is popular with fishermen, particularly after it's stocked during spring, early summer and late fall with rainbow trout.

While a visit to the lake might be underwhelming, a saunter along one of the recreation area's nature trails may provide the tranquillity you're seeking. The nature trails provide a good introduction to the natural history of the San Gabriel Mountains.

Drop in at the Crystal Lake Visitor Center (open weekends) to pick up maps, pamphlets, and the latest trail information.

DIRECTIONS TO TRAILHEAD: From the Foothill Freeway (210) in Azusa, take the Highway 39-Azusa Avenue exit. Drive north on Highway 39 for 24 miles to the turnoff for Crystal Lake Recreation Area. After a mile you'll reach the Forest Service entry station. Continue another mile to Crystal Lake Visitor Center, which is open weekends. Park in the lot next to the visitor center.

THE HIKE: Pinyon Ridge Nature Trail (1 mile) Begin southeast of the visitor center. It introduces you to several mountain ecosystems including meadowland, a yucca grove and a pinyon pine woodland. Particularly evident are the big coned trees—sugar pine, big cone spruce, and white fir. You'll also gain an appreciation for the natural forces—earthquakes, landslides, frost and flood—that have shaped the Crystal Lake Basin and the San Gabriel Mountains.

Cedar Canyon Trail follows an incense cedar-shaded canyon along a spring-fed creek. You can return via Soldier Creek Trail.

Soldier Creek Trail offers good views of San Gabriel Canyon as it winds through a mixed pine and oak forest. It connects to Cedar Canyon Trail.

Tototngna Nature Trail is an interpreted path (pick up a brochure at the visitor center) that leads through "the place of stones." You'll explore an earthquake fault and several ecologically unusual Crystal Lake communities.

Lake Trail goes where you would guess it goes—to Crystal Lake via an up-and-down route over rocky slopes. You'll appreciate the lake more if you arrive at its shores on foot.

ISLIP RIDGE

ISLIP RIDGE TRAIL
From Crystal Lake to Mt. Islip is 7.25 miles round trip with 2,200-foot gain

Trail connoisseurs appreciate the look—and feel—of hand-built Islip Ridge Trail. The moderate grade, well-engineered switchbacks, the rock work and the way the path gently crosses the land are due to the skill and hard work of many dedicated volunteers, particularly the San Gabriel Mountains Trail Builders.

This trail to Mt. Islip climbs the forested shoulder of the mountain, and intersects a summit trail which leads to the peak.

DIRECTIONS TO TRAILHEAD: From the Foothill Freeway (210) in Azusa, take the Highway 39-Azusa Avenue exit. Drive north on Highway 39 for 24 miles to the turnoff for Crystal Lake Recreation Area. After a mile you'll reach the Forest Service entry station.

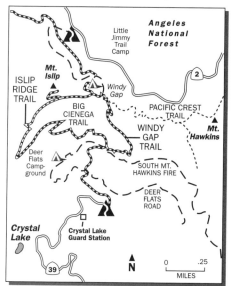

Continue another mile to Crystal Lake Visitor Center, which is open on the weekends, then another 0.5 mile to a large dirt parking lot on your right and signed Windy Gap Trail on your left.

THE HIKE: Ascend moderately on Windy Gap Trail, which passes near a campground and heads into the cool of the forest. The trail crosses a forest service road leading to Deer Flat Campground, ascends some more and reaches the dirt South Mt. Hawkins Truck Road. Cross the road and look left for the beginning of Islip Ridge Trail, which some of the trail builders like to call the Big Cienega Cut-off because it passes near Big Cienega Spring.

Enjoy the pleasant trail as it ascends moderately more or less west through pine, spruce and cedar forest. A bit more than a mile from the top, Islip Ridge Trail turns sharply north into a more sparse alpine forest.

The trail intersects the path coming from Windy Gap. Turn left and walk a short, but steep distance to the top of 8,250-foot Mt. Islip.

🦅 SAN GABRIEL RIVER'S EAST FORK

EAST FORK TRAIL
From East Fork Station to the "Bridge to Nowhere" is 9 miles round trip with 1,000-foot elevation gain; to Iron Fork is 12 miles round trip with 1,400-foot gain

Sometimes you'll see a weekend gold miner find a flash in the pan, but the real treasure of this section of the San Gabriel River lies in its beauty, its alders and tumbling waters. It's wet going; you'll be doing a lot of wading as well as walking, but you'll be well rewarded for all your boulder-hopping and stream-crossing.

This day hike takes you through the monumental middle section of the East Fork of the San Gabriel River, into the Sheep Mountain Wilderness. The dizzy chasm of the Narrows is awesome, the steepest river gorge in Southern California.

Road builders of the 1930s envisioned a highway through the East Fork to connect the San Gabriel Valley with Wrightwood and the desert beyond. The great flood of 1938 interrupted these plans, leaving a handsome highway bridge stranded far up-river, the so-called "Bridge to Nowhere." You'll pass the cracked asphalt remains of the old East Fork Road and gain access to the well-named Narrows. Expect to get wet at the numerous river crossings. High water during winter or spring means these crossings will likely be unsafe.

In the early years of this century, at the junction of Iron Fork with the main river, miner George Trogden had a home and angler's headquarters, where miners and intrepid fishermen gathered to swap tales. Up-river from Iron Fork is Fish Fork, whose waters cascade from the shoulders of Mt. Baldy. It, too, has been a popular fishing spot for generations of anglers.

DIRECTIONS TO TRAILHEAD: From the San Bernardino Freeway (10) exit on Azusa Avenue (Highway 39) and head north. Ten miles up Highway 39, turn right (east) on East Fork Road and continue eight more miles to the East Fork Ranger Station. Park below the station.

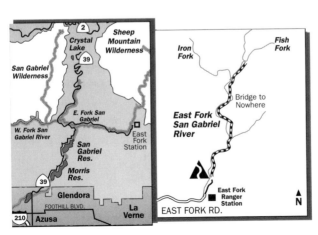

THE HIKE: Follow the service road

"The Bridge to Nowhere," East Fork of San Gabriel River

above the east side of the river 0.5 mile. Next, descend to the canyon floor and begin crossing and re-crossing the river. A bit more than two miles from the trail-head is Swan Rock, a mighty wall west of the river with the faint outline of a gargantuan swan.

As the canyon floor widens and twists northward, you'll climb up the right side of the canyon and continue up-river on the remains of East Fork Road, high above the rushing water. After ascending north a ways, you'll reach the "Bridge to Nowhere." No road meets this bridge at either end; the highway washed away in the flood of 1938.

Cross the bridge and join a slim trail that soon drops you into The Narrows. A quarter-mile from the bridge, Narrows Trail Camp is a fine place to picnic and view the handsome gorge.

Hardy hikers, like the river, will squeeze their way between towering granite walls. Iron Fork joins the river from the left, six miles from the trailhead.

Yet another mile up-river is Fish Fork, where another abandoned camp offers good picnicking. You can slosh up Fish Fork for another mile before a falls and the sheer canyon walls halt your progress.

❧ SHOEMAKER CANYON

SHOEMAKER CANYON TRAIL
From Shoemaker Canyon Road to Second Tunnel
is 5.5 miles round trip with 800-foot elevation gain

With its towering rock walls and dramatic V-shaped gorge, the East Fork of the San Gabriel River is monumental in scale, boasting some of the most rugged relief in all of Southern California.

One would logically conclude that such forbidding terrain would discourage engineers from even thinking about building a highway up the East Fork to connect with Angeles Crest Highway. But no, two generations of road-builders have attempted to bulldoze, blast and bridge a road up the East Fork.

The first attempt began in 1929 when road crews constructed a highway in the lower reaches of the great canyon. The "storm of the century" (March 1, 1938) hit the mountains and the San Gabriel River ripped the roadway to pieces.

In 1954, engineers attacked the East Fork again. This time the Los Angeles County Road Department, using inmate labor, began constructing the highway high on the west wall of the canyon in order to avoid the possibility of another flood. Despite 15 years of hard work by the prisoners of Detention Camp 14, only 4.5 miles of road were completed.

In 1969, county budget cuts and protests by conservationists led officials to halt highway construction. When the area gained wilderness status in 1984, there

was little possibilty the highway project would ever be revived.

"Convict Road," as it was known back then, stands today as a monument to bad planning. Visitors may drive the first one-third of the road and hike the balance of the "Road to Nowhere." Highlights of the hike include two very long tunnels of early 1960s vintage and grand vistas of the East Fork of the San Gabriel River.

DIRECTIONS TO TRAILHEAD: From the Foothill Freeway (210) in Azusa, take the Azusa Avenue-Highway 39 exit and head north about 11.5 miles to East Fork Road. Turn right (east) and drive 3.3 miles to a junction with signed Shoemaker Canyon Road. Bear left and follow it 2 miles to the end of the paved road, a vehicle gate and a parking area.

"Road to Nowhere"

On the return trip, hungry and thirsty hikers can stop for refreshment at Follows Camp, located just off East Fork Road, a short distance west of its junction with Shoemaker Road. The camp boasts a colorful combination restaurant-saloon-general store known as "The Fort."

THE HIKE: Step around the vehicle gate and begin a moderate ascent on the graded dirt road. Shade en route is scarce—limited to the towering walls left behind by the road cuts.

About 1.75 miles of hiking brings you to the first tunnel, an ambitious enterprise more than 1,000 feet long. The road narrows a bit, dips and climbs to a second tunnel, some 700 feet long.

Beyond the second tunnel, a brush-overgrown footpath continues 75 yards to the head of a steep ravine. It would not be a prudent move to cross over to a remaining length of road on the other side of the canyon. Shoemaker Canyon was named for grizzled gold miner Alonzo Shoemaker, who worked this small and very steep tributary of the East Fork during the 1870s and 1880s.

To take in the sights—and sounds—of the mighty East Fork of the San Gabriel River, backtrack 75 yards or so on a brushy path leading south outside the tunnel. Admire the view of the grand chasm as well as mighty Iron Mountain in the midst of the Sheep Mountain Wilderness, then retrace your steps through the tunnels back to the trailhead.

🪶 POTATO MOUNTAIN

EVEY CANYON TRAIL
Through Evey Canyon to the top of Potato Mountain is 5 miles round trip with 1,000-foot elevation gain

Hikers, for all you do, this spud's for you.

Potato Mountain, which sits above Claremont, offers the hiker great clear-day vistas of the San Gabriel Valley, eastern Los Angeles County, and parts of San Bernardino County. The 3,360-foot, russet-brown mountain, is a refuge from the busy metropolis and its far-flung suburbs.

Splitting Potato Mountain is the Evey Canyon, watered by a little creek bubbling through an oak woodland and a tangle of vines and gooseberries. Unfortunately, a devastating 2002 wildfire scorched Evey Canyon, as well as other nearby canyons and hillsides above Claremont, and thoroughly roasted Potato Mountain. Yes, the land is recovering but don't expect the pre-fire pastoral scene when you hike Evey Canyon.

Herman Garner saved the canyon from home development and gave it to Pomona College (one of the Claremont Colleges) Department of Biology with the condition that it remain pristine. Herman Garner Biological Preserve is used today for student field research, and for long walks away from it all.

The trail through Evey Canyon and up Potato Mountain consists of two fire roads (Evey Motorway and Palmer Motorway on some maps). Generally speaking, the first half of this hike is along a wide shady road through Evey Canyon and the second half is a hot ascent up a second fire road to the top of Potato Mountain.

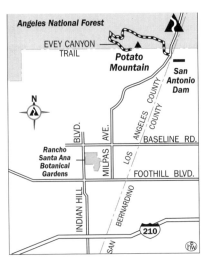

Couch potatoes and the small fry will enjoy strolling through Evey Canyon. More ambitious walkers will head for the top of the tater.

A permit is required for entry into Evey Canyon. Call the Claremont Colleges at 909-607-2993. Duplicate copies of the permit will be sent to you by mail; sign and mail back a copy, keep one for yourself.

DIRECTIONS TO TRAIL-HEAD: From the Foothill Freeway (210) in Claremont, exit on Baseline Road. Turn right (north) on Padua Avenue and travel

1.7 miles to Mt. Baldy Road. Turn right and drive 1.5 miles (that's a quarter-mile past San Antonio Dam) and look for turnouts on both sides of the road. Begin this hike on the left (west) side of the road at a locked gate.

THE HIKE: Squeeze past the locked gate (the canyon is closed to vehicle traffic) and descend into Evey Canyon. After a brief descent, the fire road begins ascending moderately through the oak- and alder-shaded canyon. Beneath the tall trees is an understory of grasses and vines.

After climbing out of the canyon and nearly two miles from the trailhead, you'll reach an unsigned junction with another fire road. Evey Motorway descends to the west, but you turn sharply left. Peel off your jacket and make the steep ascent to the top of Potato Mountain.

From the summit are metropolitan views, as well as a panorama ranging from the appallingly ugly U.S. Army Corps of Engineers-built San Antonio Dam and flood control basin to the sparkling peaks of the Angeles National Forest, including Mt. Baldy. Clear-day views also include Old Saddleback in Orange County to the south, and Mt. San Gorgonio and Mt. San Jacinto the east.

Half-baked hiker atop Potato Mountain

❧ SUNSET PEAK

SUNSET PEAK TRAIL
From Glendora Ridge Road to Sunset Peak is 7 miles round trip with 1,200-foot elevation gain

When snow covers the San Gabriel high country, consider the short hike to Sunset Peak. For most of the winter and early spring, the 5,796-foot peak seems to be strategically positioned just below the snow line and just above the smog line. You'll get great clear-day views of Claremont and the San Gabriel Valley below and of Baldy and its neighboring peaks above. Sunset views, as the name of the peak suggests, are often glorious.

DIRECTIONS TO TRAILHEAD: From Mt. Baldy Road, just short of the hamlet of Mt. Baldy, turn left on Glendora Ridge Road and drive 4 miles to a small parking lot on the left and signed Forest Service Road 2N07.

THE HIKE: Sunset Peak Trail, a Forest Service fire road closed to vehicles, ascends moderately bit steadily up the pine- and big-cone Douglas fir-shaded slopes. You'll pass a junction with another road descending to Cow Canyon and reach another junction at a saddle below the peak. Bend left with a spur road to the summit. Up top are a couple of cement pillars and other debris, remains of a Forest Service fire lookout tower that was abandoned because of several reasons: smog-hindered visibility and the Forest Service has for some years been replacing human lookouts with more automated surveillance. Also, a fire burned the peak!

The view of the metropolis below is notoriously undependable, however, the panorama of peaks above is always an inspiring sight.

STODDARD PEAK

STODDARD PEAK TRAIL
To Stoddard Peak summit is 6 miles round trip; 1,000-foot elevation gain

For most of the winter and early spring, 4,624-foot Stoddard Peak seems strategically positioned just below the snow line and just above the smog line. Its summit offers great clear-day views of Claremont and the San Gabriel Valley below, and of Baldy and its neighboring peaks above.

The peak honors William H. Stoddard who built the Baldy area's first resort in 1886. Stoddard's rustic retreat featured a dining room, cottages and cabins, plus a nearby waterfall for inspiration. San Bernardino and San Gabriel Valley families enjoyed weekend visits and week-long vacations at Stoddard Camp, which was a popular late-19th-century getaway.

Stoddard's success was a long time coming. He came from Connecticut in 1852 to try gold mining but it didn't pan out. He opened a store in Sacramento and lost both money and his health. He lived his life in the enormous shadow of his ultra-successful brother-in-law, railroad magnate Collis P. Huntington.

But Stoddard found himself—as well as a beautiful place to live and work—when he came to San Antonio Canyon. Today, he's remembered on the map by Stoddard Peak, Stoddard Canyon and Stoddard Flat.

The hike to Stoddard Peak is along a dirt fire road for most of its length. A final 0.5 mile of travel on a faint, brush-crowded path leads to the top.

DIRECTIONS TO TRAILHEAD: From the San Bernardino Freeway (10) in Upland, exit on Euclid Avenue and follow it a few miles, first through a commercial district then on a winding climb through the residential district of San Antonio Heights to Mt. Baldy Road. Turn right and follow it to the signed junction with dead-end Mountain Avenue and turn right. (The turnoff is also indicated by road paddle "1.07." Descend a short paved road to a small parking area.

THE HIKE: Ignore the old paved road heading south into the canyon and, instead, join the dirt road that heads east past a tiny hydroelectric plant.

The road crosses the creek at the

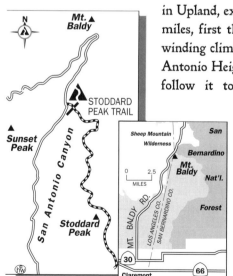

bottom of San Antonio Canyon. Three-quarters of a mile from the trailhead, you'll reach a couple of private cabins. Step over or duck under a vehicle gate and enjoy the mellow ascent through an oak woodland.

The path rounds Cascade Canyon and climbs to a saddle, a fairly level area called Stoddard Flat. Just as the dirt road reaches the flat, look sharply right for the unsigned path to Stoddard Peak.

The brushy trail plunges west into the chaparral, ascending to a ridgetop and turning south. You'll gain one false summit, then a second, before reaching the one-true Stoddard Peak. (Actually the second summit is a smidgen higher than Stoddard Peak, but the view is not-so-grand.)

Enjoy the panorama from Stoddard summit, which includes San Antonio Canyon, Mt. Baldy, San Gabriel Valley, Pomona, the Chino Hills and on especially clear days, Catalina Island and the big blue Pacific.

Winter snows turn canyons like this into wonderlands of ice.

ICEHOUSE CANYON

ICEHOUSE CANYON TRAIL
From Icehouse Canyon to Icehouse Saddle is 8 miles round trip with 2,600-foot gain

Icehouse Canyon Trail, leading from Icehouse Canyon to several 8,000-foot peaks, is an ideal introduction to the high-country delights of the Cucamonga Wilderness. The precipitous subalpine slopes of the wilderness, thickly forested with sugar pine, ponderosa pine and incense cedar, offer fresh mountain air and a network of good footpaths. The 4,400-acre wilderness, set aside by Congress in 1984, includes the Three T's—Timber Mountain, Telegraph Peak and Thunder Mountain—as well as 8,859-foot Cucamonga Peak, easternmost sentinel of the San Gabriel Mountains.

Icehouse Canyon is the hiker's only easy entry into the Cucamonga high country. The saddle and nearby peaks offer fine views to the hiker. Sierra Club peak-baggers like this trail because several peaks are within "bagging distance" of Icehouse Saddle, an important trail junction.

Icehouse Canyon was for many years known as Cedar Canyon because, as the story goes, the great cedar beams for Mission San Gabriel were logged here. The name Icehouse originated in the 1860s when ice was cut in the lower canyon and shipped to San Gabriel Valley residents.

The Chapman Trail, constructed in 1980, was named for the family that built the Icehouse Canyon resort and numerous cabins in the 1920s. The well-constructed trail heads up Cedar Canyon to Cedar Glen. The trail climbs out of Cedar Canyon, then contours on a steady grade back over to Icehouse Canyon.

DIRECTIONS TO TRAILHEAD: From the San Bernardino Freeway (10) in Upland, exit on Mountain Avenue. Head north on Mountain, which joins Mt. Baldy Road in San Antonio Canyon and winds its way to Mt. Baldy Village. Stop at the Mt. Baldy Visitor Center to obtain a free Wilderness Permit in order to enter the Cucamonga Wilderness. Go 1.5 miles past the village to Icehouse Canyon parking area.

THE HIKE: The trail leads east along the floor of the canyon. The path stays close to the oak- and spruce-shaded creek and passes some cabins. After 1.5 miles, the trail forks. You may take the "high route," the Chapman Trail, one mile to Cedar Flats and then three miles up to Icehouse Saddle, or continue straight ahead on the shorter and steeper Icehouse Canyon Trail directly up the canyon.

If you decided to continue on the Icehouse Canyon Trail, you'll pass a few more cabins. The trail climbs up the north slope of the canyon, before dropping down again and crossing the creek. The trail switchbacks steeply through pine and spruce. The tall trees frame a nice picture of Old Baldy. The Chapman Trail and the Icehouse Canyon Trail intersect and a single trail ascends a steep 0.75 mile to the top of Icehouse Saddle.

You can enjoy the view and return the same way, or pick one of the fine trails that lead from Icehouse Saddle and add to your day hike. You can continue eastward and drop down the Middle Fork Trail to Lytle Creek. A right (southeast) turn puts you on a trail that climbs two miles to Cucamonga Peak. A sharp right southwest leads 2.5 miles to Kelly's Camp and Ontario Peak. And a left on the Three T's Trail takes you past Timber Mountain, Telegraph Peak and Thunder Mountain, then drops to Baldy Notch.

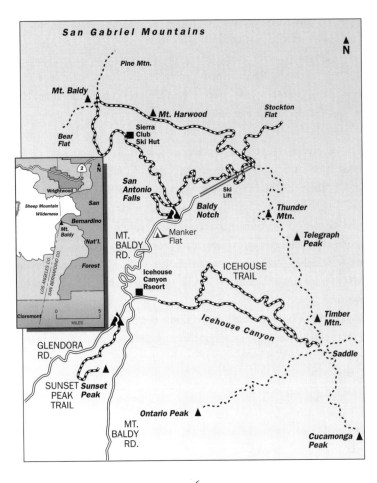

🦅 SAN ANTONIO CANYON

SKI HUT TRAIL

To San Antonio Falls is 2.5 miles round trip with 200-foot elevation gain; to San Antonio Canyon Overlook is 6.5 miles round trip with 2,600-foot gain; to Mt. Baldy summit is 8.5 miles round trip with 3,800-foot gain; Season: May-October

This day hike utilizes an attractive, but not-so-well-known trail that leads up San Antonio Canyon to the top of Baldy. Hikers of all ages and abilities will enjoy the 0.5-mile walk to San Antonio Falls. After a little rain, the three-tiered, 60-foot waterfall is an impressive sight.

Hikers who want more than the "leg stretcher" walk to the falls but aren't quite up for an assault on the peak can choose two intermediate destinations: the Sierra Club ski hut, where there's a cool spring, or a high ridge overlooking San Antonio Canyon. Hikers in top form, with good trail sense (the last mile of trail is rough and tentative), will relish the challenge of the summit climb. A clear-day view from the top offers a panorama of desert and ocean, the sprawling Southland and the southern High Sierra.

DIRECTIONS TO TRAILHEAD: From the San Bernardino Freeway in Claremont, exit on Mountain Avenue and head north, joining Mt. Baldy Road in San Antonio Canyon and winding about 11 miles to Manker Campground. About 0.3 mile past the campground entrance, look to the left for an unsigned paved road with a vehicle barrier across it. Park in the dirt lot just below the beginning of the road.

THE HIKE: Walk up the fire road, which is closed to all motor vehicles except those belonging to ski-lift maintenance workers. After a modest ascent, you soon behold San Antonio Falls. If you decide to hike down to the base of the falls, watch for loose rock and use caution on the rough trail. Resume walking along the road (unpaved beyond the falls). Soon look sharply left for an unsigned trail.

The trail ascends very steeply along the side of San Antonio Canyon. Trail connoisseurs will appreciate this path which, despite its steepness, has a hand-hewn, unobtrusive look and follows the natural contours of the land. Jeffrey pine, ponderosa pine and fir shade the path.

From the ski lift road it's 1.75 miles by trail to Sierra Club ski hut. Near the hut, constructed in 1935, is a cool and refreshing spring. Just past the ski hut the trail crosses a tiny creek, then snakes through a boulder field. Beyond the boulders the trail ascends via a 0.5-mile series of steep switchbacks to a ridgetop overlooking the headwaters of San Antonio Canyon. There's a great view from the tree-shaded ridgetop and, if you aren't up for a summit climb, this is a good picnic spot or turnaround point.

Peak-baggers will continue up the extremely rugged trail for another mile to the summit. The trail is rough and tentative in places, but rocks piled in cairns help you stay on course. You'll get a good view of Devil's Backbone, the sharp ridge connecting Mt. Harwood to Mt. Baldy.

Boulders are scattered atop Baldy's crown. Some rock windbreaks offer shelter. Enjoy the view of an assortment of San Gabriel and San Bernardino mountain range peaks, the Mojave and the metropolis.

Depending on energy or inclination, you can either return the same way or take Devil's Backbone Trail to Mt. Baldy Notch. From the Notch, follow the fire road down Manker Canyon back to the trailhead or ride down the ski lift.

MT. BALDY

DEVIL'S BACKBONE TRAIL

From Baldy Notch via ski lift, then to Mt. Baldy summit is 7 miles round trip with 2,200-foot gain; without ski lift is 13 miles roundtrip with 3,800-foot gain

Three saintly mountains—San Gorgonio, San Jacinto and San Antonio—tower over the City of the Angels. Lowest of the three, but by far the best-known is Mt. San Antonio, more commonly known as Mt. Baldy. The 10,064-foot peak, highest in the San Gabriel Mountains, is visible from much of the Southland. Its summit gleams white in winter and early spring, gray in summer and fall. Old Baldy is so big and bare that it seems to be snow-covered even when it's not.

Legend has it that the padres of Mission San Gabriel, circa 1790, named the massive stone bulwark after Saint Anthony of Padua, Italy. The 13th-century Franciscan friar was evidently a favorite of California missionaries; a number of geographical features, both in Monterey County and around Southern California, honor San Antonio. In the 1870s, San Antonio Canyon and the nearby high country swarmed with gold-seekers, who dubbed the massive peak a more earthly "Old Baldy."

Surely one of the most unique resorts in the San Gabriels was the Baldy Summit Inn, perched just below the summit of the great mountain. Gale-force winds battered the above-timberline camp, which consisted of two stone buildings and a cluster of tents. William Dewey, the owner-guide, and Mrs. Dewey, the chef, welcomed guests to their resort during the summers of 1910 through 1912. Advertised rates were one dollar a meal, one dollar a bed. The camp burned in 1913 and never reopened.

A moderate (compared to other routes up Baldy), but certainly not easy, ascent follows the Devil's Backbone Trail from Baldy Notch to the summit. This is a popular trail and the one most hikers associate with Mt. Baldy. A clear-day view from the top offers a panorama of desert and ocean, the sprawling Southland and the Southern high Sierras.

Baldy is a bit austere from afar, but up-close, the white granite shoulders of the mountain are softened by a forest of pine and fir. Dress warmly for this trip and keep an eye out for rapidly changing weather conditions.

DIRECTIONS TO TRAILHEAD: From the San Bernardino Freeway (10), exit on Mountain Avenue. Head north on Mountain, which joins Mt. Baldy Road in San Antonio Canyon and winds 12 miles to road's end just beyond Manker Campground. Park in the ski lift parking area.

If you're hiking Baldy, sans ski-lift, park on the left (west) side of Mt. Baldy Road, about 0.5 mile below the ski lift parking area. Your trailhead is the gated Baldy fire road.

Purchase a ticket and ride the ski lift up to Baldy Notch. The lift is operated weekends and holidays all year.

An alternative is to walk up a fire road to Baldy Notch. This option adds three miles each way and a 1,300-foot gain to the walk. The fire road switchbacks up the west side of the steep San Antonio Canyon, offers a good view of San Antonio Falls, then climbs northward to the top.

THE HIKE: From Baldy Notch, a wide gravel path leads to a commanding view of the desert. You then join a chair lift access/fire road, and ascend a broad slope forested in Jeffrey pine and incense cedar. The road ends in about 1.25 miles at the top of a ski lift, where a hiker's sign-in register beckons.

From the top of the ski lift, a trail leads out onto a sharp ridge known as the Devil's Backbone. To the north, you can look down into the deep gorge of Lytle Creek, and to the south into San Antonio Canyon. You'll then pass around the south side of Mt. Harwood, "Little Baldy," and up through scattered stands of lodgepole pine.

The trail reaches a tempestuous saddle. (Hold onto your hat!) From the saddle, a steep rock-strewn pathway zigzags past a few wind-bowed limber pine to the summit.

Boulders are scattered atop Baldy's crown. A couple of rock windbreaks offer some shelter. Enjoy the view of San Gabriel and San Bernardino mountain peaks, the Mojave and the metropolis, and return the same way.

STRAWBERRY PEAK

STRAWBERRY PEAK TRAIL
Red Box to Strawberry Peak summit is 6.5 miles round trip with 1,500-foot elevation gain

Named by mountaineers of a century ago—who imagined an upside-down strawberry—Strawberry Peak challenges rock-climbers and hikers. The challenge comes from the final approach to the peak, which involves some boulder-climbing when tackling the west slope or a vigorous hike along a firebreak when ascending the east slope.

At 6,164 feet, Strawberry Peak just tops its neighbor across the Angeles Crest Highway, San Gabriel Peak (6,161 feet), for the honor of being the highest peak in the front range of the San Gabriel Mountains.

Actually, Strawberry Peak seems more backcountry than front range. It offers summit panoramas, not of the city but of the Arroyo Seco and Big Tujunga watersheds, and of the crests along Angeles Crest Highway. Compared to the sometimes smoggy air clinging to other city-facing front range peaks, the air around Strawberry Peak is positively alpine.

Some hikers like Strawberry Peak because reaching the top requires more than the usual "walk-up" common to most San Gabriel Mountains. The stony ramparts, where woebegone Coulter pines cling to life, really look like a challenge when viewed from below.

And, in fact, the last mile to the summit is no walk in the park. The route is along an old firebreak, very steep—and sometimes very hot—climb. On warm days, get an early start.

DIRECTIONS TO TRAILHEAD: From the Foothill Freeway (210) in La Canada, drive 14 miles on Angeles Crest Highway (2) to Red Box Station. At the turnoff is a picnic area and parking lot; park at the easternmost (farthest) end of the lot.

THE HIKE: From the end of the picnic area, cautiously cross Angeles Crest Highway and walk 50 yards east (to the right) along the highway shoulder to a yellow-gated fire road. Follow this now-retired road, which narrows to a trail.

About 0.5 mile from the trailhead, you'll join a signed trail on your left, which switchbacks sharply up steep, chaparral-covered slopes. After providing hikers a brief workout, the trail levels and contours around Strawberry's other neighbor, Mt. Lawlor.

A bit more than two miles from the trailhead, you'll descend to a saddle. Leave the maintained trail and ascend along an unsigned but nevertheless distinct firebreak. Your up-to-now mellow hike goes ballistic here, as the brushy path

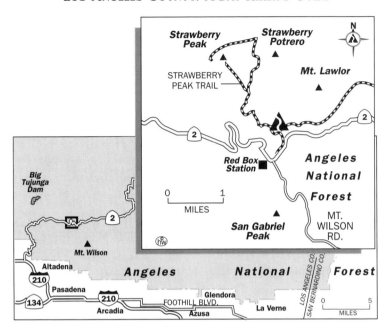

shoots steeply north toward Strawberry's summit. Alas, along the way, two dis-heartening dips mean the hiker loses hard-won elevation.

The firebreak at last angles left and you ascend west over a rocky ridge to the summit. From among wind-battered big cone spruce and pines, enjoy the Angeles National Forest panorama—you've earned it!

❧ SAN GABRIEL PEAK

SAN GABRIEL PEAK TRAIL
To San Gabriel Peak is 4.25 miles round trip with 1,300-foot elevation gain

A splendid view of high mountain summits and the wide L.A. Basin is a hiker's reward for completing the climb to the top of the San Gabriel Mountains' name-sake peak. Pyramid-shaped San Gabriel Peak, located at the crest of the front range, high above Altadena, offers a 360-degree view of basin and range.

Tote two maps to the top—one of the city, one of the Angeles National Forest—to help you identify metropolitan and mountain landmarks.

The mountain views are particularly good. From atop 6,161-foot San Gabriel Peak, you'll have the opportunity to look down on two of the Southland's most famous peaks: Mt. Lowe (5,603 feet) and Mt. Wilson (5,710 feet). Foothill Freeway commuters and other city-dwellers who are accustomed to looking up at these L.A. landmarks might enjoy seeing the two mountains from a different perspective and in a different light.

Well-engineered San Gabriel Peak Trail, built by the JPL Hiking Club in 1988, takes you to the top. The hand-built footpath switchbacks through the forest and offers a delightful alternative to the boring, paved service road (once the only way to the top) trudged by earlier generations of hikers.

The trail to San Gabriel Peak also offers the hiker a chance to easily conquer a second summit—Mt. Disappointment.

In 1873, a survey party bushwhacked through the chaparral, attempting to locate the area's highest peak in order to establish a triangulation point for future mapmaking efforts. When the surveyors reached the summit of what they adjudged to be the highest peak, they were mighty disappointed to realize that

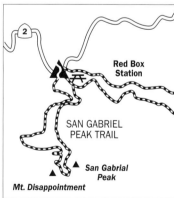

another peak—nearby San Gabriel Peak—was 100 feet higher. "Mt. Disappointment" the surveyors named San Gabriel's sister peak.

Alas, compared to lovely San Gabriel Peak, Mt. Disappointment is a homely sister. Back in the 1950s, the U.S. Army dynamited then flattened the summit, built a Nike Missile site, and bulldozed a road. Today the peak is forested with communications antennae.

Humankind has been more gentle with San Gabriel Peak. A bench is the only improvement to be found on its summit. A brisk winter or spring day is ideal for the hike and the views to be gained from the summit.

DIRECTIONS TO TRAILHEAD: From the Foothill Freeway (210) in La Canada, exit on Angeles Crest Highway (2) and drive 14 miles into the mountains to Red Box Station. Turn right on Mt. Wilson Road and proceed a short 0.5 mile to a turnout where you'll see the gated Mt. Disappointment service road and the signed trailhead for San Gabriel Peak. The trail begins 50 feet to the left of the service road.

THE HIKE: The path switchbacks southeast up the pine- and oak-forested slopes. Occasionally paralleling the Mt. Disappointment service road, the trail offers eastward views of Mt. Wilson.

About 1.5 miles from the trailhead, the trail reaches, then joins the paved service road. Climb a short 0.25 mile with the road to a junction. The service road turns sharply right (almost a U-turn) and continues another 0.25 mile to the summit of Mt. Disappointment.

From the junction, bear left and join the unsigned footpath leading to San Gabriel Peak. The trail dips and quickly comes to an unsigned junction. The right fork descends to Markham Saddle and eventually links up with the Mt. Lowe trail system. Continue on the left fork, climbing southeast, first along the saddle between Mt. Disappointment and San Gabriel Peak, then up San Gabriel Peak itself. A stiff 0.5 mile climb takes you to the summit.

❧ THE OTHER SIDE OF MT. WILSON

KENYON DEVORE, GABRIELINO TRAILS

From Mt. Wilson to West Fork Campground is 8.8 miles round trip with
2,800-foot elevation loss and gain

Most hikers think of Mt. Wilson as that perfect backdrop behind Pasadena and
the San Gabriel Valley. Almost always, we climb the storied mountain from the
south by following those classic, century-old routes—the Old Mt. Wilson Trail
and the Old Mt. Wilson Toll Road.

Few hikers think of "t'other" side (north face) of the mountain, where steep
slopes cloaked in magnificent forest await the hearty adventurer.

Does a north-slope ascent of Mt. Wilson sound intriguing?

Well, it is. But there's a catch.

Of course there's a catch. Why else would 99.9 percent of all Mt. Wilson hikers climb the great mountain from the south?

The catch is that the trailhead for a north slope climb of Mt. Wilson is . . . on
top of Mt. Wilson. Yes, that means to ascend the mountain from this side you
must first descend it. And not just a minor descent, but a steep, knee-jarring
descent all the way down to the West Fork of the San Gabriel River. Then, of
course, it's uphill all the way back to the summit where you parked your car.

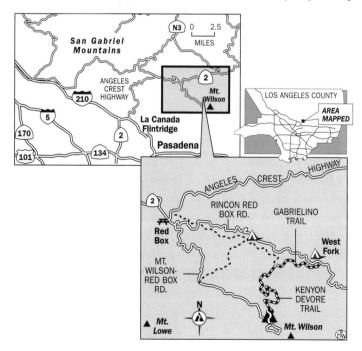

Long-time San Gabriel Mountains hikers know the reason why this trail to the top has been turned upside down: Red Box Road, which leads from Angeles Crest Highway down to West Fork Campground (a natural trail head for a north slope walk up Wilson) was closed to public traffic by the Forest Service some years ago. When (or if) this road will re-open is any hiker's guess and my guess is never.

Most maps (both older and newer) show the old Rattlesnake Trail slithering down Wilson's north slope. This serpentine path was renamed Kenyon DeVore Trail in honor of a man who spent most of the 20th century working in, and for, the San Gabriel Mountains.

Kenyon DeVore (1911-1995) was raised at his parents' trail resort on the West Fork, led mule pack trains to bring supplies to mountain dwellers, worked for the Los Angeles County Flood Control District in San Gabriel Canyon, then spent his retirement years as a Forest Service volunteer at the Chantry Flat information center.

I prefer this hike along Kenyon DeVore Trail as an out-and-back, but dogged loop-ophiles can fashion a semi-loop by returning to Mt. Wilson Road from West Fork via Valley Forge Trail. That leaves 2 miles of road-walking along Mt. Wilson Road to return to the trail head.

Kenyon DeVore Trail is in so-so shape, Expect some washouts and eroded places in the midst of the many long switchbacks.

DIRECTIONS TO TRAILHEAD: From the Foothill Freeway (210) in La Canada, exit on Highway 2, the Angeles Crest Highway and follow it 14 miles to Mt. Wilson Road. Turn right and continue 4.2 miles to just short of the summit, where the road splits and becomes one-way going in a counter-clockwise direction. At the road split, you'll spot the signed Kenyon DeVore Trail on the left; however, you will need to follow the one-way road all the way around to a small turnout for parking located about 100 yards above the beginning of the trail.

THE HIKE: The path descends among oaks, the first of many stands en route. As the trail drops farther into shadier recesses of Strayns Canyon, look for big-cone spruce, incense cedar, and plenty of pines—Jeffrey and sugar.

The trail crosses Strayns Creek, contours along the east side of the canyon wall, drops to the creek and crosses to the west side again. More descents and creek-crossings bring you to a junction with the Gabrielino Trail. Turn east and head down-canyon to West Fork Campground, which offers tables, toilets and a resting place for the long ascent back to the top of Mt. Wilson.

CHARLTON FLATS AND VETTER MOUNTAIN

VETTER MOUNTAIN, SILVER MOCCASIN TRAILS
From Charlton Flats to Vetter Mountain is 2.6 miles round trip with 700-foot elevation gain; Wolf Tree Nature Trail is 0.5 mile round trip

The first 20 miles or so of driving up the Angeles Crest Highway from La Canada into the Angeles National Forest is a pleasant enough excursion across brushy slopes and past scraggly trees, but it often leaves motorists wondering, "Where's the forest?"

Mile-high Charlton Flats is where the pine forest prevails, a tranquil gathering of tall trees that includes sugar pine, Jeffrey pine and Coulter pine, as well as big cone spruce, incense cedar and live oak.

Originally called Pine Flats, the woodsy spread was renamed for Rush Charlton, who served as national forest supervisor from 1906 to 1920. During the 1930s, the Civilian Conservation Corps constructed a sprawling campground and picnic areas at Charlton Flats, as well as a fire lookout atop 5,898-foot Vetter Mountain, a distinct summit rising above the flats.

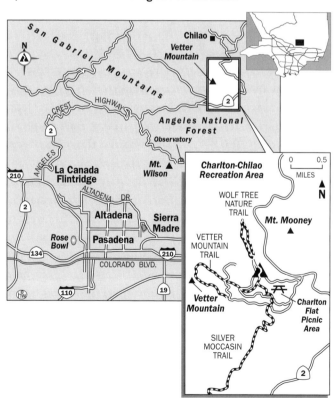

Vetter Mountain offers the hiker a good deal: a 360-degree panoramic view of the middle of the San Gabriel range for a modest climb and elevation gain. The Forest Service and volunteer groups intend to restore the old summit fire lookout and establish an interpretive center.

Wolf Creek Nature Trail shares a trailhead with the path to Vetter Mountain. The family-friendly, self-guided interpretive path tours Conifer-Land and deliver hikers to the "wolf tree," a forest-dominating Coulter pine. The Coulter boasts foot-long, five-pound pine cones—largest in the conifer family.

Winter snow conditions can prompt the Forest Service to close Charlton Flats to vehicle traffic. Hikers can walk to the trailhead if there's a modest amount of snow on the ground. More snow means great cross-country skiing or snow play at Charlton Flats.

For more information about the Charlton-Chilao Recreation Area, as it's called these days, drop by the Chilao Visitor Center located three miles up Angeles Crest Highway from Charlton Flats.

DIRECTIONS TO TRAILHEAD: From the Foothill Freeway (210) in La Canada, exit on Angeles Crest Highway (2) and drive 24 miles to the signed turnoff for Charlton Flats Picnic Area.

Follow the picnic area access road to the first intersection, turn right, and proceed 0.6 mile to a gate. Wolf Creek Nature Trail begins beyond the gate. The signed path to Vetter Mountain begins across the road to the west.

The quickest way to the top of Vetter Mountain (0.75 mile hike) is to follow the upper road (far left) all the way to the beginning of the Vetter Lookout access road. However, there's not much parking here, so be careful not to block the road.

THE HIKE: Begin your ascent and soon pass a junction with the left-branching Silver Moccasin Trail. The path proceeds through a diverse forest, crosses two paved roads, then switchbacks up to the summit lookout.

From the catwalk of the lookout, savor clear-day views to the east of the rugged San Gabriel Wilderness and mighty Mt. Baldy. To the north, are Mts. Waterman and Williamson and to the south and west such front range peaks as Strawberry and San Gabriel. The front range summits pretty well wall off the metropolis from view which, for the hiker looking to get away from it all, might not be such a bad thing.

For a slightly longer (0.75 mile) return route from the top of Vetter Mountain, take the dirt road and descend east 0.75 mile to a paved road. Follow this road 0.6 mile to where Silver Moccasin Trail crosses the road and head left on the trail. The trail crosses a paved road, then contours across a woodsy slope to meet Vetter Mountain Trail near the trailhead.

CHILAO

SILVER MOCCASIN TRAIL

From Chilao to Horse Flats Campground is 2 miles round trip with 200-foot elevation gain; to Mt. Hillyer is 6 miles round trip with 1,000-foot gain

Even on the Angeles National Forest map, the trail looks intriguing: a red dashed line zigs and zags through the heart of the San Gabriel Mountains and connects Chantry Flat and Shortcut Station, Chilao, Cloudburst and Cooper Canyon. Designed by the Los Angeles Area Council of the Boy Scouts of America, the 53-mile long Silver Moccasin Trail, extends from Chantry Flat to the mountain named for the founder of the Boy Scouts, Lord Baden-Powell. Scouts who complete the week-long trek earn the prized Silver Moccasin award.

One pretty stretch of the Silver Moccasin Trail tours the Chilao country, a region of giant boulders and gentle, Jeffrey pine-covered slopes. Another path—Mt. Hillyer Trail—leads to the top of 6,162-foot Mt. Hillyer. From the top, you'll get views to the north of the desert side of the San Gabriels.

Located just off Angeles Crest Highway near the trailhead, the Angeles

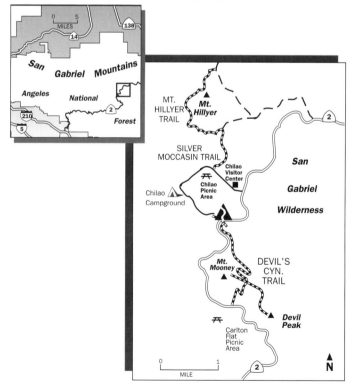

National Forest Chilao Visitor Center is well worth a visit. Exhibits interpret flora, fauna and forest history. Behind the station are three short nature trails.

DIRECTIONS TO TRAILHEAD: From the Foothill Freeway (210) in La Canada, exit on Angeles Crest Highway (2) and wind 27 miles up the mountain road to the signed turnoff for the Chilao Visitor Center. Turn left and follow the paved road past the visitor center a half-mile to signed Silver Moccasin Trail on your right. Parking at the trailhead is limited to a few cars, but there's a wide turnout located just up the road.

THE HIKE: The trail ascends a manzanita- and yucca-covered slope to the top of a minor ridge. A mile from the trailhead, the trail widens and you reach a signed junction. Here Silver Moccasin Trail swings southeast toward Angeles Crest Highway and Cooper Canyon, but you go right with a retiring dirt road one hundred yards to Horse Flat Campground. The camp, with plenty of pine-shaded picnic tables, is a good rest stop.

Just as you reach the gravel campground road, head left with the signed Mt. Hillyer Trail. The path switchbacks up pine-, incense cedar- and scrub oak-covered slopes. Some big boulders suggest a perfect hideout, whether you're fleeing the sheriff or the stresses of modern life.

Up top, Mt. Hillyer may remind you of what Gertrude Stein said of Oakland: "There's no there there." The summit is not a commanding pinnacle, but a forested flat. With all those trees in the way, you'll have to walk a few hundred yards along the ridgeline to get your view of the green country to the south and the brown, wrinkled desert side of the San Gabriels to the north.

🦅 MT. WATERMAN

MT. WATERMAN, TWIN PEAKS TRAIL
From Angeles Crest Highway to Mt. Waterman is 6 miles round trip with
1,300-foot elevation gain; to Twin Peaks is 9.5 miles round trip

Mt. Waterman is best known for its ski area. A couple of lifts carry schussers up
the north face of the mountain. Alpine scenery and decent snowfall contribute to
Waterman's popularity.

But when Mt. Waterman is snow-less, the 8,038-foot peak (and the San
Gabriel Wilderness that adjoins it) becomes the province of hikers.

Waterman's location adjoining the San Gabriel Wilderness means the
mountain shares some of the remoteness of this rough-and-rugged country. The
few trails leading around and through the San Gabriel Wilderness—even the
moderate, well-graded path to Mt. Waterman—are infrequently traveled.

Even more remote than Mt. Waterman (and offering better clear-day views)
is Twin Peaks. The boulder-strewn summits of 7,761-foot East Twin Peak and
7,596-foot West Twin Peak offer commanding panoramas of the Angeles high
country and the metropolis below.

DIRECTIONS TO TRAILHEAD: From the Foothill Freeway (210) in

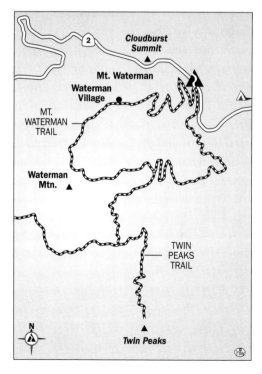

231

Tall trees grace the Angeles high country.

La Canada, exit on Angeles Crest Highway (2) and drive 33 miles. Half a mile past the Mt. Waterman ski lift, look right for road paddle 58/00, then park in the large lot on the left side of the highway. Walk carefully along the highway to a dirt road with a yellow steel gate across it. The correct path, among a couple trails and fire roads, is the easternmost (farthest to the left) one.

THE HIKE: Walk up the fire road about 50 yards, then join the unsigned footpath branching from the left side of the road. The path parallels, the rises above Angeles Crest Highway.

About 1.5 miles of ascent bring you to a dramatic crest where signs mark the boundary of the San Gabriel Wilderness.

Mt. Waterman Trail turns west 0.5 mile and brings you to a signed junction with the trail leading to Twin Peaks.

To reach Mt. Waterman: Go right and climb through the pine trees. Join an unsigned trail on your left for the final ascent to the stony, broad-shouldered summit.

To Twin Peaks: From the trail junction, descend a steep mile to Twin Peaks Saddle. A rough, steep trail contours south, then an even more steep and faint trail climbs to a ridgeline between the Twin Peaks. Ascend east to reach the eastern peak. A clear panorama includes Catalina Island and Palomar Mountain.

MT. WILLIAMSON

MT. WILLIAMSON TRAIL
From Islip Saddle to Mt. Williamson is 5 miles round trip with 1,600-foot elevation gain

Mt. Williamson stands head and shoulders above other crests along Angeles Crest Highway. The 8,214-foot peak offers grand views of earthquake country—the Devil's Punchbowl, San Andreas Fault and the fractured northern edges of the San Gabriel Mountains.

The summit of Mt. Williamson is the high point and culmination of well-named Pleasant View Ridge, a chain of peaks that rises from the desert floor to Angeles Crest Highway. It's quite a contrast to stand atop the piney peak, which is snow-covered in winter, and look down upon Joshua trees and the vast sand-scape of the Mojave Desert.

The mountain's namesake is Major Robert Stockton Williamson, who first explored the desert side of the San Gabriels in 1853. Williamson, a U.S. Army mapmakers led an expedition in search of a railroad route over or through the mountains. Certainly Williamson found no passable route through the Mt. Williamson area or any other place in the San Gabriel Mountains high country,

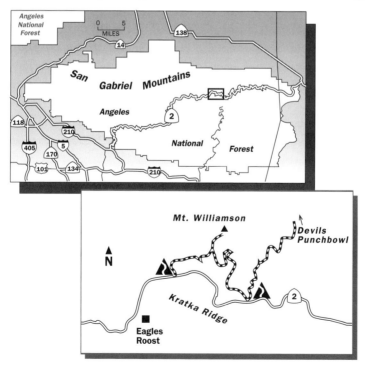

but the major did find a way around the mountains, so his mission was definitely a success. Williamson's Pacific Railroad Survey report to Congress detailed two railroad routes: Cajon Pass on the east end of the San Gabriels and Soledad Canyon on northwest.

Two fine forest service trails ascend Mt. Williamson from Angeles Crest Highway. One trail leads from Islip Saddle, the other from another (unnamed) saddle 1.5 miles farther west. Both are well-graded, well maintained routes, part of the Pacific Crest Trail.

Possibly, after a glance at a map, the idea of linking the east and west Mt. Williamson trails with a walk along Angles Crest Highway, in order to make a loop trip, will occur to you. Don't be tempted. The problem is that between the two trails, Angeles Crest Highway passes through a couple of tunnels—a definite no-no for pedestrians.

Both Mt. Williamson trails are winners; you can't go wrong. Mt. Williamson is a great place to beat the heat, and offers fine hiking in all seasons but winter, when snow covers the trail.

DIRECTIONS TO TRAILHEAD: From the Foothill Freeway (210) in La Canada, exit on Angeles Crest Highway (2) and drive about 38 miles, or 2.5 miles past (east of) the Snowcrest Ski Area. Look for the (sometimes) signed trail to Mt. Williamson on the left (north) side of the highway.

The Mt. Williamson east trail is easier to find. Continue 4 mile east of the Snowcrest Ski Area and, after you pass through the highway tunnels, you'll see the parking area at Islip Saddle on the left (north) side of the highway.

THE HIKE: At Islip Saddle, you'll spot South Fork Trail (remember this fine trail for another day) heading northeast down to South Fork Camp near Devil's Punchbowl County Park. But you'll join the trail to Mt. Williamson and begin ascending through a forest of Jeffrey and ponderosa pine.

Two miles of steep, but not brutal climbing brings you to a junction with the westerly ascending Pacific Crest Trail.

Hike north on the ridgeline along an unmaintained trail, which gets a little fainter as it nears the summit of Mt. Williamson. From the peak, savor the dramatic views of the desert below. If you have a good map along, you can pick out the many playas (dry lake beds), buttes and mountain ridges of the dry lands below. At the base of Mt. Williamson is that greatest of earthquake faults—the San Andreas Rift Zone. Most striking of all is the view of Devil's Punchbowl and its jumbled sedimentary strata.

Remember that this isn't a loop hike; return the way you came.

MT. ISLIP

MT. ISLIP TRAIL
From Angeles Crest Highway to Little Jimmy Trail Camp is 3 miles round trip with 500-foot elevation gain; to Mt. Islip is 5 miles round trip with 1,100-foot gain

Mt. Islip, (pronounced eye-slip) is not named, as you might guess, for a clumsy mountaineer, but for Canadian George Islip, who homesteaded in San Gabriel Canyon a century ago. The mountain is by no means one of the tallest San Gabriel mountain peaks, but its relatively isolated position on the spine of the range makes it stand out. The summit offers the hiker fine views of the middle portion of the Angeles National Forest high country and of the metropolis.

Mt. Islip has long been a popular destination for hikers. The mountain was particularly popular with Occidental College students who built a huge cairn (heap of boulders), dubbed the "Occidental Monument," atop the summit in 1909. The monument, which had the name Occidental on top, stood about two decades, until the Forest Service cleared the summit of Mt. Islip to make room for a fire lookout tower. Today, the monument and the fire lookout are long gone, but the stone foundation of the fire lookout's living quarters still remains.

One early visitor to the slopes of Mt. Islip was popular newspaper cartoonist Jimmy Swinnerton (1875-1974), well known in the early years of the 20th century for his comic strip "Little Jimmy." By the time he was in his thirties, hard-working, hard-drinking Swinnerton was suffering from the effects of exhaustion, booze, and tuberculosis. His employer and benefactor, William Randolph Hearst,

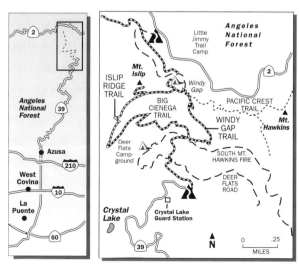

sent Swinnerton to the desert to dry out. Swinnerton, however, found the summer heat oppressive so, loading his paintbrushes onto a burro, he headed into the San Gabriel Mountains.

Swinnerton spent the summers of 1908 and 1909 at Camp Coldbrook on the banks of the north fork of the San Gabriel River. Often he would set up camp high on the shoulder of Mt. Islip near a place called Gooseberry Spring, which soon became known as Little Jimmy Spring. During the two summers Swinnerton was encamped in the San Gabriels, entertained passing hikers with sketches of his Little Jimmy character. His campsite, for many years known as Swinnerton Camp, now bears the name of Little Jimmy Trail Camp.

You can reach Mt. Islip from the south side of the mountains, the way Jimmy Swinnerton did, or start from the north side from Angeles Crest Highway. This hike follows the latter route, which is a bit easier than coming up from Crystal Lake.

DIRECTIONS TO TRAILHEAD: From the Foothill Freeway (210) in La Canada, exit on Angeles Crest Highway (2) and proceed some 41 miles to signed Islip Saddle. (At the saddle, on the north side of the highway, is a large parking area. If you want, you can start your hike to Mt. Islip at the trailhead across the road from the parking area. An old trail heads east, zigzagging up to the trees for 0.75 mile before leveling off for a mile and reaching Little Jimmy Trail camp.

From Islip Saddle, a 1.5 mile drive east on Angeles Crest Highway brings you to the signed trailhead for Little Jimmy Trail Camp on the right (south) side of the road. There's parking on both sides of the highway.

THE HIKE: Your trail, at first, is a dirt road (closed to all but Forest Service vehicles). Jeffrey and sugar pine shade the route. A half-mile ascent brings you to a three-way junction. To your right is the old crest trail coming up from Islip Saddle. The forest road you've been following continues to Little Jimmy Trail Camp.

Bear left on the signed trail to Little Jimmy. The trail stays just below and parallel to the road as it ascends a mile over forested slopes to Little Jimmy Trail Camp. The camp, popular with scout troops, has tables, stoves and restrooms. A side trail leads 0.25 mile southeast to all-year Little Jimmy Spring.

At the west end of camp, pick up the signed trail to Mt. Islip. A half-mile of switchbacks through piney woods brings you up to a sharp ridgeline. From atop the ridge, you'll enjoy great views of Crystal Lake, the San Gabriel Wilderness, and the canyons cut by Bear Creek and the San Gabriel River. The trail turns east and follows the ridge for another half-mile to the 8,250-foot peak. Summit views include the ski areas of Snowcrest and Mt. Waterman to the west and Mt. Baden-Powell to the east.

THROOP PEAK

DAWSON SADDLE, PACIFIC CREST TRAILS

From Dawson Saddle to Throop Peak is 4.5 miles round trip with 1,200-foot elevation gain

The trail to Throop Peak reveals the alpine crest of the Angeles National Forest at its best. Here's a pathway that begins among tall trees, travels among them, and even ends up on a summit shaded by them.

The trailhead for the climb to Throop (pronounced Troop) is located at Dawson Saddle, highpoint on the Angeles Crest Highway. At 7,903 feet, the saddle is positively High Sierran in height, and offers the Throop-bound hiker a great head-start into the high country. You'll appreciate this hike on a hot summer day: it can be 30 degrees F. or more cooler in temperature at Dawson Saddle than in the San Gabriel Valley, visible from the top of Throop Peak.

In 1916, four CalTech students scaled the peak, claiming it and naming it for Amos G. Throop founder of Throop University, forerunner of the California Institute of Technology.

While not unknown, Throop Peak is visited by far fewer hikers than other nearby summits. Eastern neighbor Mt. Baden-Powell (elevation 9,399 feet) attracts most of the troops—Boy Scouts, that is. Southwestern neighbor Mt.

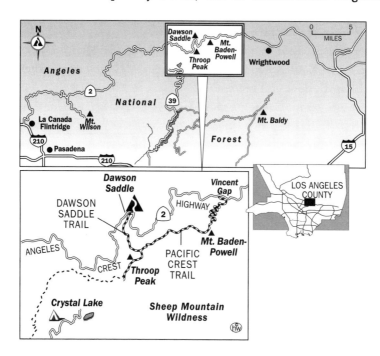

237

Hawkins (elevation 8,850 feet) lures lots of hikers because it's accessible from two major trailheads—Little Jimmy Campground and Crystal Lake.

Throop Peak, on the Sierra Club's Hundred Peaks List (summits more than 5,000 feet), does get its share of the more compulsive, goal-oriented peak-baggers among us. Many hikers walk over the shoulder of the peak along one of the most splendid stretches of the Pacific Crest Trail in the Southland, but do not detour to the top. If you do get to the top of Throop, you'll likely have the summit—and the wonderful view from the 9,138-foot peak—all to yourself.

DIRECTIONS TO TRAILHEAD: From the Foothill Freeway (2) in La Canada, exit on the Angeles Crest Highway (10) and drive some 49 miles to Dawson Saddle. In very rapid succession, the motorist will note the old trail to Throop Peak on the right, signed Dawson Saddle by a highway maintenance building on the left and Pinyon Ridge Overlook, a highway viewpoint, on the left. Continue about 100 yards down the highway past the overlook and park in an unsigned turnout on the left side of the road.

Dawson Saddle Trail, which departs from the right (south) side of the highway, is signed, but the sign is located a little bit from the beginning of the trail and difficult to see from the road.

THE HIKE: Thank the Boy Scouts for their efforts as you ascend the well-graded pathway that the scouts restored in the 1980s. Savor over-the-shoulder, conifer-framed views of the Mojave Desert; watching the desert floor shimmering in the heat far below has a way of making the hiker grateful to be walking up where the air is cool and pine-scented.

In 0.25 mile the old trail comes in from the right and joins the ascent among fine specimens of Jeffrey pine and fir. The path climbs south, then contours around the north slope of Throop Peak.

About 2 miles up Dawson Saddle Trail, you reach a signed junction with the Pacific Crest Trail. It's a two mile trek northwest on the PCT to Mt. Baden-Powell. While B-P is the second most popular high country summit in the San Gabriels (only Mt. Baldy is hiked more), not many hikers visit the peak from this direction.

Throop-bound hikers will head southwest on the PCT and admire the lodgepole pine that thrive at this elevation. After 0.25 mile along the PCT, join the unsigned summit trail that ascends the south side of the peak.

Up top is a memorial marker to Amos G. Throop (1811-1894), founder of Throop University. Sign the summit register and enjoy views of the city, the high country and the desert.

❧ MT. BADEN-POWELL

MT. BADEN-POWELL TRAIL
From Vincent Gap to summit is 8 miles round trip with 2,800-foot
elevation gain; Season: May-October

This trail and peak honor Lord Baden-Powell, a British Army officer who founded the Boy Scout movement in 1907. The well-engineered trail, grooved into the
side of the mountain by the Civilian Conservation Corps in the mid-1930s,
switchbacks up the northeast ridge to the peak.

The peak was once known as North Baldy, before Southern California Boy
Scouts lobbied the Forest Service for a name change. Mt. Baden-Powell is the terminus of the scouts' 53-mile Silver Moccasin Trail, a rugged week-long backpack
through the San Gabriels. Scouts who complete the long trail earn the Silver
Moccasin Award.

The trail follows a moderate, steady grade to the top of the mountain, where
there's a monument honoring Lord Baden-Powell. On the summit, you'll meet
those ancient survivors, the limber pines, and be treated to superb views across the
Mojave Desert and down into the Iron Fork of the San Gabriel River.

DIRECTIONS TO TRAILHEAD: Take the Angeles Crest Highway (2)
for 53 miles from La Canada to the Vincent Gap Parking Area. The signed trailhead is at the northwest edge of the parking area.

If you're coming from the east, take Interstate 15 to the Wrightwood exit,
three miles south of Cajon Pass. Proceed 8 miles west on Highway 138 to its intersection with Highway 2. Turn left on Highway 2 and follow it for 14 miles to the
trailhead.

THE HIKE: The trail immediately begins ascending from Vincent Gulch
Divide, a gap which separates the upper tributaries of the San Gabriel River to
the south from Big Rock Creek to the northwest. You begin switchbacking southwest through Jeffrey pine and fir. The trail numbers more than three dozen of
these switchbacks, but so many beautiful attractions compete for the hiker's
attention that it's hard to get an accurate count.

In 1.5 miles, a side trail (unmarked) leads a hundred yards to Lamel Spring, an
inviting resting place and the only dependable water en route.

With increased elevation, the switchbacks grow shorter and steeper and the
vegetation changes from fir to lodgepole pine. Soon, even the altitude-loving
lodgepoles give way to the heartiest of pines, the limber pine. A half-mile from
the summit, around 9,000 feet in elevation, the first of these squat, thick-trunked

limber pines come into view. Shortly, you'll intersect a side trail to the limber pine forest.

To Limber Pine Forest: A tiny sign points right (southwest) to the limber pine stand, 0.125 mile. These wind-loving, subalpine dwellers are one of the few living things that can cope with the rarefied atmosphere. *Pinus flexilis,* botanists call the species, for its long, droopy, flexible branches. They bow and scrape like hyperextended dancers and appear to gather all their nourishment from the wind.

Back on the main trail, a few more switchbacks bring you atop the ridge where Mt. Baldy can be glimpsed. You walk along the barren crest and intersect the Pacific Crest Trail. PCT swoops off to Little Jimmy Spring.

You continue past the limber pines to the summit. A concrete monument pays homage to Lord Baden-Powell. Enjoy the superb view out across the Mojave to the southern Sierra and east to Baldy, San Gorgonio and San Jacinto.

CHAPTER TWELVE

Los Angeles County Coast

Stretching some seventy-five miles from Long Beach
to Malibu, the diverse Los Angeles County coastline
includes reefs, tidepools, coves and, crescent beaches in the
south, bluffs, rocky points, coves and sandy beaches in the
north. While some beaches are virtually packed with people,
others are nearly secluded, even in the summer months.
The passing parade on the Venice Boardwalk,
the "surf city" feeling of Hermosa, the harbor of
Marina del Rey—all attract the hiker to pass through
and enjoy a coastal environment unique in all the world.

❦ Leo Carrillo Beach

LEO CARRILLO BEACH TRAIL
Leo Carrillo State Park to Ventura County line is 3 miles round trip

Angeline Leo Carrillo is best remembered for his movie role, then his television part, as the Cisco Kid's sidekick, Pancho. He and his prominent family were quite active in recreation and civic matters and it's altogether fitting that he is remembered by this beach on the Ventura/Los Angeles county line.

Leo Carrillo Beach is stabilized to some extent by minor rocky breaks in the shoreline and by extensive kelp beds offshore. Seals sometimes come ashore. (Don't disturb.) The beach is a popular locale for moviemakers, and after the property-master installs palm trees the beach doubles for a South Seas locale.

The beach trail follows an interesting and fairly natural length of coastline. At Sequit Point you'll find good surfing, swimming, skin diving and a cluster of caves and coves.

DIRECTIONS TO TRAILHEAD: Leo Carrillo State Park is located on Pacific Coast Highway just down-coast from its junction with Mulholland Highway near the Ventura/Los Angeles county line. Park along PCH (free) or the state park (fee).

THE HIKE: Head up-coast toward Sequit Point. The point bisects the beach, forming a bay to the south. Surfers tackle the well-shaped south swell, battling the submerged rocks and kelp beds.

Nearing the point, you'll pass a path which leads under the highway and connects the beach with the sycamore-shaded campground. Scramble around the rocks of Sequit Point to several rock formations, caves, coves, a rock arch and some nice tidepools.

North of the point, Leo Carrillo Beach offers good swimming with a sandy bottom. The unspoiled coast here contrasts with development in the county line area. When the beach narrows and the houses multiply, return the way you came.

❦ PT. DUME

ZUMA-DUME TRAIL

From Zuma Beach to Point Dume is 1 mile round trip;
to Paradise Cove is 3 miles round trip

Zuma Beach is one of Los Angeles County's largest sand beaches and one of the finest white sand strands in California. Zuma lies on the open coast beyond Santa Monica Bay and thus receives heavy breakers crashing in from the north. From sunrise to sunset, board and body surfers try to catch a big one. Every month the color of the ocean and the cliffs seem to take on different shades of green depending on the season and sunlight, providing the Zuma Beach hiker with yet another attraction.

During the whale-watching season (approximately mid-December through March), hikers ascending to the lookout atop Point Dume have a good chance of spotting a migrating California gray whale.

This walk travels along that part of Zuma Beach known as Westward Beach, climbs over the geologically fascinating Point Dume Headlands for sweeping views of the coast, then descends to Paradise Cove, site of a romantic little beach, a restaurant, and a fishing pier.

DIRECTIONS TO TRAILHEAD: From Pacific Coast Highway, about 25 miles up-coast from Santa Monica and just downcoast from Zuma Beach County Park, turn oceanward on Westward Beach Road and follow it to its end at a (fee) parking lot. Consult a tide table. Passage is easier at low tide.

THE HIKE: Proceed down-coast along sandy Westward Beach. You'll soon see a distinct path leading up the point. The trail ascends through a plant community of sea fig and sage, coreopsis and prickly pear cactus to a lookout point.

From atop Point Dume, you can look down at Pirate's Cove, two hundred yards of beach tucked away between two rocky outcroppings. In past years, this beach was the scene of much dispute between nude beach advocates, residents and the county sheriff.

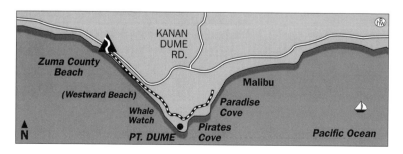

As you stand atop the rocky triangle projecting into the Pacific, observe the dense black Zuma volcanics and the much softer white sedimentary beds of the sea cliffs extending both east and west. The volcanics have resisted the crashing sea far better than the sedimentary rock and have protected the land behind from further erosion, thus forming the triangle shape of the point.

After enjoying the view and watching for whales, retrace your steps a short distance and continue on the main trail over the point, which has been set aside as a preserve under the protection of the California Department of Fish and Game. A staircase lets you descend to the beach.

A mile of beach-walking brings you to Paradise Cove, sometimes called Dume Cove. It's a secluded spot, and the scene of much television and motion picture filming. A restaurant and a private pier are located at the cove.

Zuma Beach

❦ MALIBU BEACH

MALIBU BEACH TRAIL

1 mile round trip around Malibu Lagoon, to Malibu Pier; 4 to 6 miles miles round trip up-coast

When Southern California natives say "Malibu Beach," this popular surfing spot is what they mean: the site of beach-blanket movies and Beach Boys songs. The state beach—formerly known as Surfrider—is a mixture of sand and stone. More than 200 bird species have been observed at Malibu Lagoon.

For Frederick Hastings Rindge, owner of 22 miles of Southern California coast, life in the Malibu of a century ago was divine. "The enobling stillness makes the mind ascend to heaven," he wrote in his memoir, *Happy Days in Southern California,* published in 1898.

Long before Malibu meant good surfing, a movie star colony and some of the most expensive real estate on earth, "The Malibu" was a shorthand name for Topanga-Malibu-Sequit, an early 19th-century rancho. This rancho extended from Topanga Canyon to the southeast to Ventura County on the northwest, from the tideline to the crest of the Santa Monica Mountains.

Malibu Lagoon hosts many different kinds of waterfowl, both resident and migratory. The beach is rock cobble on the ocean side of the lagoon. To the land-ward side of the lagoon stretches the alluvial fill flatland deposited by Malibu Creek. The city of Malibu is situated here.

DIRECTIONS TO TRAILHEAD: Malibu Lagoon State Beach is located at Pacific Coast Highway and Cross Creek Road in Malibu.

Malibu Lagoon

THE HIKE: First follow the nature trails around the lagoon. Next, head down-coast to the historic 700-foot Malibu Pier, built in 1903. It's a favorite of anglers and tourists. Sportfishing boats depart from the pier.

Farther down-coast is Zonker Harris Accessway, long the focus of debate between the California Coastal Commission, determined to provide access to the coast, and some Malibu residents who would prefer the public stay out. The original sign read "Zonker Harris Memorial Beach," honoring a character from the Doonesbury comic strip whose primary goal once was to acquire the perfect tan.

Up-coast, you'll pass Malibu Point; here the strong southwest swell refracts against a rock reef and creates the waves that makes Malibu so popular with surfers. Next you walk the narrow and sandy beach lined by the exclusive Malibu Colony residences, home to many a movie star. Toward the west end of The Colony, the beach narrows considerably and houses are built on stilts, with the waves sometimes pounding beneath them.

As you walk along Malibu Beach, rejoice that you do not see State Highway 60, the Malibu Freeway. In the 1960s a plan was hatched to build a causeway along Malibu Beach, supported on pilings offshore. A breakwater would have converted the open shore into a bay shore. The wonderful pounding surf would have been reduced to that of a lake.

The beach is wider and more public at Corral State Beach, located at the mouths of Corral and Solstice Canyons.

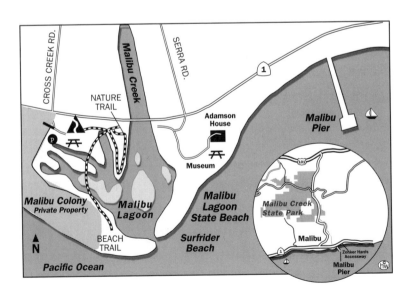

❦ MALIBU BLUFFS

MALIBU BLUFFS TRAIL

From Malibu Bluffs Park to Pacific shore is 2 miles round trip; to Malibu Lagoon State Beach is 6 miles round trip; to Dan Blocker State Beach is 6 miles round trip.

Watch for pelicans, dolphins, whales and wildflowers on a grand descent from the Malibu Bluffs to Santa Monica Bay. In addition, this hike from the heart of Malibu to the surf-line offers great vistas up and down the coast.

Malibu Bluffs Park, stunningly situated above the famed Malibu Colony, is the trailhead for a short but memorable coastal ramble. The park is operated by the city of Malibu in cooperation with the California Department of Parks and Recreation, landowner of the bluffs. (Although the city of Malibu is 27 miles long, it has no public parks of its very own.)

Six-acre Malibu Bluffs Park is mostly a Field of Dreams—that is to say, two absolutely beautiful baseball diamonds. Malibu Little Leaguers have played America's pastime on the fields for more than 20 years.

Other park amenities include a walking path, a whale-watching perch and the Michael Landon Community Building. Fans who remember that 1960s' TV horse opera, "Bonanza," will note that this hike leads from a building named for Michael Landon, the actor who played the part of Little Joe, to a beach named for Dan Blocker, who played his brother Hoss.

DIRECTIONS TO TRAILHEAD: Driving to the park can be half the fun. Malibu Bluffs Park is located at the beginning (or end, depending on how you look at things) of Malibu Canyon Road which, recently was ceremonially established as part of the Los Angeles County Scenic Highway system. A bill passed by the state legislature gave the road its scenic status.

The scenic highway begins life by the Ventura Freeway (101) as Las Virgenes Road. From Lost Hills Road in Calabasas, Malibu Canyon Road snakes eight miles through deep gorges and rugged ravines and descends into Malibu.

On approach to Pacific Coast Highway, the motorist enjoys vistas of the dra-matic sweep of Santa Monica Bay and a glimpse of world-renowned Surfrider Beach. Malibu Canyon Road winds past Pepperdine University to its terminus at Malibu Bluffs Park.

THE HIKE: Begin your lemming-like march to the sea from one of two footpaths. You'll find the first behind the center field fence of the westernmost baseball diamond. The second, better, and signed trail begins by the Michael

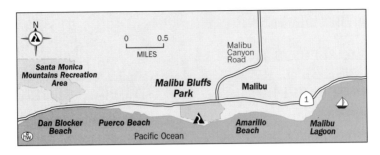

Landon Community Building. (The two trails eventually join and lead down to the water.)

Not much blooms along the state parkland trails in midsummer, but the bluffs put on quite a wildflower show in springtime, when members of the California Native Plant Society lead wildflower-appreciation hikes.

The pathway drops to Malibu Road, the access road for Malibu Colony homeowners. Directly across the road is an official coastal accessway. Take this public stairway down to the beach.

You may choose to walk up-coast or down from here along some four miles of beach.. Much of the strand in both directions is lined with expensive homes built on pilings. Respect the privacy of the beachfront property owners by walking along the tideline. You may legally walk this beach—and any beach in California—up to the mean high tide line.

Four public accessways (stairways) connect Malibu Road to the waterfront. These passages also offer an escape route for the beach hiker threatened by a rising tide.

A walk of a bit less than two miles up-coast travels Puerco City Beach to Dan Blocker State Beach (formerly Corral Beach), a mixed shore of sandy and rocky beach backed by riprap shielding the coast highway from the pounding surf.

Those opting for a down-coast route will enjoy a beach hike of a bit more than two miles to Malibu Lagoon State Beach. From here, you can follow nature trails around the lagoon, continue along the shore to historic Malibu Pier, or return the same way.

♛ Santa Monica Bay

CALIFORNIA COASTAL TRAIL
20 to 40 miles

Fringed by palm trees, with the Santa Monica Mountains as dramatic backdrop, the wide sandy beaches along Santa Monica Bay draw visitors from around the world.

Locals tend to get a bit blasé about this beauty in their backyard, and often fail to take advantage of what is, in my opinion, one of the world's great beach walks.

Favorite bay walks enjoyed by tourists include Venice Beach and the Venice Boardwalk, the Santa Monica Pier and Palisades Park in Santa Monica. These are pleasant enough excursions, but I would suggest something more ambitious: a walk around the entire bay.

Such a hike will surely be a very long day—or a weekend—to remember. You'll get a real feel for the bay, not only as a collection of beaches and seashore sights, but as a living, dynamic ecosystem whose health and well-being depends heavily on government and citizen action.

Geographically, Santa Monica Bay is a mellow intrusion by the Pacific Ocean into the western edge of the Los Angeles lowlands. The bay's magnificent curving beaches are cooled by a prevailing ocean breeze, which protects the coast from the temperature extremes—and smog—that are characteristic of the interior.

Alas, all views along Santa Monica Bay are not picture-perfect; huge smokestacks from power plants tower over some South Bay beaches, while jets departing LAX fly low and loud over others.

And the bay has its share of well-documented environmental problems, too. Sewers and storm drains empty into the bay. Organizations such as Heal the Bay have undertaken the Herculean task of educating the public and public officials that the bay is not merely a series of sand strands, but a complex ecosystem.

Pick a brisk fall or winter weekend to walk the bay and you'll be surprised at how much shoreline solitude you'll enjoy. It's possible to walk the bay from Torrance to the Santa Monica Pier in a very long day, but the 20-mile beach hike is more comfortably completed in two days.

If bay-walking agrees with you, consider walking the rest of the bay—another 20 miles from the Santa Monica Pier to Pt. Dume.

You can arrange a car shuttle or use the bus system to return to your day's start point. Better yet, leave a bicycle at the end of your walk and cycle back to the trailhead along the South Bay Bicycle Trail. Super-jocks will relish the challenge of what I call the Triathlon Trail: Walk the 20 miles from Torrance County Beach to the Santa Monica Pier, cycle the South Bay Bicycle Trail, then take a long refreshing swim.

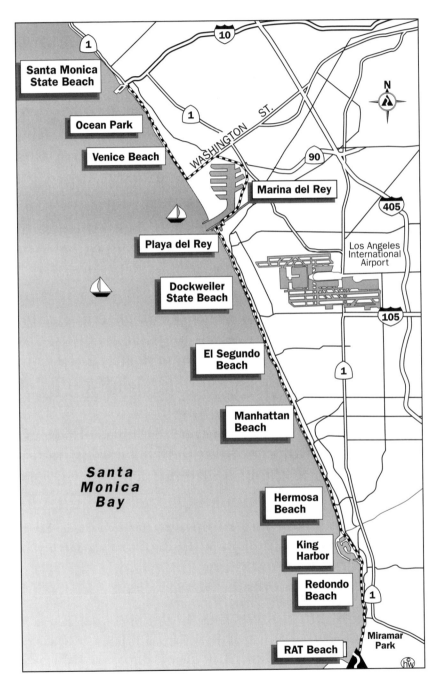

❦ SOUTH COAST BOTANIC GARDEN

SOUTH COAST TRAIL
1 mile or so round trip

Beginning in the 1920s, diotomaceous earth (used in abrasives, filtering systems, insulation) was dug from a huge Palos Verdes Peninsula pit. When the diatomite were exhausted, the County of Los Angeles acquired the site for a landfill, burying 3.5 million tons of trash during the 1960s.

After the landfill was filled, a decision was made to create a garden. Numerous horticultural problems had to be overcome: soil settling (which is why the land was unsuitable for building), lack of compost (diotomaceous earth has none), and root-wrecking heat and gases given off by buried vegetable matter.

Major plant collections include roses, succulents, flowering fruit trees and even redwoods. Among the specialized sections are an herb garden, a vegetable garden and an English garden. South Coast also has impressive groupings by color—blue, pink and yellow. The garden particularly emphasizes plants from Australia, the Mediterranean and southern Africa—flora that thrive in Southern California's similar climate.

For the hiker, a system of trails leads through the garden over to a manmade lake. The garden's high points offer superb clear-day panoramas of Los Angeles. Joining hikers and garden buffs, horticulturists and reclamation experts travel from near and far to study this innovative project.

DIRECTIONS TO TRAILHEAD: From the Harbor Freeway (110) in Wilmington, exit on Pacific Coast Highway. Go west 3 miles to Crenshaw Boulevard, then turn south to the South Coast Botanic Garden.

Taking root in the South Coast

❦ PALOS VERDES HILLS

PORTUGUESE BEND TRAIL
From Del Cerro Park to Badlands Slide Area is 2.5 miles round trip
with 400-foot elevation gain

The little-known and infrequently traveled trails of Palos Verdes Peninsula offer the walker a tranquil escape from metropolitan life. During the spring, the hills are colored an emerald green and sprinkled with wildflowers.

This short loop trip, suitable for the whole family, explores the hills above Portuguese Bend, one of the most geologically interesting (and unstable) areas in Southern California. Earth movement from 1956 to 1957 wrecked approximately 100 homes. The rate of movement was more than an inch a day!

Portuguese Bend takes its name from the men who practiced the risky, but lucrative, business of shore whaling. Most of the hardy whalers who worked the waters off Palos Verdes Peninsula from the 1850s to the 1880s were of Portuguese descent. Many a whale was slaughtered, but the Peninsula whaling operation was abandoned; not for lack of gray whales, but because of a shortage of the fuel necessary to process blubber into oil.

The route I've dubbed Portuguese Bend Trail links various paths and fire roads and offers great clear-day views of the Peninsula and Catalina Island.

DIRECTIONS TO TRAILHEAD: From the San Diego Freeway (405) in Torrance, exit on Crenshaw Boulevard and head south. Continue on Crenshaw past Pacific Coast Highway and into the hills of Rancho Palos Verdes. Park at boulevard's end at the side of the road or at nearby Del Cerro Park.

THE HIKE: Head down the unsigned fire road, which is officially named Crenshaw Extension Trail. Leaving red-roofed huge haciendas behind, you'll look ahead to a million-dollar view. The green hills, bedecked with lupine in the spring, roll to the sea. Geology students will observe the Peninsula's unique blend of native brush and imported flora gone wild.

A half-mile descent from the trailhead brings you to a water tank and an unsigned three-way intersection. The leftward trail climbs to a fire station. The trail dead-ahead will be your return route on this walk. Continue right with Crenshaw Extension Trail, which soon drops into a wildflower-splashed meadow known as Peacock Flats. It's doubtful you'll see a peacock here, but you might here the shrill call of the "watchdog of the Peninsula" from other parts of the trail. The aggressive birds are popular pets around here, but they do get on the nerves of local residents, some of whom favor banishing them from the area.

Above Peacock Flats, two short trails lead up a hill topped with a dozen pine

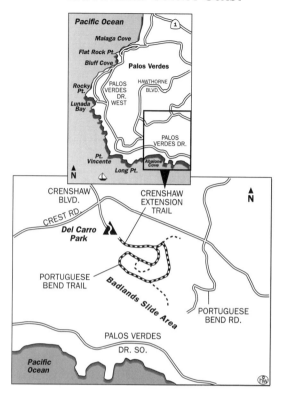

trees. From the crest of the hill, known as Eagle's Nest, you'll have grand clear-day views of Catalina. The nest is close to the southwestern-most point of the Peninsula, meaning Catalina is but 17 nautical miles away; often many of the island's geographical features are identifiable.

Return to the main trail which heads northwest then makes a long horseshoe bend to the southeast. After descending past a stand of eucalyptus and a water tank, you'll begin crossing the geologically unstable terrain known as Badlands Slide Area.

A water pipe on the left parallels the dirt road at this point. Look sharply left for an unsigned trail that climbs to the east. After a steep and tentative start, the trail widens and ascends at a more moderate pace atop a canyon wall. Sweet-smelling fennel lines the path, which turns north and climbs to the above-mentioned three-way trail junction. Retrace your steps on Crenshaw Extension Trail to the trailhead.

❦ PALOS VERDES PENINSULA

PALOS VERDES PENINSULA TRAIL

From Malaga Cove to Rocky Point is 5 miles round trip; to Point Vincente
Lighthouse is 10 miles round trip

Palos Verdes Peninsula is famous for its rocky cliffs, which rise from 50 to 300 feet
above the ocean and for its thirteen wave-cut terraces. These terraces, or plat-
forms, resulted from a combination of uplift and sea-level fluctuations caused by
the formation and melting of glaciers. Today the waves, as they have for so many
thousands of years, are actively eroding the shoreline, cutting yet another terrace
onto the land.

While enjoying this walk, you'll pass many beautiful coves, where whaling
ships once anchored and delivered their cargo of whale oil. Large iron kettles, used to
boil whale blubber, have been found in sea cliff caves. Native Americans, Spanish
rancheros and Yankee smugglers have all added to the Peninsula's romantic history.
Modern times have brought mansions to the Peninsula bluffs, but the beach
remains almost pristine. Offshore, divers explore the rocky bottoms for abalone and
shellfish. Onshore, hikers enjoy the wave-scalloped bluffs and splendid tidepools.

Hiking this beach is like walking over a surface of broken bowling balls. The
route is rocky and progress slow, but that gives you more time to look down at the
tidepools and up at the magnificent bluffs.

Check a tide table and hike only at low tide.

DIRECTIONS TO TRAILHEAD: Take Pacific Coast Highway to Palos
Verdes Boulevard. Bear right on Palos Verdes Drive. As you near Malaga Cove
Plaza, turn right at the first stop sign (Via Corta). Make a right on Via Arroyo,
then another right into the parking lot behind the Malaga Cove School. The
trailhead is on the ocean side of the parking area where a wide path descends the
bluffs above the Flat Rock Point tidepools. A footpath leaves from Paseo Del
Mar, 0.1 mile past Via Horcada, where the street curves east to join Palos Verdes
Drive West.

THE HIKE: From the Malaga Cove School parking lot, descend the wide
path to the beach. A sign indicates you're entering a seashore reserve and asks you
to treat tidepool residents with respect. To the north are sandy beaches for seden-
tary sun worshipers. Active rock-hoppers clamber to the south. At several places
along this walk you'll notice that the great terraces are cut by steep-walled
canyons. The first of these canyon incisions can be observed at Malaga Cove,
where Malaga Canyon slices through the north slopes of Palos Verdes Hills, then
cuts west to empty at the cove.

The coastline curves out to sea in a southwesterly direction and Flat Rock Point comes into view. The jade-colored waters swirl around this anvil-shaped point, creating the best tidepool area along this section of coast. Above the point, the cliffs soar to 300 feet. Cloaked in morning fog, the rocky seascape here is reminiscent of Big Sur.

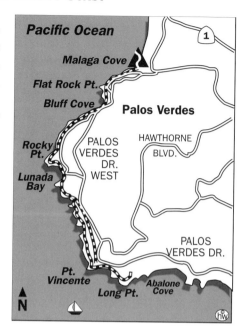

Rounding Flat Rock Point, you pick your way among the rocks, seaweed and the flotsam and jetsam of civilization to Bluff Cove, where sparkling combers explode against the rocks and douse the unwary with their tangy spray. A glance over your right shoulder brings a view of Santa Moncia Bay, the Santa Monica Mountains in gray silhouette and on the far horizon, the Channel Islands.

A mile beyond Bluff Cove, Rocky (also called Palos Verdes) Point juts out like a ship's prow. Caught fast on the rocks at the base of the point is the rusting exoskeleton of the Greek freighter *Dominator,* a victim of the treacherous reef surrounding the peninsula.

Trek around Rocky Point to Lunada Bay, a good place to observe the terrace surfaces. From here you'll walk under almost perpendicular cliffs that follow horseshoe-shaped Lunada Bay. Shortly you'll round Resort Point, where fishermen try their luck. As the coastline turns south, Catalina can often be seen glowing on the horizon. Along this stretch of shoreline, numerous stacks, remnants of former cliffs not yet dissolved by the surf, can be seen.

The stretch of coast before the lighthouse has been vigorously scalloped by thousands of years of relentless surf. You'll have to boulder-hop the last mile to Point Vincente. The lighthouse has worked its beacon over the dark waters since 1926.

Passage is usually impossible around the lighthouse at high tide; if passable, another half-mile of walking brings you to an official beach access (or departure) route at Long Point.

ABALONE COVE SHORELINE PARK

ABALONE COVE TRAIL
From Palos Verdes Drive to Portuguese Point is 2 miles round trip with 180-foot elevation gain.

Abalone Cove offers the hiker a fine sampling of the pleasures of the PV shoreline: tidepools, sandy beaches and dramatic 180-foot high bluffs laced with trails. The excellent vistas from the top of the bluffs include Sacred (Smugglers) Cove and Inspiration Point, Catalina Island and the wide blue Pacific, and inland to the Portuguese Bend landslide zone.

Mile-long Abalone Cove Shoreline Park boasts two beaches—East Beach, a sandy beach at the east end of the cove and Upper Beach, an artificially raised rocky and sandy beach created in the 1930s for a resort hotel, whose former clubhouse now serves as a lifeguard facility. An ecological reserve protects the rich tidepools and offshore kelp beds.

DIRECTIONS TO TRAILHEAD: From the end of Hawthorne Boulevard at the coast, head south on Pacific Coast Highway (1) two miles to the signed entrance of Abalone Cove Shoreline Park. Turn right and park (fee required) in the lot.

THE HIKE: From the parking lot, head east (up-coast) across the picnic area to a wide path that leads to the park service road. Fork left on this road and ascend a narrow path that parallels Palos Verdes Drive South.

You reach—and hike briefly up—another park service road to a trail junction. Bear left to begin a clockwise exploration of Portuguese Point. After looping around and savoring the views (watch for dolphins surfacing just outside the surf zone), you'll return to the trail junction and this time take the west fork. The path leads down to the shoreline below the point and connects to a coastal trail that you'll follow a half-mile up-coast along Abalone Cove. At Upper Beach and the lifeguard station, ascend the park road to a junction with a footpath that climbs through the coastal scrub back to the trailhead.

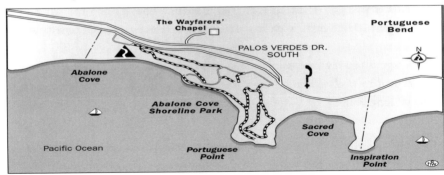

❦ CABRILLO BEACH

CABRILLO BEACH TRAIL
From Cabrillo Beach to White Point is 3.5 miles round trip

This coastal hike has a little of everything: Cabrillo Beach, the only real sand beach for miles to the north and south; the family-friendly Cabrillo Marine Aquarium; historic White Point, an intriguing chapter from coastal SoCal's history.

The mission of the Cabrillo Marine Aquarium is to promote knowledge and conservation of marine life in Southern California and this it does well, with exhibits interpreting the region's mudflats, kelp forest, sandy beach and other environments. The aquarium sponsors tidepool walks, grunion watches and is a coordinating point for whale-watching cruises. Open daily except Mondays, the aquarium attracts scores of school groups.

All but forgotten today, the rocky cove just down-coast from White Point in San Pedro once flourished as a Roaring Twenties health spa and resort. All that remains today are some sea-battered cement ruins and lush overgrown gardens.

White Point was originally settled at the turn of the century by immigrant Japanese fishermen who harvested the bountiful abalone from the waters off Palos Verdes Peninsula. Tons of abalone were shipped to the Far East and tons more were consumed locally in Los Angeles' Little Tokyo. In a few years the abalone was depleted, but an even greater resource was discovered at White's Point—sulfur springs.

In 1915 construction of a spa began. Eventually the large Royal Palms Hotel was built at water's edge. Palm gardens and a golf course decorated the cliffs above. The sulfur baths were especially popular with the Japanese population of Southern California.

The spa boomed in the 1920s, but the 1933 earthquake closed the springs. The cove became part of Fort McArthur during World War II, the Japanese-American settlers were incarcerated in internment camps, and the resort was soon overwhelmed by crumbling cliffs and the powerful sea.

Some maps and colorful local histories refer to White's Point, as a place named for a 19th century sailor who jumped ship and swam ashore to this point. Other sources say the point name honors Senator Stephen White, who led the fight to locate the Port of Los Angeles in San Pedro. The definitive word from the San Pedro Historical Society is that the white shale of White Point has made it a landmark for generations of mariners, and hence the name.

Look for the new White Point Natural Preserve on the inland side of Paseo

Del Mar across from Royal Palms County Beach. Plans call for nature trails and rejuvenation of the coastal scrub and coastal prairie habitats. Other trails will interpret the fascinating local history, explore the hills and lead to overlooks for whale-watching.

DIRECTIONS TO TRAILHEAD: Take the Harbor Freeway south to San Pedro and exit on Gaffey Street. Follow Gaffey seaward to 1st Street, turn left and travel a quarter-mile to Pacific Avenue. Turn right and travel south 2.5 miles to 36th Street. Fee parking is available in the large lot that serves Cabrillo Beach and the Cabrillo Marine Aquarium.

THE HIKE: March up sandy Cabrillo Beach, which has a monopoly on the grunion, since the sand-seeking fish have few other spawning options along Palos Verde Peninsula. You'll soon pass the San Pedro breakwater and reach the Cabrillo Bath House.

Just up-coast from Cabrillo Beach is the rocky shoreline of Point Fermin Marine Life Refuge. Cabrillo Coastal Park Trail (a concrete path across the beach and a boardwalk along the cliffs) assists visitors of all abilities to reach the rocky shores of the Point Fermin Marine Life Refuge and the sandy shore of the inner beach.

After rock-hopping among the tidepools, you must double-back on Cabrillo Coastal Park Trail because it is all but impossible to walk around Point Fermin via the shoreline route.

Follow a dirt path or the paved road up to the top of the coastal bluffs; walk steeply uphill along Bluff Place through a residential area to a parking lot at the terminus of Pacific Avenue. Join a blufftop trail, which soon leads past the remains of "Sunken City," a 1930s housing tract built on bluffs that soon collapsed. Palm trees and huge chunks of asphalt are all that remain of the oceanside housing tract.

The dirt path delivers the hiker to Point Fermin Park. Continue on the park's paved pathway past the puzzlingly named Point Fermin Cetacean & Community Building to the handsome Victorian-style Point Fermin Lighthouse. Built in 1874 from materials shipped around Cape Horn, the lighthouse was a welcome beacon to approaching sailors. Lighthouse tours are offered every afternoon except Monday at 1, 2 and 3 P.M.

At the up-coast edge of the park, take the walkway paralleling Paseo Del Mar. On the inland side of the roadway lies Joan Milke Flores Park, where paths depart to such attractions as the Korean Friendship Bell and the Fort MacArthur Military Museum, as well as Angels Gate Park and Lookout Point Park.

From atop the landscaped bluff, a coastal access-way at the foot of Meyler Street and another at the foot of Barbara Street lead down to the rocky shores. At low tide, plucky rock-hoppers can reach White Point in this way.

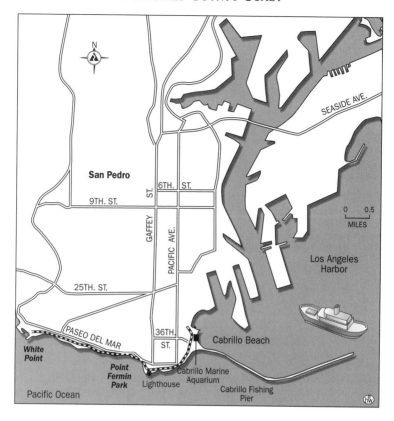

Bluff-top hikers will continue to the end of the linear park and continue another 0.4 mile the White Point Bluff Park. A combination of paved and dirt pathways advance toward White Point. Look across Paseo Del Mar for the entrance to the new White Point Nature Preserve.

An unsigned coastal access-way leads to the cobbled beach on the down-coast side of White Point however most hikers will prefer to continue across the bluffs and enjoy the fabulous clear-day vistas of Catalina Island. Along the way, interpretive plaques describe the natural and cultural attractions of White Point. An entry kiosk heralds your arrival at Royal Palms County Beach. Motorists pay for the privilege of driving down to park at the beach, but hikers may enter for free.

Near White Point, you'll see a palm garden with fire pits. Royal Palms Hotel was once situated here until overcome by the sea. Storm-twisted palms and curious cement remains reminders of the resort and flush times long passed.

Beyond the point stretch the rugged cliffs and cobblestone shores of Palos Verdes Peninsula. Return the same way or, if you have the time, and the tide is right, walk on. The difficult terrain will ensure that few follow in your footsteps.

❦ SIGNAL HILL

SIGNAL HILL TRAIL
4-mile loop of Signal Hill with 300-foot elevation gain

Signal Hill has long been synonymous with oil. Atop this Long Beach prominence a great oil field was discovered in 1921. Alamitos #1, as the discovery well was known, produced 600 barrels a day. Soon Signal Hill was covered with derricks, which produced 250,000 barrels a day.

The hill is a quieter place now, though a number of active wells are still pumping black gold. Because Signal is the only hill for miles around, it has long drawn walkers trying to stay in shape or get a view.

Signal Hill achieved worldwide recognition for the petroleum and profits produced, but the hill has never been known as a model oil field. Haphazard development and excessive drilling led to an ugly and dangerous environment.

Signal Hill—the mountain—has been cleaned up since its heyday, and its slopes now host more houses than oil wells; in fact, subdivisions are now he greatest environmental threat to the hill. There isn't a single path around the hill; rather, you improvise a route on Signal's dirt and paved roads.

DIRECTIONS TO TRAILHEAD: From the San Diego Freeway (405) in Long Beach, take the Cherry Avenue/Signal Hill exit. Head south on Cherry 0.5 mile to Willow. Turn right and after one mile, make a right on Redondo, then right on aptly named Hill Street. Proceed to the base of Signal Hill. Depending on your time and/or inclination, you can park at the base of the hill or closer to the top.

THE HIKE: Follow Panorama Drive or the dirt road below it in a counterclockwise direction. You'll pass oil wells, get a view to the north of the San Diego Freeway, the planes arriving and departing from Long Beach Airport, and many square miles of suburbia. Eucalyptus and palm trees line the up-and-down dirt roads. Lemon grass and California poppies add a little color to the hillsides.

Your route crosses Burnett Street and you join a dirt road on the west side of the hill. Growing on this slope is a zany mixture of flora—banana palms and California fan palms, Canary Island pines, lemonade berry and brittle bush.

Only the hawks (!) circling, overhead have a better view than you. The view west takes in the Palos Verdes Peninsula. Catalina Island, thirty miles away, is visible on a clear day. Looking south and west you can identify the *Queen Mary* and its three stacks and count a number of man-made oil islands. Dominating the coast is the massive Los Angeles/Long Beach harbor complex and the tall cranes used for loading containerized cargo. After circling the hill and seeing the sights, you'll end up at the corner of Hill and Temple streets.

EL DORADO NATURE CENTER

EL DORADO NATURE TRAIL
2-mile loop through El Dorado Nature Center

Southern Californians have long lamented the destruction of the natural world caused by freeway construction. But in one community, freeway building resulted in the formation of a unique nature center.

Back in the mid-1960s, during construction of the San Gabriel River/San Diego Freeway interchange, earth movers moved millions of cubic yards of earth. Thanks to conservationists, some of that earth was moved to form 800-acre El Dorado Regional Park and 80-acre El Dorado Nature Center. The park has wide lawns, ball fields and picnic areas. The Nature Center is a surprise—an oasis in the midst of the metropolis.

Surely this land has undergone a strange evolution: from San Gabriel River floodplain to bean fields to freeway interchange to nature preserve. Only in Southern California!

Several ecological zones are represented in the nature preserve which, for the most part, emphasizes native California flora. Hikers can tour oak woodland, grassy meadow, and chaparral zones representative of Southland plant communi-

El Dorado Nature Center: Bridge over the tranquil waters.

ties, and can meander among redwoods and a white alder grove—vegetation typical of the northern part of the state.

El Dorado Nature Center, a small museum perched on an island, is a good place to learn about local plant life and wildlife. This satellite museum of Los Angeles County features a "hands-on" ecology exhibit and a gallery that displays the work of nature artists and photographers.

Kids will particularly enjoy a visit to the nature center. The museum's exhibits, interpretive walks and even the pint-sized drinking fountains were designed with kids in mind.

Two miles of easy trail circle El Dorado. A one-mile nature trail is keyed to a pamphlet available from the museum. Another mile of trail loops around the preserve's two ponds.

Bird-watchers flock to the preserve because more than 150 resident and migratory bird species have been sighted. A bird checklist is available at the museum.

DIRECTIONS TO TRAILHEAD: From the San Diego Freeway (405), exit on Studebaker Road and travel north about 2.5 miles to Spring Street. Take a right on Spring and proceed 0.75 mile to the entrance of El Dorado Park Nature Center. Park in the lot by the nature center for a fee or for free along Spring Street.

THE HIKE: Pick up a nature trail interpretive pamphlet from the museum, then head out across the bridge into the reserve. Enjoy the native plant communities, including a cattail-lined creek and a chaparral-cloaked hillside. And keep an eye out for two nonnatives that have been part of rthe Southland scene for more than a century and seem like natives—the large, plume-like pampas grass from South America and the ubiquitous eucalyptus. Be sure to get the "big picture" from the Observation Tower, the preserve's highest point.

When you reach a trail junction, you can proceed straight ahead on the "One Mile" nature trail or bear right for a two-mile hike. The second mile of trail meanders past the park's ponds before returning to the nature center building.

⚜ Long Beach

LONG BEACH TRAIL
From Long Beach Aquarium to Long Beach City Beach is 3 miles
round trip; to Belmont Pier is 6 miles round trip; to Naples is 8 miles round
trip; to Alamitos Bay is 10 miles round trip

The Long Beach Aquarium of the Pacific and nearby waterfront revitalization efforts mean a Long Beach that's easier on the eye, and much more pleasant for the adventurer afoot. From the aquarium, take a short walk along a rejuvenated waterfront now called Rainbow Harbor to the Shoreline Village shopping center or opt for a more ambitious sojourn along long, Long Beach.

During the first mile of this shoreline saunter, the walker gets various views of the *Queen Mary,* at one time known as the largest passenger liner ever built. Once past Shoreline Village and the city marina, the explorer can continue on the paved beach/bicycle/pedestrian path or hit the beach and walk along water's edge. You can certainly take a very long walk along Long Beach; the well-named strand is very long—and quite wide in places as well.

Long Beach City Beach extends nearly five miles from the city's downtown marina to Alamitos Bay. The beach, 100 yards wide in places, offers some of the most gentle ocean swimming in Southern California.

Those preferring a one-way ramble along Long Beach, can return to the

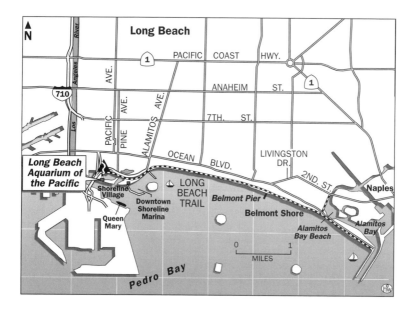

aquarium by Long Beach Transit bus, or check out the schedules for the AquaBus or AquaLink for a ride on the waterways.

DIRECTIONS TO TRAILHEAD: Head south on the Long Beach Freeway (710) to its end and follow the Downtown Long Beach/Aquarium signs. The signs lead you onto Shoreline Drive and to the Aquarium's multi-level, 1,500-vehicle parking structure on the right.

THE HIKE: Leaving the wave-shaped aquarium behind, follow the beige-and brown-brick road along Rainbow Harbor. The soothing strains of classical music emanating from the loudspeakers lining the esplanade add to the Oz-like quality of the waterfront.

Follow the promenade as it travels under the pedestrian overpass that links the convention center to the waterfront and you'll soon arrive at Shoreline Village, a waterside shopping center. Two detours beckon: (1) Follow the board-walk past the shops and eateries of Shoreline Village. (2) Head out on the Long Beach Marina breakwater for good views of the pleasure craft and the *Queen Mary*.

Continue a less-than-scintillating 0.5 mile or so down-coast along the inland side of the marina to a second breakwater and the beginning of Long Beach City beach. At the south breakwater, the bike-pedestrian path continues beneath the bluffs, but the better, quieter walking is right along the beach.

Walk along the wide sandy Long Beach Strand, past the downtown area. On summer weekends, you'll pass brigades of beach-goers; at other times, in other seasons, the walk is a more tranquil one, often in the company of curlews, godwits, sandpipers and other shorebirds.

Cross into the trendy Belmont Shores and reach the 1,620-foot long Belmont Pier. From the pier, a mile's walk brings you to the foot of Bay Shore Avenue. For a fun side trip, follow the avenue a mile around the horseshoe of Alamitos Bay to Appian Way Bridge and Naples, a residential community of three islands sepa-rated by canals.

Those determined to complete the last leg of the Long Beach walk will head out onto Alamitos Peninsula, which extends from 54th Place to the entrance channel of Alamitos Bay. You can stick with the sandy and rocky beach or join Bay Shore Walk, a public walkway that extends along the bay from 55th to 65th Place.

CHAPTER THIRTEEN

Santa Monica Mountains

Bordered by two of the busiest freeways in the world, and within easy reach of nearly seventeen million people, the Santa Monica Mountains remains a near-wilderness area offering much-needed solitude and green space. With long stretches of chaparral, oak woodlands, fern glens, grasslands and seasonal creeks, this diverse land beckons the hiker to explore its many parks, preserves and very special places. Home to the Chumash, and later part of a huge ranchland, the history of this natural land awaits discovery by today's outdoors enthusiast.

WILL ROGERS STATE HISTORIC PARK

WILL ROGERS TRAIL
To Inspiration Point is 2 miles round trip with a 300-foot elevation gain

Will Rogers, often called the "Cowboy Philosopher," bought a spread in the Santa Monica Mountains in 1922. He and his family eventually enlarged their weekend cottage to 31 rooms.

The Oklahoma-born Rogers toured the country as a trick roper, punctuating his act with humorous comments on the news of the day. His roping act led the humorist to later fame as a newspaper columnist, radio commentator and movie star.

Today, the ranch and grounds of the Rogers Ranch is maintained as Will Rogers State Historic Park, set aside in 1944. You can see a short film on Rogers' life at the park visitor center and tour the ranch house, still filled with his prized possessions.

Rogers himself designed the riding trails that wind into the hills behind his ranch. The path to Inspiration Point is an easy family walk.

DIRECTIONS TO TRAILHEAD: From Sunset Boulevard in Pacific Palisades, 4.5 miles inland from Sunset's junction with Pacific Coast Highway, turn inland on the access road leading to Will Rogers State Historic Park. Park your car near the polo field or near Rogers' house.

THE HIKE: Join the path near the tennis courts west of park headquarters and begin ascending north into the mountains. (You'll see a couple of different trails; join the main, wide bridle path.)

Rogers Trail ascends a ridge overlooking nearby Rivas Canyon and leads to a junction, where you take the turnoff for Inspiration Point. Not really a point at all, it's actually more of a flat-topped knoll; nevertheless, clear-day views are inspiring: the Santa Monica Bay, the metropolis, the San Gabriel Mountains, and even Catalina Island.

Will Rogers and family

❦ SULLIVAN CANYON

SULLIVAN CANYON TRAIL
8-mile loop with 1,100-foot elevation gain

Sullivan Canyon is one of the gems of the eastern portion of the Santa Monica Mountains. Stately oaks and sycamores shade a seasonal creek and a fine trail travels the length of the canyon.

The canyon was very attractive to its former owner—the Los Angeles County Sanitation District—and was long near the top of the list as a potential landfill site. Protests by environmentalists derailed the dump and these days Sullivan Canyon is a beautiful place to roam.

Sullivan's high and narrow canyon walls display handsome sandstone outcroppings, as well as a blue-gray bedrock known as Santa Monica slate. During winter and spring, the canyon walls are colored with clusters of ceanothus.

Casual hikers will enjoy a nearly flat stroll for a mile or three along the canyon floor. More energetic hikers will make a loop trip by climbing out of the canyon and traveling Sullivan's west ridge. Views from the ridge are quite good.

DIRECTIONS TO TRAILHEAD: From the San Diego Freeway (405) in west Los Angeles, exit on Sunset Boulevard and head west 2.5 miles to Mandeville Canyon Road. Turn right and after 0.25 mile turn left on Westridge Road, which you'll travel a bit more than a mile to Bayliss Road. Make a left, travel 0.25 mile, make another left on Queensferry Road and follow this road another 0.25 mile to its end. Park near the end of the road.

THE HIKE: The trail begins near the end of Bayliss Road, where a frequently traveled equestrian trail, ascending from the wilds of Brentwood, joins the road. Walk down an asphalt road (closed to vehicles) a hundred yards to a cement flood control apron, then turn right and enter Sullivan Canyon.

The wide trail meanders near a willowy streambed, beneath the boughs of antiquarian oaks and across carpets of lemongrass. Three miles of tranquil trail brings you to a couple of eucalyptus trees on your left. This is a good turnaround point.

Those hikers wanting to complete this loop trip will continue up canyon on an old dirt road. After a 0.5 mile ascent, the road forks. The right fork leads to Mulholland Drive, which you can see about a 0.5 mile away. Take the left fork and ascend a little farther to an unsigned junction with dirt Fire Road 26. A right turn offers another route to Mulholland Drive, but you'll turn left and begin descending the west ridge of Sullivan Canyon. Occasionally you'll get a glimpse to the east of Sullivan, but the better views are to the west of Rustic Canyon and the bold slopes of Topanga State Park. If it's not foggy, the coastal views are pretty good too.

The only shade on the ridge route occurs about halfway down, where you'll find a small clump of oaks and a little bench. Farther down the ridge, you'll reach a gate and a paved road leading down to the Boy Scouts' Camp Josepho.

A few hundred yards past this turnoff, you'll walk under some telephone lines—your clue to begin looking sharply to the left for the unsigned connector trail that will return you to the bottom of Sullivan Canyon. As the road bears right, you'll head left for a telephone pole, pass directly under the pole's two guide wires and join the footpath. The steep trail drops several hundred feet in 0.25 mile and deposits you back on the canyon floor. Turn down-canyon and travel 0.5 mile back to the trailhead.

Rustic Canyon

❀ RUSTIC CANYON

RUSTIC CANYON TRAIL
Loop through Will Rogers State Historic Park and Rustic Canyon is 6 miles round trip with 900-foot elevation gain

Rustic Canyon is every bit as woodsy and secluded as its name suggests. The surprisingly rugged little enclave is located in the Pacific Palisades section of the Santa Monica Mountains.

For the hiker, Sullivan Canyon (see description in this guide) and neighboring Rustic Canyon are an interesting contrast. Sullivan is a gently sloping canyon with a wide flat floor shaded by sycamores. Rustic is wild, narrow, steep, with dramatic rock walls. One way to reach Rustic Canyon is to descend via Sullivan Canyon; another way (this hike) is via Will Rogers Park.

Rustic Canyon has a storied past. In the late 19th century, the Santa Monica Forestry Station was established adjacent to the canyon. The many eucalyptus in and around the canyon are a result of tobacco millionaire-builder-of-Venice-forestry pioneer Abbot Kinney's efforts. The eucalyptus, an Australian import, thrived in Southern California but to Kinney's disappointment proved to be a miserable source of timber.

Most of Rustic Canyon remained undeveloped until the 1920s when it became the woodsy retreat of a group of Los Angeles businessmen known as The Uplifters. The group, at first an offshoot of the Los Angeles Athletic Club, was chartered "to uplift art, promote good fellowship, and build a closer acquaintance among its members." It was L. Frank Baum, author of the Wizard of Oz books who came up with the name "The Lofty and Excellent Order of the Uplifters."

Cabins, clubhouse buildings and an outdoor theater were built in the canyon. The club went strong during the 1920s, slowed during the Depression years, and came to an end after World War II.

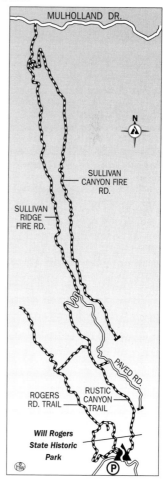

269

This hike begins in Will Rogers State Historic Park. You'll follow the trail to Inspiration Point, march a mile or two up the Backbone Trail, then descend into Rustic Canyon and loop back to Will Rogers.

One highlight of Rustic Canyon is Rustic Creek. Most Santa Monica Mountains watercourses flow only after rains, but Rustic Creek is one of the few that's spring-fed and thus usually flows all year round through the lower reaches of the canyon. About a mile of the trail through Rustic Canyon can be wet going.

DIRECTIONS TO TRAILHEAD: From Sunset Boulevard in Pacific Palisades, turn north on the access road leading to Will Rogers State Historic Park. There is a state park day use fee.

THE HIKE: From Will Rogers's home, on the east side of a wide field, take the paved road leading past a line of eucalyptus trees to a riding ring. Soon you'll intersect a dirt road. Turn left on this road (actually, right is okay, too, because the roads join). If you head left, be sure to stay on the main fire road and ignore rightward turns on lesser roads. The fire road ascends to a junction just below Inspiration Point. Continue to Inspiration Point for inspiring clear-day views of the city if you wish, but this hike joins a trail to the left.

Climbing Chicken Ridge, the beginning of famed Backbone Trail offers great views of downtown, Century City, the sweep of Santa Monica Bay and Catalina Island. After a mile's climb along the ridge, the trail crests, then descends another 0.25 mile to an unsigned three-way junction. The two leftward trails are high and low route continuations of the Backbone, but you'll turn sharply to the right and begin a steep descent on a connector trail. This manzanita-lined trail wastes no time descending 0.5 mile to the bottom of Rustic Canyon. Ahead is a white barn and an unsigned intersection with Rustic Canyon Trail. Left up Rustic Canyon leads to Camp Josepho, the Boy Scout camp. You bear right, down-canyon.

Rustic Canyon Trail stays at the canyon bottom, crossing and re-crossing the creek. You'll pass the ruins of some homes that have suffered the ravages of fire and flood. Rustic Canyon flora includes the usual riparian growth plus some stray exotics such as cactus, aloe, jade and periwinkle. German ivy, a pretty but invasive plant with little yellow flowers, has really taken over in spots.

You'll pass a small dam. The trail narrows, the canyon walls close in. Nearing the state park, you'll follow an elaborate trail, fashioned with enough wooden trestles to support a freight trail, then cross a white bridge over a culvert, and spy a parking lot and Rogers's house where you began the hike.

❧ TEMESCAL CANYON

SUNSET, TEMESCAL CANYON, TEMESCAL RIDGE TRAILS
Canyon loop is 4.4 miles round trip with 700-foot gain;
to Skull Rock is 5.4 miles round trip

Park agencies in the Santa Monica Mountains have combined forces to open a number of "gateways" to the mountains. For hikers (particularly those of us accustomed to beginning hikes at the end of dirt roads greeted by trail signs nailed to trees), these gateways are deluxe trail heads indeed: restrooms, picnic grounds, water fountains, native plant gardens and more.

I have a particular fondness for Temescal Gateway Park in Pacific Palisades. Not only does this park have it all, park pathways quickly leave it all behind.

Temescal Canyon is an ideal Santa Monica Mountains sampler. You get an oak- and sycamore-shaded canyon, a seasonal waterfall and terrific views from the ridge crest.

Temescal has long been a canyon that inspired nature lovers and enlightenment-seekers. During the 1920s and 1930s, the canyon hosted Chatauqua assemblies—large educational and recreational gatherings that featured lectures, concerts and stage performances. The canyon was purchased by the Presbyterian Synod in 1943 and used as a

Skull Rock

retreat center until 1995 when the Santa Monica Mountains Conservancy purchased the property.

DIRECTIONS TO TRAILHEAD: From Los Angeles, head west on the Santa Monica Freeway (10) to its end and continue up-coast on Pacific Coast Highway. Turn north (right) on Temescal Canyon Road and drive 1.1 miles. Just after the intersection with Sunset Boulevard, turn left into the (fee) parking area for Temescal Gateway Park.

(Sidewalks, picnic grounds, and an intermittent greenbelt along Temescal Canyon Road might tempt intrepid hikers to stride the mile from the beach to the trailhead.)

THE HIKE: Walk up-canyon on the landscaped path past the restrooms.

The footpath takes on a wilder appearance and soon crosses a branch of Temescal Creek via a wooden footbridge.

At a signed junction, save Temescal Ridge Trail for your return route and continue through the canyon on Temescal Canyon Trail. Travel among graceful old oaks, maples and sycamores to the "doggie turnaround" (no dogs beyond this point) and enter Topanga State Park.

The path ascends moderately to another footbridge and a close-up view of the small waterfall, tumbling over some large boulders. Leaving the canyon behind, the path steepens and climbs westward up Temescal Ridge to a signed junction with Temescal Ridge Trail.

I always enjoy heading uphill on this trail a half mile or so to distinctly shaped Skull Rock. The rock is a good place to rest, cool off, and admire the view.

As you return down Temescal Ridge Trail, you'll get excellent views of Santa Monica Bay, Palos Verdes Peninsula, Catalina Island, and downtown Los Angeles. The view to the southwest down at the housing developments isn't too inspiring, but the view of the rough, unaltered northern part of Temescal Canyon is.

After serving up fine views, the path descends rather steeply and tunnels into tall chaparral. Continue past junctions with Bienveneda and Leacock trails and follow the narrow ridgeline back to a junction with Temescal Canyon Trail. Retrace your steps on Sunset Trail back to the trailhead.

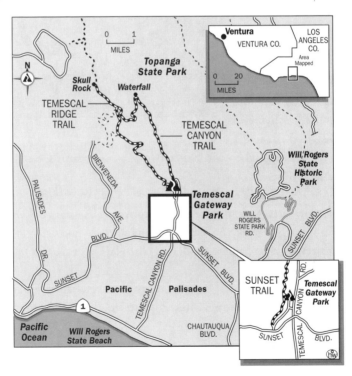

❁ LOS LIONES CANYON

LOS LIONES CANYON, EAST TOPANGA FIRE ROAD TRAILS

From Los Liones Drive to The Overlook is 6 miles round trip
with 1,500-foot elevation gain; from Paseo Miramar to The Overlook
is 5 miles round trip with 1,200-foot gain

Rugged Los Liones Canyon is but a mile from Sunset Boulevard, but very much apart from the Westside city scene. "The Overlook" offers grand views of West Los Angeles and Santa Monica Bay.

This hike explores the coastal slopes of Topanga State Park. Your goal is a viewpoint sometimes called Parker Mesa Overlook, sometimes called Topanga Overlook, but most often simply called The Overlook. Views of West L.A. and the sweep of Santa Monica Bay are superb. Sunset (the descending day star not the winding boulevard) views are often inspiring.

Two trails help you reach the inspiring view. Los Liones Canyon trail travels through its namesake canyon to East Topanga Fire Road which in turn leads to Topanga Overlook. Or the walker may head directly for The Overlook via the fire road.

From The Overlook, the ambitious hiker can trek into the main part of Topanga State Park.

DIRECTIONS TO TRAILHEAD: To Los Liones Drive trailhead: From Pacific Coast Highway in Pacific Palisades, turn inland on Sunset Boulevard for 0.25 mile. Turn left on Los Liones Drive and follow it to road's end and a small parking area. Don't park in the adjacent church lot.

To Paseo Miramar: From Sunset Boulevard, proceeding inland, the next left after Los Liones Drive is Paseo Miramar. Follow this winding road through a residential area to its end at a vehicle gate across East Topanga Fire Road. Park safely and considerately on Paseo Miramar.

THE HIKE: From Los Liones Canyon: March past the vehicle gate and follow the trail into the canyon. After 0.25 mile, the trail begins to climb in earnest, switchbacking through the chaparral.

After leveling out for a stretch, the path then switchbacks even more earnestly through thickets of ceanothus. Los Liones Trail intersects East Topanga Fire Road about 0.25 mile from the road's beginning at Paseo Miramar.

Turn left (northwest) on the fire road and continue your ascent. For a short while the road travels a cool, north slope and you get good over-the-right-shoulder views of neighboring Santa Ynez Canyon, a canyon that's wild and dramatic in its upper reaches (in the state park) and atrociously subdivided in its lower reaches outside park boundaries.

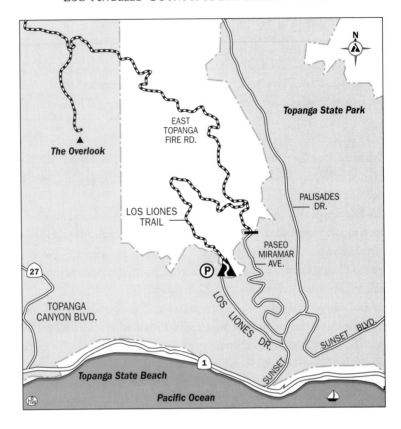

A two-mile ascent along the fire road brings you to a junction with a trail leading south along a bald ridge. Join this trail, which travels 0.5 mile to The Overlook.

Enjoy clear-day panoramas of Westside L.A., Santa Monica Bay, Palos Verdes and Catalina Island.

❦ SANTA YNEZ CANYON

SANTA YNEZ TRAIL
From Trippet Ranch to Santa Ynez Canyon is 6 miles round trip with 1,000-foot elevation gain

Ferns, falls, wildflowers and dramatic sandstone cliffs are some of the delights of a ramble through Santa Ynez Canyon. The canyon—and its waterfalls—can be reached from two trailheads; one is located at the edge of the tony Palisades Highlands development, the other is found in the heart of Topanga State Park.

Santa Ynez Trail descends a ridge into Santa Ynez Canyon, then heads upstream to a 15-foot waterfall. Remember that the uphill part of this hike comes last; pace yourself accordingly.

DIRECTIONS TO TRAILHEAD: From Topanga Canyon Boulevard, turn east on Entrada Road; that's to the right if you're coming from Pacific Coast Highway and to the left if you're coming from the Ventura Freeway (101). Follow Entrada Road by turning left at every opportunity until you arrive at Topanga State Park. There is a state park day-use fee.

You can easily reach Santa Ynez Canyon via the Palisades Highland trailhead. From Sunset Boulevard in Pacific Palisades, a short distance inland from Pacific Coast Highway, turn north on Palisades Drive. As you enter the Palisades Highlands community, turn left on Verenda De La Montura. Park near the signed trailhead.

THE HIKE: From Topanga State Park: From the parking lot, you may proceed up the wide main trail or join the park's nature trail (a prettier way to go) and ascend past some oaks. Blue-eyed grass, owl's clover and lupine splash some springtime color on the grassy slopes. Both the nature trail and the main trail out of the parking lot lead a short 0.25 mile to Fire Road 30A. Turn left on the dirt fire road and travel a short distance to signed Santa Ynez Trail. Start your descent into Santa Ynez Canyon.

High on the canyon wall, you'll get good views of the canyon and of the ocean beyond. A 0.5 mile descent brings you to an outcropping of reddish sandstone. The main route of Santa Ynez Trail stays atop a ridgeline, but you'll notice a few steep side trails that lead to the right down to the canyon floor.

Soap plant, a spring bloomer with small, white, star-like flowers is abundant along the trail. This member of the lily family was a most useful plant to early residents of the Santa Monica Mountains. Native Americans cooked the bulbs to concoct a glue for their arrows. Later settlers stuffed mattresses with the plant's fiber.

Enjoy the views of tilted sandstone and the great bowl of Santa Ynez Canyon. As the trail nears the canyon floor it descends more precipitously.

❀ TOPANGA STATE PARK

EAGLE ROCK LOOP TRAIL (BACKBONE TRAIL)
To Eagle Rock via Eagle Rock/Eagle Springs Loop is 6.5 miles round trip
with 800-foot elevation gain; to Will Rogers SHP via Eagle Rock, Fire
Road 30, Rogers Road is 10.5 miles one way with a 1,800-foot loss

Topanga Canyon is a quiet retreat, surrounded by L.A. sprawl but retaining its
rural character. The state park is sometimes billed as "the largest state park within a city limit in the U.S."

The name Topanga is from the Shoshonean dialect. These people and their
ancestors occupied the canyon on and off for several thousand years until the
Spanish evicted them and forced them to settle at the San Fernando Mission.

Until the 1880s, there was little permanent habitation in the canyon. Early
settlers tended vineyards, orchards, and cattle ranches. In the 1920s, the canyon
became a popular weekend destination for Los Angeles residents. Summer cabins
were built along Topanga Creek and in subdivisions in the surrounding hills. For
one-dollar round-trip fare, tourists could board a Packard auto stage in Santa
Monica and be driven up Pacific Coast Highway and Topanga Canyon Road to
the Topanga Post Office and other, more scenic spots.

Most Topanga trails are good fire roads. On a blustery winter day, city and
canyon views are superb.

In the heart of the state park, the hiker will discover Eagle Rock, Eagle
Spring and get topographically oriented to Topanga. The energetic will enjoy the
one-way journey from Topanga to Will Rogers State Historic Park. The lower
reaches of the Backbone Trail offer a fine tour of the wild side of Topanga Canyon
while the ridgetop sections offer far-reaching inland and ocean views.

DIRECTIONS TO TRAILHEAD: From Topanga Canyon Boulevard,
turn east on Entrada Road; that's to the right if you're coming from Pacific Coast
Highway. Follow Entrada Road by turning left at every opportunity until you
arrive at Topanga State Park. The trailhead is at the end of the parking lot. (For
information about the end of this walk, consult the Will Rogers State Historic
Park write-up and directions to the trailhead in this guide.)

THE HIKE: From the Topanga State Park parking lot, follow the distinct
trail eastward to a signed junction, where you'll begin hiking on Eagle Springs
Road. You'll pass through an oak woodland and through chaparral country. The
trail slowly and steadily gains about 800 feet in elevation on the way to Eagle
Rock. When you reach a junction, bear left on the north loop of Eagle Springs
Road to Eagle Rock. A short detour will bring you to the top of the rock.

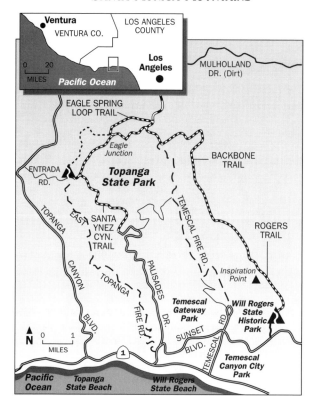

To complete the loop, bear sharply right (southwest) at the next junction, following the fire road as it winds down to Eagle Spring. Past the spring, you return to Eagle Spring Road and retrace your steps back to the trailhead.

Three-mile long Musch Ranch Trail, which passes from hot chaparral to shady oak woodland, crosses a bridge and passes the park pond, is another fine way to return to the trailhead.

To Will Rogers State Historic Park: Follow the loop trip directions to the northeast end of Eagle Rock/Eagle Spring Loop, where you bear right on Fire Road 30. In 0.5 mile you reach the intersection with Rogers Road. Turn left and follow the dirt road (really a trail) for 3.5 miles, where the road ends and meets Rogers Trail. Here a level area and solitary oak suggest a lunch stop. On clear days enjoy the spectacular views in every direction: To the left is Rustic Canyon and the crest of the mountains near Mulholland Drive. To the right, Rivas Canyon descends toward the sea.

Stay on Rogers Trail, which marches up and down several steep hills for about two more miles until it enters Will Rogers Park near Inspiration Point.

✿ UPPER TOPANGA CANYON

SUMMIT VALLEY LOOP TRAIL
2-mile loop with 200-foot elevation gain; to Summit to Summit Motorway
is 3.5 miles round trip with 400-foot elevation gain

Just a few miles from the Ventura Freeway, at the head of Topanga Canyon, lies
Summit Valley, a new park likely to become a favorite of local hikers. The park is
perched just over the 1,560-foot high ridge that walls off Topanga Canyon from
the hustle and bustle of the San Fernando Valley.

Not so long ago, it seemed Summit Valley was about to resemble the San
Fernando Valley. Developers intended to construct 967 homes, three artificial
lakes and a golf course. More than three million cubic acres of earth were to be
graded; in effect, all the summits and valleys of Summit Valley would have been
obliterated.

Santa Monica Mountains' conservation groups, along with vociferous
Topanga Canyon residents, battled developers for 16 years—by some accounts the
longest running major development dispute in Los Angeles County history. The
Santa Monica Mountains Conservancy purchased the 659-acre property in 1994

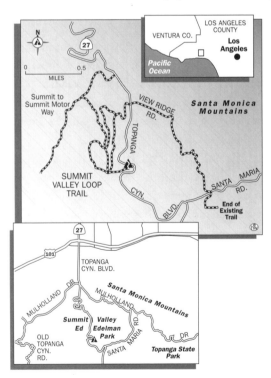

for $20 million. Then-county supervisor Edmund Edelman helped broker the deal between developers and environmentalists, which may suggest why the preserve's official name is Summit Valley Edmund Edelman Park.

Summit Valley's botanical highlights include some impressive old oaks that, the eagle-eyed hiker will notice, have numbers on their trunks. When developments were afoot, state law required an accounting of each oak prior to its fate: preservation, relocation, or destruction. Two of my favorites—Oak #131 and Oak #225—and hundreds more remain to inspire us, their numbers serving as a wry reminder of the long struggle to save Summit Valley.

DIRECTIONS TO TRAILHEAD: From the Ventura Freeway in Woodland Hills, exit on Topanga Canyon Boulevard and drive south five miles to the signed (Summit Valley Edmund Edelman Park) turnout on the right (west) side of the road. If you're coming from Coast Highway 1, drive 8 miles inland on Topanga Canyon Boulevard to the trailhead.

The turnout is on a tightly winding segment of Topanga Canyon Boulevard; use caution when entering and exiting the parking area.

THE HIKE: The path descends into a draw and crosses the headwaters of Topanga Creek. You'll soon encounter a right-forking path (the loop trail's return leg) that leads north along the bottom of Topanga Canyon. Continue straight (west) on the original path, which soon bends north as it climbs gently through tall mustard plants.

About 0.75 mile out, a steep, left branching connector trail offers the opportunity to climb to Summit to Summit Motorway (a dirt road). Rewards for the ascent are excellent views of the mountains and the metropolis. For the astute map-reading hiker, the motorway adds many trail options.

Summit Valley Loop Trail meanders through a thicket of mallow and soon reaches a junction with the east leg of the loop. The return to the trailhead is via an easy creekside saunter down Topanga Canyon on a wide path.

Those hikers wishing to explore the more rudimentary trail network on the east side of Summit Valley will continue east at the above-mentioned junction and hike through a eucalyptus grove to Topanga Canyon Boulevard. Carefully cross the road, join the pedestrian walkway alongside Viewridge Road for a modest 0.3 mile ascent to the trailhead at road's end opposite the gated and guarded Summit Pointe subdivision.

A splendid mile of trail leads across oak-studded hill and grassy dale to Santa Maria Road. The developed trail ends a few hundred yards past Santa Maria Road at a precipitous rock outcropping that offers spectacular canyon views.

❀ HONDO CANYON

BACKBONE TRAIL
From Saddle Peak Road to Topanga Canyon is a bit over five miles one way
with 1,200-foot elevation loss

"With the possible exception of Zuma Canyon, Hondo is the most dramatic
canyon in the Santa Monica Mountains," stated Ron Webster, who designed the
footpath through Hondo Canyon.

One look over the canyon rim at Hondo (which means "deep" in Spanish)
will convince most hikers what a daunting task Webster and his crews faced in
forging a footpath through the canyon. While the trail was being built, Hondo
Canyon experienced fire, flood, and even the Northridge Earthquake.

Completed in 1994, Hondo Canyon ranks as one of the most scenic segments
of the Backbone Trail. The Hondo Canyon hike can be a five-mile one way, mostly downhill jaunt from Saddle Peak Road to Topanga State Park or a ten-mile
round trip walk. The state park trailhead is only 0.25 mile from Topanga Center,
where restaurants and a grocery store offer food and provisions for hikers.

DIRECTIONS TO TRAILHEAD: From the Ventura Freeway (101) in
Woodland Hills, exit on Topanga Canyon Boulevard and proceed south, winding a
few hilly miles into the canyon. Turn left at the signed entrance to Topanga State
Park on Entrada Road. A short distance up Entrada, turn left into a state park parking lot. (Don't continue driving up Entrada to the main entrance of the state park.)

To reach the Saddle Peak Road trailhead: From the intersection of Topanga Canyon
Boulevard and Old Topanga Road, proceed 5.5 miles up the latter road to Mulholland
Highway. Turn left and drive 4.5 miles to Stunt Road, turn left, and continue 4 more
miles to a junction with Schueren Road. Park off Stunt Road (which assumes a new
name—Saddle Peak Road and continues east) in one of the wide dirt turnouts.

THE HIKE: Begin at the yellow fire gate on the north side of Stunt Road.
Walk one hundred yards and look rightward for a sign (an arrow) that directs you
onto the footpath.

The ridgetop you're following has long been known informally as Fossil
Ridge and if you look sharply at the rocks, you'll see why. A quarter-mile from
the trailhead, embedded in a pink-hued rock, are what appear to be (at least to we
nonscientists) giant clam fossils.

As the trail drops off the ridgetop you get a view of the clear-day view of
Warner Center area of the San Fernando Valley, then begin to lose sight of civilization as you descend into Hondo Canyon. Flower-lovers will note the abundant
tree poppy and bush lupine and mariposa lily growing on this slope.

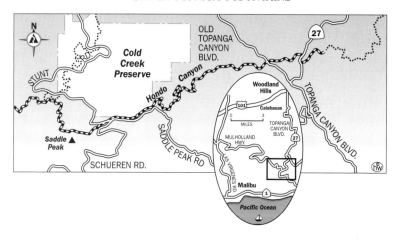

After a 0.5 mile descent from top of the canyon, you'll reach the site of a one-time mega-marijuana garden, discovered and destroyed by authorities.

The trail drops to the bottom of the canyon, cool in the shade of bay laurel, oak and sycamore. A seasonal stream and waterfall at the canyon bottom come to life after a good rain.

The path climbs briefly along the south canyon wall, then descends to what looks to be the scene of a minor avalanche, but is really the work of the great quake of 1994. Shattered oaks and dislodged boulders are other evidence of the quake's power.

Iron wagon parts, kerosene cans and an old stove, mark the site of an old cabin. Past the cabin, the path crosses lush Topanga Meadows, where helpful signs keep you on the Backbone Trail and steer you away from a complication of horse paths that cross the meadow.

Soon after crossing the meadow, the trail leads across the (usually) shallow waters of the creek flowing next to Old Topanga Road. If you're seeking refreshment, the Topanga Center is 0.25 mile down the road at its junction with Topanga Canyon Boulevard.

Those hikers continuing to the Dead Horse Trailhead in Topanga State Park will cross Old Topanga Road and join the moderately steep path (signed "Horse Trail") that climbs a low hill, passes a water tank and descends to Topanga Elementary School. Walk past the school, down Topanga School Road to Topanga Canyon Boulevard.

Very carefully cross the boulevard (not a particularly safe street crossing, but better than anything ahead). Walk two hundred yards up Topanga Canyon Boulevard to Entrada Road, turn right and ascend briefly to the trailhead in Topanga State Park.

🌺 MULHOLLAND GATEWAY

MULHOLLAND GATEWAY
3.5 miles round trip with 500-foot elevation gain;
longer loops possible

Marvin Braude Mulholland Gateway Park, located on the San Fernando Valley side of the Santa Monica Mountains above Tarzana, is sure to attract lots of hikers. The park provides all the basics for the hiker about to hit the trail—water fountains, toilets and (free!) parking. Grassy hillsides offer superb picnic sites. A walkway leads around a native plant landscaped vista point, where a dozen handsome rock benches offer places to contemplate the mountains above and metropolis below.

Park namesake and long-time Los Angeles City Councilman the late Marvin Braude was an inspirational and influential supporter of Santa Monica Mountains parklands. Braude (unlike some other former L.A.-area politicians with question-able conservation credentials) actually deserved to have a park named in his honor. The "Mulholland Gateway" in the park name is apropos, too, because a long, unpaved section of famed Mulholland Drive is easy to access from the trailhead.

MBMG Park offers several different hiking opportunities. Area trails are well maintained and major junctions are way-marked. For a fine family hike and a good introduction to hiking the valley side of the Santa Monicas, I recommend a 3.5 mile loop from the park to the Mulholland Drive ridgecrest, then back down Caballero Canyon.

DIRECTIONS TO TRAILHEAD: From the Ventura Freeway (High-

Dirt Mulholland Drive looks much the same today as it did in the 1920s.

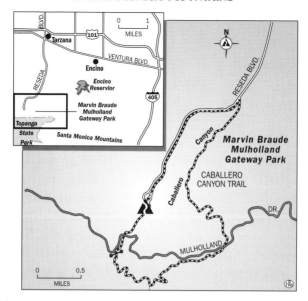

way 101) in Tarzana, exit on Reseda Boulevard and head north 3 miles to road's end and Marvin Braude Mulholland Gateway Park.

THE HIKE: Walk up the fire road 50 yards and look left for the distinct but unsigned footpath that branches right from the road. Follow this path on a 0.3 mile mellow ascent to meet dirt Mulholland Drive. Turn right and walk 0.1 mile to meet a gated fire road (closed to vehicles)on your left.

Walk the fire road into Topanga State Park. The fire road curves south then east and, after 0.6 mile, leads past a junction with signed Garapito Trail and almost immediately reaches a second junction.

The fire road bends south, but you head north and east on signed Bent Arrow Trail, which dips 0.25 mile into heavy brush then rises 0.25 mile out of it to meet Mulholland Drive.

Turn right and walk briefly along Mulholland until a parallel footpath appears on the right side of the road. Follow the footpath (or Mulholland) 0.3 mile to a signed junction at the top of Caballero Canyon.

Caballero Canyon Trail descends north into the canyon, and soon keeps company with a sycamore-lined, seasonal creek. The pleasant downhill jaunt reaches the "old" Caballero Canyon trailhead, a still popular starting place for many Sierra Club outings.

Close the loop and return to the trail head with a sidewalk saunter up Reseda Boulevard past new gated residential communities. As you walk and survey Caballero Canyon below and the mountain crest above, it's rather obvious what the epic conservation struggles of the 1970s, 1980s and 1990s preserved—and what they did not.

❀ SAN FERNANDO VALLEY TO THE SEA

LEMMING TRAIL
From Caballero Canyon to Will Rogers State Beach
is 12 miles one way with 2,000-foot elevation gain

You won't find any lemmings along the Southern California coast; the furry, short-tailed, mice-like creatures inhabit Arctic, not Mediterranean climes. The Lemming Trail takes its name not from the rodent's presence in the Santa Monica Mountains, but from its proclivity to rush headlong into the sea.

A crisp, cool winter or spring day is a great time to make like a lemming and hike from the San Fernando Valley to the sea. The Lemming Trail offers a grand tour of the Santa Monica Mountains, from Tarzana to Topanga to Temscal to the Pacific on a network of trails and fire roads and treats the hiker to superb coastal vistas.

Though the Lemming Trail was named for a small rodent, be assured that this is no Mickey Mouse hike. Be prepared for a very long and strenuous day.

DIRECTIONS TO TRAILHEAD: Leave one car at Will Rogers State Beach (fee) or along Pacific Coast Highway (free) near the intersection of the Coast Highway and Temescal Canyon Road. Next proceed up-coast on PCH to Topanga Canyon Road (27) and drive inland through the canyon to Ventura Boulevard. Turn right (east) and head into Tarzana. Turn right on Reseda Boulevard and follow this road to the signed trailhead on the left side of the road. (A quick route to the Lemming trailhead is to exit the Ventura Freeway [101] on Reseda Boulevard. Shave a mile or so off the hike by beginning at Marvin Braude Mulholland Gateway Park at the very end of Reseda Boulevard.)

THE HIKE: Descend to the dirt road (Fire Road 28) that meanders up the bottom of Caballero Canyon. The sycamore-dotted canyon bottom hosts an intermittent stream. After a mile, the fire road veers left and climbs to a locked gate on Mulholland Drive.

Turn right onto Mulholland and after walking 0.5 mile, look leftward for the Bent Arrow Trail, which will take you into Topanga State Park. Follow this trail, which at first parallels Mulholland, for 0.5 mile as it contours around a steep slope and reaches Temescal Fire Road (Fire Road 30). Turn left and begin a moderate descent. After 1.5 miles, you'll pass junctions with fire roads on your right leading to Eagle Rock and Eagle Spring. Continue straight ahead past these junctions on the sharp ridgeline separating Santa Ynez and Temescal Canyons. You'll pass the junction with Rogers Road which leads to Will Rogers State Historic Park. Near the intersection of Rogers Road and Temescal Fire Road is Temescal Peak (2,126 feet), highest peak in Topanga State Park. If you wish, scramble up a short and steep firebreak to the top for a fine view.

After 1.5 miles of mostly level walking beyond the Rogers Road intersection, you'll pass Trailer Canyon Road and a mile farther south, Split Rock Road. A microwave tower, atop what locals have dubbed "Radio Peak," stands halfway between the points.

As you descend along the ridge, you'll spot rock outcroppings and Skull Rock, where you can climb inside the wind-formed (aeolian) caves to cool off or picnic. From the ridgetop, the view to the southwest down at the housing developments isn't too inspiring, but the view of the rough unaltered northern part of Temescal Canyon is superb.

Temescal Fire Road narrows and switchbacks down into Temescal Canyon. Stop and cool off at the small waterfall here at the Temescal Creek crossing at the bottom of the canyon. Your route crosses over to the east side of the canyon and descends the canyon bottom on a trail shaded by oaks, willows, and sycamores.

Continue to Temescal Gateway Park and down to Sunset Boulevard. Walk the sidewalk or through a narrow greenbelt along Temescal Canyon Road for an easy mile to Pacific Coast Highway. Across Coast Highway is Will Rogers State Beach. Local mountaineering tradition dictates that you emulate the lemming and rush into the sea.

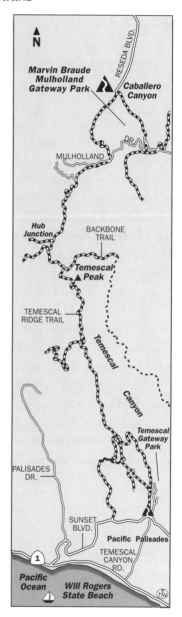

❦ COLD CREEK CANYON PRESERVE

COLD CREEK TRAIL
5 miles round trip with 900-foot elevation gain

Cold Creek Canyon is one of the secret treasures of the Santa Monica Mountains. A year-round stream and a protected north-facing canyon nurture a rich variety of ferns and flowering plants in the 600-acre preserve.

Cold Creek Canyon was once part of a ranch, homesteaded in the early years of this century. It later served as a ranch/retreat for the Murphy family members who donated their ranch to The Nature Conservancy in 1970s, stipulating that Cold Creek be forever preserved in its natural state.

The natural world of Cold Creek Canyon is diverse. Lining Cold Creek are ferns, flowers and cattails. Winter rains swell the creek, creating a dozen small waterfalls. A hundred bird species have been sighted within the preserve, including golden eagles. Hikers may encounter a squirrel raccoon, deer or even a bobcat.

Wildflower-lovers will find much to admire. Early bloomers (February to April) include the white blossoms of the milkmaid. Later in spring, look for the bright yellow canyon sunflower and the yellow-orange-spotted Humboldt lily.

Remember that this is an upside-down hike; the elevation gain occurs during your return. Save some energy.

DIRECTIONS TO TRAILHEAD: From the Ventura Freeway (101) in Calabasas, exit on Las Virgenes Road. Head south to Mulholland Highway, turn east and continue to Stunt Road. Turn right and drive 3.38 miles (watch the road

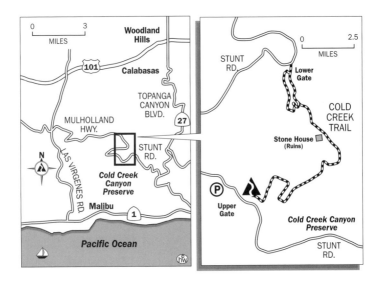

Hot rocks at Cold Creek.

paddles for mileage indicators) to the signed Cold Creek Canyon Preserve entrance on your left.

THE HIKE: Head through the gate and down the trail. One of the first shrubs you'll encounter along the trail is red shank, a floral cousin to the far more prolific chamise. You'll recognize it by its characteristic peeling bark. It's a late bloomer—August is its prime time.

An old pickup truck mired in the middle of the trail suggests that the path was once a road. Occasional breaks in the brush offer views of Calabasas Peak dead-ahead, and a sandstone formation to the right known as Fossil Ridge.

As the path, shaded by oak and bay, nears the canyon bottom, the vegetation becomes more lush. Woodwardia and bracken ferns thrive along Cold Creek. The towering sandstone walls that form Cold Creek absorb rainfall, then slowly release water throughout the year.

A bit more than a mile from the trailhead is the remains of an old house. Sandstone boulders formed the walls of the structure. Quite an ingenious use of materials at hand.

Beyond the rock house, the trail drops steeply into a marshy world of ferns and Humboldt lilies. You'll cross Cold Creek on a wooden footbridge and spot a fern-surrounded waterfall. The trail leads uphill for a time, then returns to the creek.

The trail forks. The right fork heads a short distance up-creek to a small waterfall, while the left dead-ends at the preserve's lower gate on Stunt Road.

❀ RED ROCK CANYON PARK

CALABASAS PEAK, RED ROCK CANYON TRAILS
4 miles round trip with 600-foot elevation gain

Hooray for the red, white and blue in the Santa Monica Mountains. Vistas of towering red rocks, along with floral clouds of white and blue-hued ceanothus are bound to stir the heart and stimulate the senses of any American hiker on the trail to Red Rock Canyon Park near Topanga Canyon.

Huge red sandstone outcroppings remind the traveler of the American Southwest. For geologists, the rock record displays a complex history of river-deposited sandstone and conglomerates that have been folded and faulted and sculpted by wind and water.

The tan, red and pale purple rocks are joined by colorful wildflowers in the spring. Look for cliff aster, clarkia, golden bush and many more blooms on the canyon walls near the trail.

Oaks and sycamores occupy the bottom of the sandstone gorge, which ecologists consider a very special microhabitat. Red Rock Canyon, strategically located between Topanga and Malibu Creek state parks, acts as a wildlife corridor and habitat linkage between the larger parklands.

Angelenos seeking the country life began constructing homes in Red Rock Canyon in 1906. One early resident, James Slauson willed 80 acres to the Boy Scouts of America. Camp Clauson was a popular weekend scout camping area for many years. The Santa Monica Mountains Conservancy purchased the property, opened it to the public as Red Rock Canyon Park, and placed it under the stewardship of the Mountains Recreation and Conservation Authority.

The park offers drinking water and a small picnic area but is otherwise undeveloped. I hope your hiker's sense of discovery is not diminished too drastically by the revelation that one can drive most of the way to Red Rock Canyon by entering the park via Old Topanga Canyon Road.

But then you'd miss some exercise and a fine hike. . . .

DIRECTIONS TO TRAILHEAD: From Highway 101 (Ventura Freeway) in Woodland Hills, exit on Topanga Canyon Road and head south a mile to Mulholland Highway. Turn west and proceed 6 miles. As Mulholland curves west, turn east on Stunt Road and travel exactly one mile to a large turnout on the right side of the road at mile-marker 1.0. The trail, a gated fire road, begins on the opposite side of the road.

To reach Red Rock Canyon Park directly by road, exit the Ventura Freeway in Woodland Hills on Topanga Canyon Road and head south a mile to

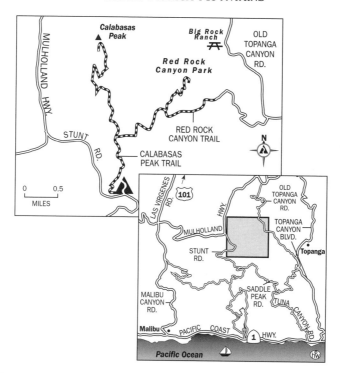

Mulholland Highway. Turn west and drive 2.2 miles to Old Topanga Canyon Road. Head 3.6 miles south, then turn west on Red Rock Road. Drive 0.8 mile (the last 0.2 mile is unpaved) to Red Rock Canyon Park.

THE HIKE: Walk up the fire road across chaparral-blanketed slopes dominated by toyon, laurel sumac, mountain mahogany and ceanothus. These larger shrubs are joined by a host of smaller ones including buckwheat, black sage, bush sunflowers and sagebrush.

After a 0.75 mile ascent, Calabasas Peak Fire Road delivers you to saddle and a junction. The left fork is a continuation of the road and leads to some fascinating rock formations and namesake Calabasas Peak. Take the right fork and begin a 0.75 mile long descent to the bottom of Red Rock Canyon. The canyon narrows and appears more and more intriguing as you near the bottom.

At the 1.5 mile mark, signed Red Rock Canyon Trail offers an intriguing option. The footpath crosses a trickle of a creek and climbs among the rock formations on the north wall of the canyon. It's a fun detour if the temperature isn't too hot.

The major trail continues along the canyon bottom another 0.5 mile to the heart of Red Rock Canyon Park. It's worth extending your hike with a short stroll among the impressive red-rock formations stacked up along the dirt segment of the park's entry road.

❁ CALABASAS PEAK

CALABASAS PEAK TRAIL
To Calabasas Peak is 4 miles round trip with 900-foot elevation gain

Calabasas Peak (2,163 feet high) stands head and shoulders above neighboring summits and offers great clear-day views of the Santa Monica Mountains, the San Fernando Valley, and San Gabriel Mountains.

After a serious 1993 fire scorched the peak, the native chaparral recovered in truly remarkable fashion. These days the slopes are cloaked with laurel sumac, a six- to 12-foot evergreen shrub with smooth, reddish-brown bark. Also much in evidence along Calabasas Peak Trail is the humble, homely Santa Susana tarweed.

In springtime, look for white and blue ceanothus blossoms, Indian paint-brush and Catalina Mariposa lily.

DIRECTIONS TO TRAILHEAD: From the Ventura Freeway, (U.S. 101) in Calabasas, exit on Las Virgenes Road and travel 3.25 miles south to Mulholland Highway. Turn left (east) and proceed four miles to Stunt Road, bear right and drive exactly a mile to the parking area on the right side of Stunt Road. The trailhead is on the left side of Stunt Road by road paddle "1.0"

THE HIKE: Ascend north on the fire road. Behind you is a view of Cold Creek Canyon. Trailside geology is fascinating: large, tilted slabs and fins of sand-stone have been sculpted by erosion into weird shapes.

About 0.75 mile from the trailhead is a saddle, sometimes known as Red Rock Saddle, and a three-way road junction. The right-forking road descends two miles through Red Rock Canyon to Old Topanga Canyon Road.

A very rough, bulldozed road ascending from the saddle leads to a narrow ridge. A trail-less, mile-long, ridgetop route winds among sandstone rocks, then joins a dirt fire road for another 0.5 mile ascend to Topanga Lookout. From the lookout are views of downtown Los Angeles, the San Fernando Valley and Santa Monica Bay. (Don't try this route if it's wet; it gets slippery.)

Your path, Calabasas Peak Trail, is the fire road that continues north from the three-way junction, leading another mile past intriguing sandstone forma-tions. After a couple of very sharp bends in the fire road, you'll gain the top of a ridge and stand just south of Calabasas Peak.

The road edges a bit east, but you join a left-branching fire break leading directly to the peak. Enjoy the view east to Topanga Canyon, west to the famed Goat Buttes towering over Malibu Canyon, and north to the metropolis.

 SADDLE PEAK

BACKBONE TRAIL
From Saddle Peak Road to Saddle Peak is 4 miles round trip with 900-foot elevation gain. From Piuma Road to Saddle Peak is 10 miles round trip with 2000-foot gain

Handsome sandstone formations, commanding coastal and metropolitan views, and botanically intriguing Dark Canyon are some of the highlights of a hike to Saddle Peak. A superb stretch of the Backbone Trail crosses the boulder-strewn crest of the mountains east of Malibu Creek State Park and leads to the peak.

The peak—actually two peaks with a "saddle" in between—is one of the highest points in the central part of the Santa Monica Mountains. Saddle Peak West is forested with communications antennae and off-limits to hikers, but Saddle Peak East, an easy summit climb, offers great vistas.

The commanding promontory stands about 2,800 feet high and often pokes above the coastal clouds that blanket lesser peaks and ridges. Located only about 2.5 miles as the cliff swallows (look for these birds among the peak's sandstone outcroppings) fly from the coast, Saddle Peak is a superb perch for gazing out at Santa Monica Bay and the Channel Islands. Eastern views include downtown Los Angeles and way out to snowcapped Mt. San Jacinto.

Enjoy either a short or long climb to Saddle Peak. From Saddle Peak Road, a family-friendly jaunt offers a little bit of everything: sandstone formations for the kids to climb, an ocean view, a sampling of the Backbone Trail.

Experienced hikers will relish the challenge of a longer, and quite steep trek on the Backbone Trail. (When a trail gains 500 feet or more in a mile, I automatically classify it as "strenuous") Expect a vigorous workout on the trail from Piuma Road to Saddle Peak. One highlight of this hike is Dark Canyon, a lovely retreat with quiet pools shaded by bay and alder.

DIRECTIONS TO TRAILHEAD: (Short hike) From Highway 101 (the Ventura Freeway) in Agoura, exit on Las Virgenes Road and head 3 miles south to Mulholland Highway. Turn left and drive 4 miles west to Stunt Road and veer right, proceeding 2.9 miles, to the signed trail head on the right and sparse parking on the left side of the road. Look for better parking at mileage marker 3.0 on the left side of Stunt Road.

(Long Hike) From Highway 101 (Ventura Freeway) in Agoura, exit on Las Virgenes Road and drive 4.7 miles south to Piuma Road. Turn left and drive 1.2 miles (0.2 mile past Piuma's intersection with Cold Canyon Road) to the signed trailhead.

THE HIKE: (short way) A brief (0.2 mile) walk on the connector trail extending southwest through the chaparral leads to a signed junction. The right fork leads 3 miles to Piuma Road but you head left on the Backbone Trail. The path ascends Saddle Peak's brush-covered slopes, brightened at this time of the year by the bright red berries of the toyon or California holly.

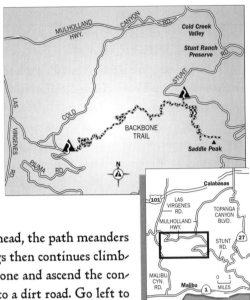

About 1.5 miles from the trailhead, the path meanders among bold sandstone outcroppings then continues climbing to a junction. Leave the Backbone and ascend the connector path right (south) 0.1 mile to a dirt road. Go left to the top of East Peak or right to the saddle of Saddle Peak and enjoy the views.

To Saddle Peak (the long way): From Piuma Road, the Backbone Trail drops into Dark Canyon. Ferns, Humboldt lily and tangles of a rare native grape thrive in the canyon bottom.

Leave behind the cool, moist sycamore- and alder-shaded canyon and begin a long, switchbacking ascent among ceanothus and manzanita. When you pause to catch your breath on this earnest ascent, look back to admire a dramatic view to the west: Malibu Creek State Park and the impressive canyon cut by its namesake creek.

The trail winds among great boulders, which frame views of Cold Creek Canyon to the northeast and Calabasas Peak to the north. About 2.5 miles from the trail head, you'll pass a minor saddle and small meadow, then continue another mile to intersect the connector trail leading down to Saddle Peak Road. Continue on the Backbone Trail and follow the "short way" description above to reach Saddle Peak.

❁ MALIBU CREEK

MALIBU CREEK TRAIL

To Rock Pool is 3.5 miles round trip with 150-foot elevation gain;
to Century Lake is 4.5 miles round trip with 200-foot elevation gain

Before land for Malibu Creek State Park was acquired in 1974, it was divided into three parcels belonging to Bob Hope, Ronald Reagan and 20th Century-Fox. Although the park is still used for moviemaking, it's primarily a haven for day hikers and picnickers.

Today the state park preserves more than 7,000 acres of rugged country in the middle of the Santa Monica Mountains. Malibu Creek winds through the park. The creek was dammed at the dawn of the 20th century to form little Century Lake.

The trail along Malibu Creek explores the heart of the state park. It's an easy, nearly level walk that visits a dramatic rock gorge, Century Lake and several locales popular with moviemakers.

DIRECTIONS TO TRAILHEAD: From Pacific Coast Highway, turn inland on Malibu Canyon Road and proceed 6.5 miles to the park entrance, 0.25 mile south of Mulholland Highway. If you're coming from the San Fernando Valley, exit the Ventura Freeway (101) on Las Virgenes Road and continue four miles to the park entrance.

THE HIKE: From the parking area, follow the wide fire road. You'll cross the all-but-dry creek. The road soon forks into a high road and a low road. Go right and walk along the oak-shaded high road, which makes a long, lazy left arc as it follows the north bank of Malibu Creek. You'll reach an intersection and turn left on a short road that crosses a bridge over Malibu Creek.

You'll spot the Gorge Trail and follow it upstream a short distance to the gorge, one of the most dramatic sights in the Santa Monica Mountains. Malibu Creek makes a hairpin turn through 400-foot volcanic rock cliffs and cascades into aptly named Rock Pool. The "Swiss Family Robinson" television series and some Tarzan movies were filmed here.

Return to the trailhead or retrace your steps back to the high road and bear left toward Century Lake. As the road ascends you'll be treated to a fine view of Las Virgenes Valley. When you gain the crest of the hill, you'll look down on Century Lake. Near the lake are hills of porous lava and topsy-turvy sedimentary rock layers that tell of the violent geologic upheaval that formed Malibu Canyon. The lake was scooped out by members of Crag's Country Club, a group of wealthy businessmen who had a nearby lodge.

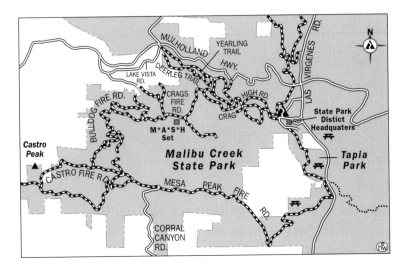

Call it a day here, or continue on the fire road past Century Lake. You'll pass the location of the now-removed set for the "M*A*S*H" television series. The prominent Goat Buttes that tower above Malibu Creek were featured in the opening shot of each episode.

❀ REAGAN RANCH

REAGAN RANCH TRAIL
4-mile loop through Malibu Creek State Park

Before Ronald Reagan purchased what was to become the most well-known ranch in the world—Rancho del Cielo in the Santa Ynez Mountains above Santa Barbara—he owned another spread in the Santa Monica Mountains. Reagan's Ranch, now part of Malibu Creek State Park, is a delight for hikers, who can enjoy the ranch's rolling meadowland and grand old oaks, and even probe the origins of the former president's conservative political philosophy.

During the 1950s when Reagan hosted television's "Death Valley Days," he desired a more rural retreat than his home in Pacific Palisades. He bought the 305-acre ranch as a place to raise thoroughbred horses. Land rose greatly in value, and taxes likewise; the tax increases really piqued Reagan and influenced his political philosophy. From this point on, he would be hostile toward government programs that required more and more tax dollars to fund.

Reagan's Ranch boosted his political career in another way: it was the locale of many a barbecue and gathering attended by the well-heeled politicos who supported his gubernatorial campaign. When Reagan was elected governor in 1966, he moved to Sacramento, and sold his ranch to a movie company. Today the ranch makes up the northwest corner of Malibu Creek State Park. When the property was acquired, the Reagan ranch house was in such grim condition that it had to be destroyed. The Reagan barn still stands and is now used for offices and storage by state park employees.

Trails loop through the Reagan Ranch and connect with the main part of the state park. One path, which I've dubbed Reagan Ranch Trail, uses a combination of trails—Yearling, Deer Leg, Lookout, Crag's Road and Cage Canyon—to explore Reagan country and the heart of the park.

Winter, after rains put a little green in the grassy meadows, and spring, when lupine, larkspur and poppies pop out all over, are the best seasons for a visit.

DIRECTIONS TO TRAILHEAD: From Santa Monica, take Pacific Coast Highway up-coast to Malibu Canyon Road, turn inland and proceed to Mulholland Highway. Turn left and drive 3 miles to the ranch entrance at the corner of Mulholland and Cornell Road. Or from the Ventura Freeway (101) in Agoura, exit on Kanan Road and head south. Make a left on Cornell Road and follow it to its intersection with Mulholland Highway. The trailhead is on the southeast corner. Park carefully alongside Cornell Road.

THE HIKE: Walk into the park on Yearling Road. The dirt road leads 0.25

mile past a row of stately eucalyptus and soon arrives at the old Reagan barn. Continue on the road which passes a corral and heads across a meadow. Soon you'll pass the first of a couple of side trails leading rightward into a grove of oaks and linking up with Deer Leg Trail. Continue straight ahead on the meadow trail.

During spring, wildflowers color the field, a long grassy strip. At the east end of the meadow, the trail dips in and out of a canyon, tunnels through some high chaparral and ascends an oak crowned ridge. Atop the ridge is a great view of Malibu Creek and the main features of the state park. Also on the ridgetop is an unsigned trail junction. You'll take the left-leading trail and begin descending southeast on well-named Lookout Trail. The trail drops to Crag's Road, the state park's major trail, near Century Lake.

Crag's Road leads east-west with Malibu Creek and connects to trails leading to the site of the old "M*A*S*H" set, the Backbone Trail and the park visitors center. More immediately, when you make a right on the road, you pass close to Century Lake. Near the lake are hills of porous lava and topsy-turvy sedimentary rock layers that tell of the violent geologic upheaval that formed Malibu Canyon. The man-made lake was scooped out by members of Crag's Country Club, a group of wealthy, turn-of-the-20th-century businessmen who had a nearby lodge.

Walk up Crag's Road about 200 hundred yards and join unsigned Cage Canyon Trail on your right. The trail makes a short and rapid ascent of the oak- and sycamore-filled canyon and soon brings you to an unsigned intersection with Deer Leg Trail. Bear left and begin traveling under a canopy of oaks. You'll get occasional glimpses of the rolling grassland of the Reagan Ranch below. One attractive oak grove shades a barbecue area where the Reagans once entertained. This grove is a good place for a picnic.

Soon you'll bear leftward at a trail junction and begin ascending the cool north slope of a hillside above the ranch. Leaving the oaks behind, the trail climbs a brushy hillside to an overlook. Enjoy the view of Malibu Lake and Paramount Ranch. The trail intersects a fire road, which you take to the right on a steep descent to the meadow near park headquarters. The road vanishes here, so walk 50 yards across the meadow to Yearling Road, which leads back to the trailhead.

❀ MALIBU LAKE AND MORE

CRAGS ROAD TRAIL

From Malibu Lake to former "M*A*S*H" set is 2 miles round trip; to Century Lake is 4 miles round trip; to Visitor Center is 5.6 miles round trip

Crags Road, Malibu Creek State Park's most popular path and everyone's idea of a family hike, offers a mellow ramble through the heart of the Santa Monica Mountains. The time-honored route alongside Malibu Creek from the park entrance on Las Virgenes to the visitor center, "The Gorge," and the location of the former "M*A*S*H" television series, is one of the Southland's most classic hikes.

There's no improving such a hike, but there is the possibility of hiking it "backward" for a variation on a lovely theme. For experienced hikers looking for something a little different, I suggest beginning at Malibu Lake and entering the state park through the back door. This rarely used trailhead coupled with a car shuttle might suggest a one-way hike along Malibu Creek.

Malibu Lake was created for a country club and real estate development in the early 1920s when a dam was built to impound the waters of Malibu Creek. The Mountain Club, established on the lakeshore in 1922, still stands and is available for rent on the weekends.

During the 1930s and 1940s, the lake was a popular location for movies, particularly Westerns. *Wells Fargo* (1937) and *The Adventures of Tom Sawyer* (1938) were among the films that featured Malibu Lake.

Except for its usefulness to hikers as an obscure state park trailhead, Malibu Lake has little attraction for the traveler. There's absolutely nowhere to park around the lake, which boasts more no trespassing signs than trees on its shores. The lake looks far more attractive from distant mountaintops and aerial photos than it does up-close.

DIRECTIONS TO TRAILHEAD: From the Ventura Freeway in Calabasas, exit on Las Virgenes Road and drive 3 miles south to Mulholland Highway. (The main state park entrance is off Las Virgenes, just a little bit farther south.) Turn right (west) on Mulholland and drive 3.2 miles to an intersection with Cornell Road (extending west) and Lake Vista Drive (which you follow southwest) a short distance to Malibu Lake and 0.6 mile to Crags Road. Turn left on Crags Road and continue 0.8 mile to a vehicle gate and the state park boundary. Best parking is about a quarter-mile back on Crags Road from the trail head. Park is a safe, legal and courteous manner in the neighborhood along Crags Road.

THE HIKE: Walk east on the dirt road 0.3 mile to an unsigned junction.

(Detour left, north, along Malibu Creek past some handsome rock-framed pools. This path deadends in a quarter mile at a picnic table perched near Malibu Dam. A nice place to eat your lunch!)

Continue on Crags Road past a signed intersection with Bulldog Road, then another 0.3 mile to the "M*A*S*H" site, marked by the charred exoskeleton of an old Jeep. The prominent Goat Buttes that tower above Malibu Creek were featured in the opening shot of each episode.

Crags Road offers many more attractions. Another mile of easy hiking brings you to Century Lake, a man-made lake scooped out by members of the Crags Country Club, a group of wealthy, early 20th-century businessmen, who had a nearby lodge. Near the lake are hills of porous lava and topsy-turvy sedimentary rock layers that tell of the violent geologic upheaval that formed Malibu Canyon.

Continue another 0.8 mile past the lake to the park visitor center. Enjoy the interpretive displays on the weekends when the center is open, and the picnic area out front anytime.

Take Crags Road through the heart of the park.

❀ Liberty Canyon

LIBERTY CANYON, TALOPOP TRAILS
Talopop Loop Trail is 3 miles; Liberty Canyon walk is 3 miles round trip

Across Mulholland Highway from the main body of Malibu Creek State Park is an arm of park land called Liberty Canyon, as lonely a place as you'll find in the popular state park.

It's an area rich in history, believed to have been continuously inhabited by prehistoric peoples and more recently by the Chumash from 6000 B.C. to the early 1800s. Talopop was the name of the native Chumash village located here; it's now the name of the loop trail that circles the tribe's ancestral land.

In 1834, the land along Las Virgenes Creek became part of the Las Virgenes Rancho belonging to Domingo Carrillo and Nemisio Dominguez. Dominguez's daughter Maria married Pedro Sepúlveda in 1859 and the couple built an adobe near the banks of the creek. They raised twelve children in the two-room adobe that still stands near the corner of Malibu Canyon Road and Mulholland Highway.

While the story of an early California Hispanic family in the last half of the 19th century would likely have a great deal of interest to park visitors, the Sepúlveda adobe remains unrestored, deteriorating behind a chain-link fence. Sepulveda Adobe is located near another closed-to-the-public treasure, the White Oak Farm, an early 20th century dairy and ranch. James Hope, brother of entertainer Bob, lived here and managed the ranch for more than twenty years.

The Liberty Canyon hiker will be better rewarded than the history buff, but still experiences one frustration: the two major trails—Liberty Canyon Trail and Talopop Trail don't connect. From the crest of Talopop Trail, the hiker looks down at lovely Liberty Canyon (so near, yet so far!) with consternation: Alas, you can't get there from here.

Explorer Juan Bautista de Anza's expedition camped on the San Fernando Valley side of the Santa Monica Mountains while enroute from Baja to Monterey. Anza's namesake park, operated by the city of Calabasas, boasts a state-of-the-art kid's playground, superb basketball courts and picnic facilities, and offers hikers offers new and improved access to Liberty Canyon. The east fork of Talapop Trail leads south to a junction with Liberty Canyon Trail and to the historic Sepúlveda Adobe.

DIRECTIONS TO TRAILHEAD: From the Ventura Freeway (101) exit on Las Virgenes Road and drive 3.5 miles south to Mulholland Highway. Park in the small lot at the southwest corner of Las Virgenes and Mulholland or (carefully) in one of the small turnouts along Mulholland.

To reach Juan Bautista de Anza Park, you'll drive 1.5 miles from the freeway exit on Las Virgenes Road to Lost Hills Road. Turn right. The park is on the left side of the road.

THE HIKE: Walk west along Mulholland over the pedestrian-friendly bridge over Las Virgenes Creek and join the unsigned trail on the north side of the road leading toward the Sepulveda Adobe. Continue past the off-limits historic site, crossing a meadow and heading toward the tiny Crater Substation powerplant. At the paved powerplant road, turn right, walk 200 feet, then join the dirt road on your left which soon leads past the ranch house and barn of White Oak Farm, skirts an oak-dotted meadow, then crosses a footbridge over Las Virgenes Creek.

Arriving at a junction, you briefly join Liberty Canyon Trail before coming to a second signed junction. Liberty Canyon Trail continues straight ahead (more about this path later) while Talopop Trail veers right, rising above the canyon floor and following a grassy ridge that offers excellent vistas of the area. To the north you can see housing developments creeping south toward the park boundaries. South, pretty as a picture, is White Oak Farm nestled in a green hollow, with the wilder parts of Malibu Canyon providing a dramatic backdrop.

The trail dips and climbs a couple times before descending a sage- and scrub oak-smothered hillside east to a junction. The left fork leads a quarter-mile east, then bends north to the state park boundary and Lost Hills Road.

From the junction, Talopop Trail leads an easy mile back to White Oak Farm, where you can either return to the trailhead or join Liberty Canyon Trail for further exploration.

Liberty Canyon Trail: From its junction with Talopop Trail, the wide path heads up the oak-filled canyon, bends around a private ranch and continues to the state park boundary. At trail's end is Patrick Henry Place and suburbia. Off to the left is an unsigned junction with Stagecoach Trail, which heads south back to Mulholland Highway (at a point a mile or so west of the trailhead).

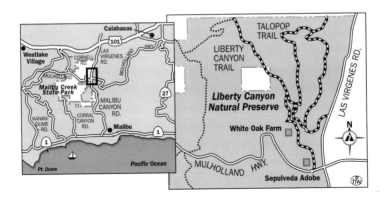

❀ LAS VIRGENES VIEW PARK

LAS VIRGENES VIEW TRAIL
4.8 miles round trip with 500-foot elevation gain

For good vistas of the central portion of the Santa Monica Mountains, ascend the Las Virgenes View Trail.

The trail is yet another successful project of the busy Santa Monica Mountains Conservancy, in partnership this time with the Las Virgenes Municipal Water District and the city of Calabasas.

The path traverses the similarly named Las Virgenes View Park, located just a stone's throw east of famed Malibu Creek State Park. The park is managed by the Mountains Recreation and Conservation Authority.

No trail sign marks the beginning of the path, but a veritable thicket of other signs have much to proclaim: Calabasas, population 27,165. Wow. Not so long ago that little town had a population less than its elevation (796 feet). Tree City, USA. Good show! Environmental Enhancement Mitigation Program Site. Say what? Watch for Future Trails Planning. We will!

A trailhead interpretive display proved to be right on target with its description of flora and fauna found along the trail. While hiking the path, I observed a surprising number of animals: a Western fence lizard basking on a sunny rock, a red-tailed hawk soaring over the grasslands, mule deer browsing the brush, an acorn woodpecker rat-a-tat-tatting against a tree trunk, a coyote jogging along a high ridge. What seemed to me so incongruous about this wildlife drama is that it plays out within sight of the Ventura Freeway.

The trailhead natural history display left out one animal: the cow. Cattle graze Las Virgenes View Park and the private property surrounding it. One black-and-white bovine blocked a narrow part of the path for some time while we negotiated who would continue along the trail and who would climb off-trail into the brush. (The heaviest, most patient animal, the one with the horns, prevailed in this standoff.)

The new park preserves several of the major plant communities common to the Santa Monica Mountains, including chaparral, oak woodland, and a riparian zone highlighted by sycamore, black cottonwood, willow and bay. A rare valley grassland contains purple needle grass and blue-eye grass, two native species that have managed to survive two centuries of cattle grazing.

DIRECTIONS TO TRAILHEAD: From the Ventura Freeway (101) in Calabasas, exit on Las Virgenes Road. Head south 3 miles to a stop-lighted intersection with Mulholland Highway. Las Virgenes View Trail begins at the north-

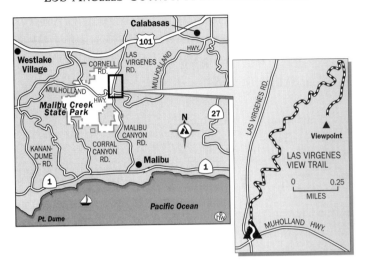

east corner of the intersection, where there's limited parking. More parking is available at the southwestern corner, on the border of Malibu Creek State Park.

Use caution at this intersection. Traffic moves at very high speeds in all directions.

THE HIKE: Las Virgenes View Trail ascends north on a more or less parallel course to Las Virgenes Road. Contemplate the scene from a trailside bench located a quarter-mile out. After another half-mile, an intriguing section of trail wanders across a narrow ledge.

As the path twists and turns, civilization's cacophony recedes, though views of that civilization—Calabasas, the Ventura Freeway and more—actually get more distinct. Reaching a ridgeline, the trail bends south along a wire fence. Enjoy the stirring views, which include Castro Peak and Goat Buttes in Malibu Creek State Park and Saddle Peak to the southeast. The trail makes a tight loop atop the ridgeline and you return the way you came.

 CASTRO CREST

BACKBONE TRAIL
From Malibu Canyon Road to Castro Crest is 7 miles one way with 2,000 foot gain; return via Bulldog Motorway, and Century Road is 14 miles round trip

The Backbone Trail route through Malibu Creek State Park has been finished for quite some time and has proved very popular. Both a primary and alternate route lead through the state park. The high "primary" route follows a dramatic ridgetop toward Castro Crest while the "alternate" route meanders along with Malibu Creek through the heart of the state park.

This day hike connects the two branches of the Backbone Trail and provides a grand tour of Malibu Creek State Park. Fine ocean and island views are offered along the first half of the hike and a chance to explore geologically and ecologically unique Malibu Creek Canyon on the second half.

DIRECTIONS TO TRAILHEAD: From Pacific Coast Highway, turn inland on Malibu Canyon Road and proceed 5 miles to Tapia County Park, located a short mile south of Malibu Creek State Park.

THE HIKE: Mesa Peak Motorway, as this dirt road is known, ascends steeply at first, gaining 1,500 feet in 2.5 miles. With the elevation gain comes sweeping panoramic views of Point Dume, Santa Monica Bay, and Palos Verdes Peninsula. On clear days, Catalina, Anacapa and Santa Cruz Islands float upon the horizon.

The trail veers left toward Mesa Peak (1,844 feet) and continues climbing in a northwesterly direction through an area rich in fossilized shells. Hillside road-cuts betray the Santa Monica Mountains' oceanic heritage. As you hike the spine of the range, a good view to the north is yours: the volcanic rocks of Goat Butte tower above Malibu Creek gorge and the path of Triunfo Canyon can be traced.

The road passes through an area of interesting sandstone formations and intersects paved Corral Canyon Road, which is termed Castro Motorway from this point. Continue west on Castro Motorway for one mile, reaching the intersection with Bulldog Motorway.

Clinging to life in the Castro Crest area is the humble Santa Susana tarweed, a plant only a botanist could love—or even find. *Hemizonia minthornii*, a low mass of woody stems and dull green herbage, was believed to exist only in the Santa Susana Mountains before its discovery in the late 1970s atop Castro Crest and in other isolated locales high in the Santa Monica Mountains.

Backbone Trail continues west toward the forest of antennae atop Castro Peak (2,824 feet).

Return via Bulldog Motorway: For a nice loop trip back through Malibu

Creek State Park, bear right on Bulldog Motorway. Descend steeply under transmission lines, veering east and dropping into Triunfo Canyon. In 3.5 miles, you reach Century Road. Turn right and soon pass what was once the location of the exterior sets used by the "M*A*S*H" television series. (The set is now on display in the Smithsonian Institution.) The prominent Goat Buttes that tower above Malibu Creek are featured in the opening shot of each episode.

The road passes Century Lake, crosses a ridge, then drops down to Malibu Creek and comes to a fork in the road. Take either the left (high road) or continue straight ahead over the bridge on the low road; the roads meet again downstream, so you may select either one. One-half mile after the roads rejoin, you approach the park's day use parking area.

Follow a dirt road that skirts this parking area, leads past a giant valley oak and approaches the state park's campground. Bear right on a dirt road that leads a short distance through meadowland to the park's Group Camp. Here you'll join a connector trail that will take you a mile up and over a low brushy ridge to Tapia Park. Hike through the park back to your car.

Along the crest of the Santa Monicas.

 CORRAL CANYON

BACKBONE TRAIL
6-mile loop along Castro Crest and through upper Solstice Canyon with
1,000-foot elevation gain

Stalk the rare Santa Susana tarweed—and some genuinely pretty flowering plants—
on a nice loop trail along the Castro Crest area of the Santa Monica Mountains.

Geologically minded hikers will also enjoy tramping along Castro Crest.
Towering above the parking area is the gray sandstone/mudstone Sespe Formation,
formed 40 to 25 million years ago. Down in Solstice Canyon is the Coal Canyon
Formation, of marine deposition, laid down 60 to 50 million years ago. Many mol-
lusks are visible in the long rock slabs. Even those hikers without interest in botany
or earth science will enjoy this outing. It samples both high and low segments of the
Backbone Trail, provides great views and a good aerobic workout.

DIRECTIONS TO TRAILHEAD: From Pacific Coast Highway, about 2
miles up-coast from Malibu Canyon Road, turn inland on Corral Canyon Road.
Proceed 5.5 miles to road's end at a large dirt parking lot.

THE HIKE: From the parking area, head past the locked gate up the wide
dirt road, Castro Motorway. (You're walking the nearly complete Backbone Trail
that extends 65 miles across the spine of the range.) After a short climb, enjoy a
fine clear-day view of Mt. Baldy and the San Gabriel Mountains, as well as of the
Santa Susana Mountains—home of the elusive tarweed. A great place to look for
the plant is about 0.75 mile from the trailhead on the north side of the dirt road
near the junction of Castro Motorway with Bulldog Motorway.

Bulldog Motorway on you right leads to Malibu Creek State Park and its
many miles of trail, but you continue climbing another 0.75 mile to a junction
with Newton Canyon Motorway, which you'll join by bearing left. (Castro
Motorway descends to a junction at a saddle. You could go straight, south that is,
here and drop into Upper Solstice Canyon; this would cut off about two miles
from the six-mile round trip distance of this hike.)

Bear right on the stretch of Backbone Trail called Castro Trail and head west
for a mile to paved Latigo Canyon Road. Walk along the road for a short while and
join Newton Motorway on your left, which passes by a private residence then
descends to the saddle discussed above and the connector trail leading back toward
Castro Motorway. Continue east, meandering along the monkeyflower- and paint-
brush-sprinkled banks of Solstice Creek. Watch for a lovely meadow dotted with
Johnny jump-ups and California poppies. The trail turns north with the creekbed
then climbs west for a time up a chaparral-covered slope back to the trailhead.

❀ SOLSTICE CANYON PARK

SOLSTICE CANYON TRAIL
3 miles round trip

Solstice Canyon Trail leads visitors along a year-round creek and introduces them to the flora and history of the Santa Monica Mountains. The path is a narrow country road—suitable for strollers and wheelchairs—which offers an easy family hike in the shade of grand old oaks and towering sycamores.

Solstice Canyon in the Santa Monica Mountains is enjoyable year-round, but autumn and winter are particularly fine times to ramble through the quiet canyon. In autumn, enjoy the fall color display of the sycamores and in winter, from the park's upper slopes, look for gray whales migrating past Point Dume.

Solstice Canyon Park opened on summer solstice, 1988. The Santa Monica Mountains Conservancy purchased the land from the Roberts family and transformed the 550-acre Roberts Ranch into a park. Ranch roads became foot trails. Milk thistle, castor bean and other assorted nonnative plants were almost eliminated (but since returned); picnic areas and a visitor contact station were built. Today National Park Service rangers are the stewards of Solstice Canyon.

Solstice Canyon's strangest structure resembles a futurist farm house with a

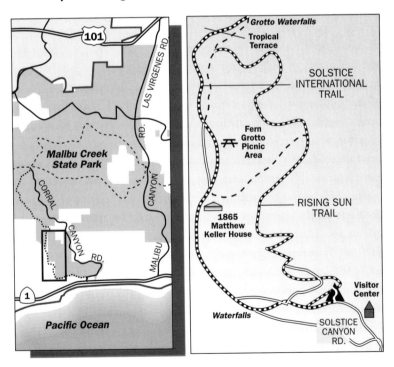

silo attached, and really defies architectural categorization. Bauhaus, maybe. Or perhaps Grain Elevator Modern. From 1961 to 1973 Space Tech Labs, a subsidiary of TRW used the building to conduct tests to determine the magnetic sensitivity of satellite instrumentation. The Santa Monica Mountains Conservancy was headquartered here for many years.

Creature of the canyon.

DIRECTIONS TO TRAILHEAD: From Pacific Coast Highway, about 17 miles up-coast from Santa Monica and 3.5 miles up-coast from Malibu Canyon Road, turn inland on Corral Canyon Road. At the first bend in the road, you'll leave the road and proceed straight to the very small Solstice Canyon parking lot.

THE HIKE: Stop at the bulletin board, pick up a trail brochure.

About halfway along, you'll pass the 1865 Mathew Keller House and in a few more minutes, Fern Grotto. The road travels under the shade of oak and sycamore to its end at the remains of the old Roberts Ranch House. Palms, agave, bamboo and bird of paradise and many more tropical plants thrive in the Roberts' family garden gone wild. A waterfall, fountain and an old dam are some of the other special features found in this paradisiacal setting known as Tropical Terrace.

Across the creek from Tropical Terrace is signed Rising Sun Trail, which climbs a ridge for rewarding canyon and ocean views. The two-mile trail offers an excellent, but more difficult return route.

🌸 CORRAL CANYON PARK

CORRAL CANYON LOOP TRAIL
2.5-mile loop with 400-foot elevation gain.

Corral Canyon Loop Trail is a footpath for the whole family to enjoy. In this era of budget cutbacks and bean-counting bureaucrats it's a pleasure to report that a modest expenditure of public monies has created something quite lovely, something enduring, a way to enjoy nature that will be treasured by today's hikers and generations to follow.

Corral Canyon is the last remaining coastal canyon in the Los Angeles County portion of the Santa Monica Mountains with an uninterrupted band of natural land from the ocean to the crest of the range. A mixed woodland of alder, sycamore, willow and coastal live oak lines Corral Creek, which flows from its headwaters high in Malibu Creek State Park down to its mouth at Dan Blocker Beach.

The footpath has a hand-built quality that I really appreciate. It's certainly not the kind of trail that I see all too often these days: a big and wide swath bulldozed over the land by a huge park bureaucracy out-of-touch with hikers and with the great outdoors.

"My goal was to design a trail that really fit in with the terrain," explained Larry Chirico, designer of the Corral Canyon Loop Trail, told me.

Chirico, Special Projects Leader for the Mountains Recreation and Conservation Authority, spent a month beating around the bush and flagging a route up Corral Canyon with yellow ribbons. "To design a good trail, one in keeping with the spirit of the land, you almost have to think like a coyote."

Corral Canyon Trailhead, complete with parking, picnic areas and restrooms, is another marvelous accomplishment of the Santa Monica Mountains Conservancy. Park officials and trails advocates hope the path will one day soon connect to planned trails across adjacent coastal bluffs and up into the wild heart of upper Corral Canyon.

When I hiked the path early on a perfect summer day, I spotted lots of wildlife, including deer, rabbits, ground squirrel and lots of California quail scurrying about. Red-tailed hawks rode the thermals high above Corral Canyon.

The lower part of Corral Canyon was once owned by the late entertainer Bob Hope who, in the early 1990s, intended to build a luxury home development and golf course in Corral Canyon. In 1998, the Santa Monica Mountains Conservancy acquired the land and formed Corral Canyon Park.

DIRECTIONS TO TRAILHEAD: You'll find the trailhead for Corral

Canyon Loop Trail located between Malibu Canyon and Kanan Dume Roads on Pacific Coast Highway. The trailhead is next to Malibu Seafood Fresh Fish Market and Patio Café at 25653 Pacific Coast Highway, 1.5 miles up-coast from Pepperdine University.

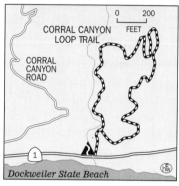

After your hike you can sit at the café for fish and chips, a squid steak and a cool one. Add to the fine trail and good eats a sunset stroll on the beach across the Coast Highway from the trailhead, and you have a great date or family outing.

Those tired of always having to drive to the start of a hike will be happy to learn they can take the bus. An MTA bus stop is located on Pacific Coast Highway right by the entrance to the trailhead.

THE HIKE: The trail crosses Corral Creek on funny-looking cement posts, which seem like they belong on an obstacle course. Just down-creek by the highway bridge is a tiny marsh defined by low, salt-tolerant shrubs.

You'll soon reach an unsigned trail junction. I decided on the right fork and to hike the loop in a counterclockwise direction. The path ascends to an ancient marine terrace, and across native bunchgrass-covered coastal bluffs.

The path climbs north in the coastal sage community among purple sage, buckwheat and coyote brush to the divide with Puerco Canyon. Reward for the ascent comes in the form of fine views of Santa Monica Bay and the Ventura County coastline.

Bending west, the trail drops back into Corral Canyon. The last leg of the hike is an easy ramble along the riparian corridor of the canyon back to the trailhead.

❀ PARAMOUNT RANCH

COYOTE CANYON TRAIL
0.75-mile interpretive path

Even in 1921, Burbank was too busy a place for filming Western movies on location, so Paramount Studios purchased a 2,700-acre spread in the then-remote Agoura area. Paramount Ranch had many a desirable location: mountains, meadows, creeks, canyons, oak and walnut groves. One dramatic mountain—Sugarloaf Peak—is said to have inspired the famous Paramount logo.

Besides innumerable westerns, such 1930s classics as *The Adventures of Marco Polo* and *Tom Sawyer* were filmed here.

Paramount sold the ranch in 1948 but a smaller part of it, including Western Town, continued to be used for filming. The ranch was particularly popular during the 1950s heyday of the television Western when "The Cisco Kid," "Bat Masterson," "Have Gun Will Travel" and many more horse operas were filmed here. The ranch substituted for Colorado in the long-running television series "Dr. Quinn, Medicine Woman."

The National Park Service purchased the ranch in 1980. Today, filmmakers continue to use the Western town and the surrounding hills for features, television series and commercials.

The park doubled in size with the acquisition of the Historic Oaks portion of the old ranch by the National Park Service. It was long cherished by the public, who knew it as the site of the Renaissance Pleasure Faire.

For the walker, Paramount Ranch offers a stroll through Western Town, a loop around what used to be a sports car race track, and a couple of miles of hiking trail. Runners will note the ranch's 5K route that links the race track and a couple of paths.

DIRECTIONS TO TRAILHEAD: From the Ventura Freeway (101) in Agoura, exit on Kanan Road. Drive south 0.75 mile, forking left onto Cornell Road, then proceeding 2.5 miles to Paramount Ranch.

THE HIKE: Coyote Canyon Trail begins behind Western Town and meanders among some handsome oaks. Halfway along the trail, there's a good hilltop view back at Western Town and of Goat Buttes towering above nearby Malibu Creek State Park. Interpretive brochures are available at the ranger station or bulletin board.

You can join Stream Terrace Trail south of the parking lot by the old race track. The path ascends a hill for vistas of Western Town, Malibu Lake and Sugarloaf Peak.

❦ PARAMOUNT TO MALIBU CREEK

PARKLINK TRAILS
From Paramount Ranch to Malibu Creek State Park is 6 miles one way with 400-foot elevation gain

If there's anything I love as much as a loop trail, it's a one-way hike.

When my time is limited and there's much to see in a particular area, I jump at the chance of taking a one-way hike. So I was delighted to learn about the ParkLink Shuttle, a bus service that transports you to parks and trailheads in the Santa Monica Mountains. With the shuttle schedule in hand, you can plan a one-way walk, knowing you can bus back to where you started your hike.

I've enjoyed taking one-way hikes with the help of shuttle buses in other national parks such as Zion, Bryce Canyon and Yosemite and used the public bus service in and around the Golden Gate National Recreation Area. There's something very special about arriving at or departing from a trailhead by bus: meeting other visitors, the sense of embarking on special adventure, and simply a break from the same-old-same-old drive to the trailhead, get out of your car and do an out-and-back hike routine.

I got started in the Santa Monica Mountains with a one-way jaunt from Paramount Ranch, a national park site, to Malibu Creek State Park. We learned a lot about movie and TV show locations as we hiked from an old Western town film set to the "M*A*S*H" site. It was an easy to moderate hike, a bit more than 6 miles in length, with very little elevation gain.

We concluded our hike at the main parking lot at Malibu Creek State Park. Here we boarded a ParkLink shuttle bus for the ten-minute ride back to Paramount Ranch and the trailhead. The buses run very conveniently and the cost is very low.

The shuttle bus system currently runs on the weekends from 8 A.M. to 5 P.M. and on some holidays. Destinations along the coast include Zuma Beach, Solstice Canyon, Corral Canyon, Malibu Beach, and Malibu Village. The shuttle travels Malibu Canyon Road with stops at Malibu Creek State Park and Tapia Park; along Mulholland with stops at Paramount Ranch and Peter Strauss Ranch; and along Kanan-Dume Road with a stop at one of the Backbone Trailheads.

The shuttle is sponsored by the National Park Service, the Santa Monica Mountains Conservancy, California State Parks and Los Angeles County Beaches and Harbors. For more ParkLink Shuttle information, call 1-888-734-2323, or visit www.parklinkshuttle.com

❀ PETER STRAUSS RANCH

PETER STRAUSS TRAIL
0.6 mile round trip

"The largest swimming pool west of the Rockies." That was once the boast of Lake Enchanto, a resort and amusement park popular in the 1930s and 1940s. Sometimes 5,000 Southlanders a weekend would come to swim, fish, picnic and enjoy the amusement rides. A Big Band-style radio program was broadcast live, while L.A. notables and Hollywood stars danced the night away.

During the 1960s a plan was hatched to develop a theme park—Cornell World Famous Places—that would replicate Egyptian pyramids and Mt. Fuji. Meanwhile, Lake Enchanto itself disappeared when the dam backing up Triunfo Creek washed away in a flood. These plans never materialized, the property was sold for back taxes, and finally ended up in the hands of actor-producer Peter Strauss, who purchased the former resort in 1977. After Strauss restored and improved the property, it was acquired by the Santa Monica Mountains Conservancy, who deeded it to the National Park Service.

DIRECTIONS TO TRAILHEAD: From the Ventura Freeway (101) in Agoura, exit on Kanan Road. Proceed south 2.75 miles to Troutdale Road and turn left. At Mulholland Highway, turn left again, cross the bridge over Triunfo Creek and turn into the Peter Strauss Ranch parking area. After parking, hike back to Mulholland, cross the bridge over Triunfo Creek, then join the signed trail behind the ranch house.

THE HIKE: The trail begins near a eucalyptus grove and a former aviary, switchbacks up the hillside behind the ranch house, then loops back down the slope. Chaparral and some creekside oaks are the chief habitats.

 ROCKY OAKS

ROCKY OAKS TRAIL
1 mile round trip

Until the late 1970s, Rocky Oaks Park was a working cattle ranch. The grassland (pasture) and pond (for cattle) are remnants of that era.

Rocky Oaks, acquired by the National Park Service in 1981, is one of those little places perfect for a picnic or a little leg-stretcher of a hike.

DIRECTIONS TO TRAILHEAD: From the Ventura Freeway (101) in Agoura, exit on Kanan Road and drive south. Turn right (west) onto Mulholland Drive, then right into the park.

THE HIKE: From the parking area, a signed path leads to the oak-shaded picnic area; another path heads for directly for the pond. Rainfall determines the depth—indeed, the existence of—the pond. These two paths intersect, and ascend a brushy hillside to an overlook, which offers views of the park and surrounding mountains.

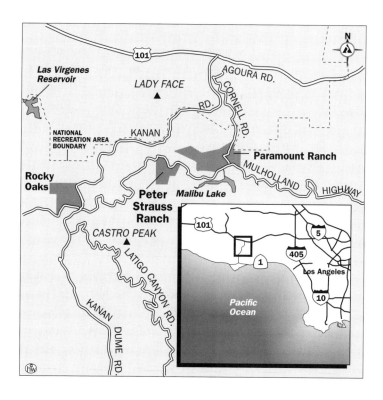

313

❁ ZUMA CANYON

ZUMA LOOP, ZUMA RIDGE TRAILS

Around Zuma Canyon is 2-mile loop; via Zuma Ridge Trail is 9.8-mile loop with 1,700-foot elevation

At first, when you turn inland off Pacific Coast Highway onto Bonsall Drive and enter Zuma Canyon, the canyon looks like many others in the Santa Monica Mountains: huge haciendas perched on precipitous slopes, accompanied by lots of lots for sale. But the road ends and only footpaths enter Zuma Canyon.

Malibu, Topanga, Temescal and Santa Ynez—perhaps these canyons and others in the Santa Monica Mountains looked like Zuma a century ago: a creek cascading over magnificent sandstone boulders, a jungle of willow and lush streamside flora, fern-fringed pools and towering rock walls.

Hikers can partake of Zuma Canyon's grandeur via three routes: For an easy family hike join 2-mile Zuma Loop Trail, which explores the canyon mouth; hardy hikers will relish the challenge of the gorge—two miles of trail-less creekcrossing and boulder-hopping—one of the most difficult hikes in the Santa Monicas; Zuma Ridge Trail, lives up to the promise of its name. Hikers ascend Zuma Canyon's west ridge for grand ocean and mountain views, then follow a series of fire roads and footpaths to circle back to the trailhead.

This loop around Zuma Canyon's walls is a great workout and conditioning hike because of two major ascents and descents en route. Bring lots of water. Water is available at the Bonsall Drive trailhead but nowhere else on the hike.

DIRECTIONS TO TRAILHEAD: From Pacific Coast Highway in Malibu, head up-coast one mile past an intersection with Kanan-Dume Road and turn right on Bonsall Drive (this turn is just before the turnoff for Zuma Beach). Drive a mile (the last hundred yards on dirt road) to road's end at a parking lot.

To start the hike on Zuma Ridge Trail, continue very briefly up-coast past the Bonsall Drive turnoff on Pacific Coast Highway to the next major right turn—Busch Drive. Travel a bit over a mile to the small dirt parking lot and signed trail.

THE HIKE: Just before you join Zuma Ridge Trail (a dirt road, gated to prevent vehicle entry) note the signed footpath (Ridge Canyon Access Trail) just to the east. This path will return you to the trailhead on the very last leg of your long loop.

Begin your shadeless ascent, following the dirt road below some water tanks. Up, up, up you go along the ridge between Zuma Canyon on your right and Trancas Canyon on your left. Look behind you at the sparkling blue Pacific and the Malibu Riviera.

Three miles of vigorous ascent brings you to a junction with the right-forking Zuma Edison Road. What goes up must come down, and down east you go toward the floor of Zuma Canyon. After a mile's descent you'll pass a horse guzzler, then continue the steep descent another mile or so to the sycamore-shaded canyon bottom. By all means take a break here and marshal your energy for this hike's second major climb.

The road climbs southeasterly out of the canyon. Far below is Kanan-Dume Road, about a mile to the east. Zuma Edison Road bends north for 0.25 mile to intersect Zuma Canyon Connector Trail, a footpath that turns south to travel along a knife-edge ridge. This engaging path takes you 0.7 mile down to meet Kanan-Edison Road. Coast coastward as you descend this dirt fire road 1.3 miles to a junction with Canyon View Trail, a path that descends into the heart of Zuma Canyon. You could branch off on this pleasant trail, but in keeping with the ridge-route theme of this walk I prefer to continue on Kanan-Edison Road just 0.1 mile more to meet Ocean View Trail. This path descends westward 1.1 miles to the canyon bottom while serving up fine ocean views.

When you meet Zuma Canyon Trail, go left about 100 feet to meet Ridge-Canyon Access Trail. Join this 0.7 mile long footpath on a climb from the canyon bottom up and over a low hill to return to the Busch Drive trailhead.

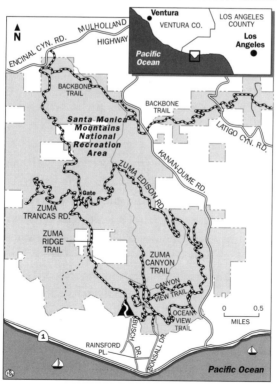

🌿 Charmlee Park

Ocean Vista Trail
3-mile loop

Charmlee, perched on the bluffs above Malibu, often has outstanding spring wildflower displays. Most of the park is a large open meadow; the flower display, given timely rainfall, can be quite colorful. Lupine, paintbrush, larkspur, Mariposa lily, penstemon and California peony bust out all over.

Stop at Charmlee's small nature center and inquire about what's blooming where. Also pick up a copy of a brochure that interprets the park's Fire Ecology Trail. This nature trail interprets the important role of fire in Southern California's chaparral communities.

Good views are another reason to visit Charmlee. The Santa Monica Mountains spread east to west, with the Simi Hills and Santa Susana Mountains rising to the north. Down-coast you can see Zuma Beach and Point Dume and up-coast Sequit Point in Leo Carrillo State Park. Offshore, Catalina Island and two of the Channel Islands–Anacapa and Santa Cruz–can sometimes be seen.

Beginning in the early 1800s this Malibu meadowland was part of Rancho Topanga-Malibu-Sequit and was used to pasture cattle. For a century and a half, various ranchers held the property. The last of these private landholders– Charmain and Leonard Swartz–combined their first names to give Charmlee its euphonious name. Los Angeles County acquired the Charmlee property in the late 1960s and eventually opened the 460-acre park in 1981.

For the hiker, Charmlee is one of the few parks, perhaps even the only park, that actually seems to have a surplus of trails. Quite a few paths and old ranch roads wind through the park, which is shaped like a big grassy bowl.

Because the park is mostly one big meadow fringed with oak trees, it's easy to see where you're going and improvise your own circle tour of Charmlee. Bring a kite and a picnic to this undiscovered park and take it easy for an afternoon.

DIRECTIONS TO TRAILHEAD: From Pacific Coast Highway, about 12 miles up-coast from the community of Malibu, head into the mountains on Encinal Canyon Road 4.5 miles to Charmlee Natural Area County Park.

THE HIKE: Walk through the park's picnic area on a dirt road, which travels under the shade of coast live oaks. The trail crests a low rise, offers a couple of side trails to the left to explore, and soon arrives at a more distinct junction with a fire road leading downhill along the eastern edge of the meadow. This is a good route to take because it leads to fine ocean views.

Follow the road as it skirts the eastern edge of the meadow and heads south.

Golden Stars bloom throughout the Santa Mountain Mountains in the spring.

Several ocean overlooks are encountered but the official Ocean Overlook is a rocky outcropping positioned on the far southern edge of the park. Contemplate the coast, then head west to the old ranch reservoir. A few hundred yards away is an oak grove, one of the park's many picturesque picnic spots.

You may follow any of several trails back to the trailhead or join Fire Ecology Trail for a close-up look at how Southern California's Mediterranean flora rises phoenix-like from the ashes.

🌸 ESCONDIDO CANYON

WINDING WAY, ESCONDIDO CANYON TRAILS
4.2 miles round trip with 300-foot elevation gain

Escondido means "hidden" in Spanish—a perfect characterization of this lovely canyon ensconced in the hills above Malibu. Escondido Canyon is hidden from easy view and hidden from better-known Malibu destinations along the coast.

For years it was hidden from hikers, too, because of private property-public use disputes. These tussles have been settled; there is now legal access to this gem of a canyon.

The creek bubbling through Escondido Canyon runs all-year; rain-swollen, it's an impressive little watercourse. At the end of the trail through this box canyon is the hiker's payoff—Escondido Falls, which cascades over limestone rock into a handsome grotto.

Escondido Canyon is but a hop, skip and short hike from neighboring Ramirez Canyon, where two conservation groups—the state's Santa Monica Mountains Conservancy and the nonprofit Mountains Conservancy Foundation— are headquartered in Barbra Streisand's former estate.

The first mile of the hike is along Winding Way, a road that leads by several huge haciendas on high. Mile 2 of the sojourn is altogether different—along a well-maintained footpath that meanders creekside under a canopy of oak and sycamore.

Winter and spring rains seem to make at least one group of Escondido Canyon dwellers very happy—the resident newts—who can often be observed slithering along the trail. Be on the lookout for newt sunbathers and be sure to take lots of newt photos.

DIRECTIONS TO TRAILHEAD: From inland locales, exit Highway 101 in Agoura Hills on Kanan Road and head south 12 miles to Pacific Coast Highway in Malibu. Turn left (down-coast) and drive 1.5 miles to Winding Way. Turn left, then make an immediate right into the signed, 10-space parking lot.

If you're heading up Pacific Coast Highway, you'll spot the Winding Way turnoff about 5 miles up-coast from Malibu proper.

THE HIKE: From the parking lot at the base of Winding Way, walk up the paved road. You can follow a sketchy footpath on the left, then the right side of the road, but it's hardly worth the effort.

As you climb, gawk at the houses ahead of you, then about-face and savor the ocean vistas behind you. About a mile from the trailhead, you'll close-in on a distinct, tree-lined canyon. Join a footpath that traverses a modest-size meadow and follow it to the bottom of Escondido Canyon.

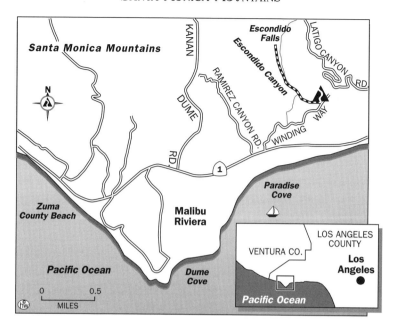

After the trail crosses Escondido Creek, it junctions. The right fork heads down-creek and over toward Ramirez Canyon. Take the left branch of the trail and walk up-creek.

A couple of side trails wander over the chaparral-cloaked slopes, but stick with the main trail that follows the creek. A half-mile into the canyon, look heavenward and observe the big waterfall ahead; this glimpse should prove more than sufficient motivation to hike the last half-mile or so to the base of Escondido Falls. The falls cascades into a peaceful, fern- and moss-lined grotto.

Very skilled scramblers can reach a second falls, nearly three times as high as the first, with a 15-minute climb; however, the slippery canyon slopes make this a difficult, even dangerous, proposition, and there are some long-standing private property concerns.

On your return trip, enjoy an optional tour of lower Escondido Canyon via a couple of unsigned footpaths crisscrossing National Park Service land.

❀ ARROYO SEQUIT

ARROYO SEQUIT LOOP TRAIL
2-mile loop with 200-foot elevation gain

Wildflowers, waterfalls, and a hike to remember are the attractions of Arroyo Sequit Park, a gem of a little preserve located just off Mulholland Highway in the Santa Monica Mountains.

Hikers can experience the park's considerable charms via a lollipop-shaped trail system that loops through open meadows and dips in an out of the gorge cut by the headwaters of the east fork of Arroyo Sequit. Along the way are grand views of Boney Mountain, western sentinel of the Santa Monicas.

Despite a treasure trove of flowering plants, this 155-acre mountain hideaway, now under the stewardship of the National Park Service, receives few visitors. One reason for Arroyo Sequit's anonymity is its isolation from other parks. Long-planned trails intended to link the park with nearby National Park Service properties such as Malibu Springs and Circle X Ranch have not got off the drawing board and onto the ground. Should the park ever get connected by trail to surrounding destinations, Arroyo Sequit will emerge as a compelling destination or superb trailhead for long rambles through the wild west end of the Santa Monica Mountains.

For now at least, Arroyo Sequit is a family-friendly destination for a nature walk and a picnic. Visit in winter after a rainstorm to view the park's small waterfalls or hike in spring to marvel at the many wildflowers.

The loop around Arroyo Sequit is an excellent wildflower hikes. Some 50 to 75 species of flowers bloom during the spring.

Spring celebrants include lupine, large-flowered phacelia, monkeyflowers, owl's clover and thickets of California roses. Look for white star lily and bleeding heart along the trail heading out of Arroyo Sequit gorge. Hardy inhabitants of the park's nutrient-poor volcanic rock region include blue larkspur, shooting star, fuchsia and ferns.

DIRECTIONS TO TRAILHEAD: From Pacific Coast Highway, just up-coast from Leo Carrillo State Park on the Los Angeles-Ventura county line, drive north and then west on Mulholland Highway 5.6 miles. Turn right (south) at the Arroyo Sequit entry gate and park in the lot. Those journeying from the San Fernando Valley side of the mountains, may exit the Ventura Freeway on Westlake Boulevard (23) in Westlake Village, and head south to Mulholland Highway, continuing south, then west on Mulholland to the park.

THE HIKE: Follow the paved road 0.25 mile to the ranch house (now a caretaker's residence) and old barn. You'll pass a Santa Monica College astronom-

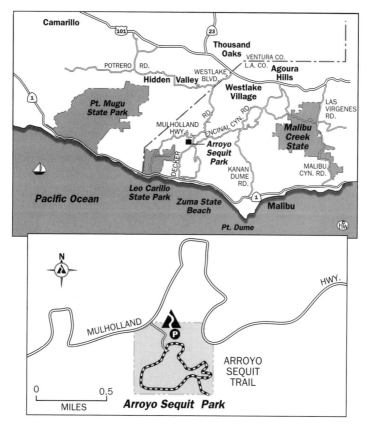

Arroyo Sequit Park

ical observation site; star-gazing is excellent here, far from the lights of the big city. Join the signed path (which boasts a couple of plant identification plaques) that soon crosses a meadow and leads to the rim of the canyon. Savor the particularly dramatic view of Boney Mountain.

The trail descends rather steeply, with the help of some switchbacks, to the bottom of Arroyo Sequit. The trail crosses and re-crosses the creek a couple times as it follows the canyon bottom. Just as it seems as if this hike is about to dead-end in a box canyon, the path crosses the creek a final time and begins climbing the wall of the gorge.

The moderately steep, but well-graded trail returns you to the top of the gorge then heads west to the park's picnic area. Continue on the trail back to the paved road and then on to the parking area.

🌸 NICHOLAS FLAT

NICHOLAS FLAT TRAIL
From Leo Carrillo State Beach to Nicholas Flat is 7 miles round trip
with 1,600-foot elevation gain

Leo Carrillo State Beach has always been a popular surfing spot. Surfers tackle
the well-shaped south swell, while battling the submerged rocks and kelp beds. In
recent years, the state added a large chunk of Santa Monica Mountains parkland,
prompting a name change to Leo Carrillo State Park.

The park's Nicholas Flat area is one of the best spots in the Santa Monica
Mountains for spring wildflowers because it's a meeting place for four different
plant communities. Chaparral, grassland, coastal scrub and oak woodland all converge near the flat. Another reason for the remarkable plant diversity is Leo
Carrillo's elevation, which varies from sea level to nearly 2,000 feet.

Along park trails, look for shooting star, hedge nettle, sugar bush, hollyleaf
redberry, purple sage, chamise, blue dick, deer weed, burr clover, bush lupine,
golden yarrow, fuschia-flowered gooseberry, and many more flowering plants.
Around Nicholas Pond, keep an eye out for wishbone bush, encelia, chia, Parry's
phacelia, ground-pink, California poppy, scarlet bugler and goldfields.

Even when the wildflowers fade away, Nicholas Flat is worth a visit. Its
charms include a big meadow and a pond patrolled by coots. Atop grand boulders
you can enjoy a picnic and savor Malibu coast views.

Nicholas Flat Trail can also be savored for
one more reason: In Southern California, very
few trails connect mountains to the sea. Get
an early start. Until you arrive at oak-dotted
Nicholas Flat itself, there's not much shade en
route.

DIRECTIONS TO TRAILHEAD:
From the west end of the Santa Monica
Freeway in Santa Monica, head up-coast on
Pacific Coast Highway about 25 miles to Leo
Carrillo State Beach. There's free parking
along Coast Highway, and fee parking in the
park's day use area. Signed Nicholas Flat trailhead is located a short distance past the park
entry kiosk, opposite the day use parking are.

THE HIKE: Soon the trail splits. The

322

Nicholas Flat

right branch circles the hill, climbs above Willow Creek, and after a mile, rejoins the main Nicholas Flat Trail. Enjoy this interesting option on your return from Nicholas Flat.

Take the left branch, which immediately begins a moderate to steep ascent of the grassy slopes above the park campground. The trail switchbacks through a coastal scrub community up to a saddle on the ridgeline. Here you'll meet the alternate branch of Nicholas Flat Trail. From the saddle, a short side trail leads south to a hilltop, where there's a fine coastal view. From the viewpoint, you can see Point Dume and the Malibu coastline. During the winter, it's a good place to bring your binoculars and scout the Pacific horizon for migrating whales.

Following the ridgeline, Nicholas Flat Trail climbs inland over chaparral-covered slope. Keep glancing over your right shoulder at the increasingly grand coastal views, and over your left at the open slopes browsed by the park's nimble deer.

After a good deal of climbing, the trail levels atop the ridgeline and you get your first glimpse of grassy, inviting Nicholas Flat. The trail descends past a line of fire-blackened, but unbowed, old oaks and joins an old ranch road that skirts the Nicholas Flat meadows. Picnickers may unpack lunch beneath the shady oaks or out in the sunny meadow. The trail angles southeast across the meadow to a small pond. The man-made pond, used by cattle during the region's ranching days, is backed by some handsome boulders.

Return the way you came until you reach the junction located 0.75 mile from the trailhead. Bear left at the fork and enjoy this alternate trail as it descends into the canyon cut by Willow Creek, contours around an ocean-facing slope, and returns you to the trailhead.

Information Sources

ANGELES NATIONAL FOREST
Supervisor's Office
701 N. Santa Anita Ave.
Arcadia, CA 91006
(626) 574-5200

Los Angeles River Ranger District
12371 N. Little Tujunga Canyon
Road
San Fernando, CA 91342
(818) 899-1900

Chilao Visitor Center
Angeles Crest Highway (Hwy 2)
La Canada, CA 91011
(626) 796-5541

Mt. Baldy Visitor Center
Mt. Baldy Road
Mt. Baldy, CA 91759
(909) 982-2829

San Gabriel River Ranger District
110 N. Wabash Avenue
Glendora, CA 91741
(626) 335-1251

Grassy Hollow Visitor Center
Angeles Crest Highway (Hwy 2)
Wrightwood, CA 92397
(626) 821-6737

Clear Creek Information Center
Angeles Crest Highway (Hwy 2)
La Canada, CA 91011
(626) 821-6764

Big Pines Information Center
Angeles Crest Highway (Hwy 2)
Wrightwood, CA 92397
(760) 249-3504

BONELLI REGIONAL PARK
120 Via Verde Park Road
San Dimas, CA 91773
(909) 599-8411

BRAND PARK
1601 West Mountain Street
Glendale, CA 91201
818.548.2000

CABRILLO MARINE AQUARIUM
3720 Stephen White Drive
San Pedro, California USA 90731
(310) 548-7562

CHARMLEE NATURAL AREA
2577 S. Encinal Canyon Road
Malibu
(310) 457-7247

COLD CREEK CANYON PRESERVE
Stunt Road between Schueren &
Mulholland
Malibu
(310) 456-5627

DESCANSO GARDENS
1418 Descanso Drive
La Cañada Flintridge, CA 91011
818.949.4200

DEUKMEJIAN WILDERNESS PARK
3429 Markridge Road
La Crescenta, CA 91214
(818) 548-3795

EATON CANYON NATURE CENTER
1750 North Altadena Drive
 Pasadena, California 91107
 (626) 398-5420

EL DORADO PARK NATURE CENTER
7550 E. Spring St.
Long Beach
570-1745

ELYSIAN PARK
835 Academy Road
Los Angeles, CA 90012
(213) 485-5054

FRANKLIN CANYON PARK
2600 Franklin Canyon Drive
Beverly Hills
(310) 858-7272

GRIFFITH PARK
4730 Crystal Springs Drive
Los Angeles, CA 90027
(323) 913-4688

KENNETH HAHN STATE RECREATION AREA
4100 South La Cienega Boulevard
Los Angeles, CA 90056
(323) 298-3660

LAMOUNTAINS.COM
(Santa Monica Mountains
Conservancy)
(310) 589-3200 or (323) 221-8900

LEO CARRILLO STATE PARK
35000 W. Pacific Coast Highway
Malibu, CA 90265
(818) 880-0350

LOS ANGELES ARBORETUM & BOTANIC GARDEN
301 N. Baldwin Avenue
Arcadia, CA 91007
(626) 821-3222

LOS ANGELES RIVER CENTER & GARDENS
570 West Avenue Twenty-Six,
Suite 100
Los Angeles, CA 90065
Tel: (323) 221-8900

MALIBU CREEK STATE PARK
1925 Las Virgenes Road
Calabasas, CA 91302
(818) 880-0350

MONROVIA CANYON PARK
200 N. Canyon Blvd
Monrovia
(626) 256-8282.

O'MELVENY PARK
17300 Sesnon Blvd.
Granada Hills
(818) 368-5019

PARAMOUNT RANCH
2813 Cornell Road
Agoura
805-370-2301

PLACERITA CANYON PARK AND NATURE CENTER
19152 Placerita Canyon Rd.
Newhall, CA 91321
(661) 259-7721

POINT MUGU STATE PARK
9000 W. Pacific Coast Highway,
Malibu, CA 90265
(818) 880-0350

PUENTE HILLS LANDFILL NATIVE HABITAT AUTHORITY
7702 Washington Avenue, Suite C
Whittier, CA 90602
(562) 945-9003

RANCHO SANTA ANA BOTANIC GARDEN
1500 North College Avenue
Claremont, CA 91711
(909) 625-8767

RANCHO SIMI RECREATION & PARKS DISTRICT
1692 Sycamore Drive
Simi Valley, California 93065
(805) 584-4400

RUNYAN CANYON PARK
(213) 485-5572

SANTA MONICA MOUNTAINS CONSERVANCY
(310) 589-3200, (323) 221-8900

SANTA MONICA MOUNTAINS NATIONAL RECREATION AREA
401 Hillcrest Dr.
Thousand Oaks, CA 91360
(805) 370-2301

SCHABARUM COUNTY PARK
17250 East Colima Road
Rowland Heights, California 91748
(626) 854-5560

SOUTH COAST BOTANIC GARDEN
26300 Crenshaw Blvd.
Palos Verdes Peninsula, CA
(310) 544-6815

TEMESCAL GATEWAY PARK
15601 Sunset Blvd.
Pacific Palisades, CA 90272
Tel: (310) 454-1395

TOPANGA STATE PARK
(310) 455-2465

THEODORE PAYNE
FOUNDATION
10459 Tuxford St.
Sun Valley, CA 91352
(818) 768-1802

WILLIAM S. HART PARK
24151 San Fernando Road
Newhall, California 91321
Museum (661) 254-4584
Park (661) 259-0855

WILL ROGERS STATE
HISTORIC PARK
1501 Will Rogers Park Road
Pacific Palisades, CA 90272
310-454-8212

The Trailmaster Index

CELEBRATING L.A. COUNTY'S SCENIC, SUBLIME AND RIDICULOUS POINTS OF INTEREST

HIGHEST PEAK WITHIN LOS ANGELES CITY LIMITS
Mt. Lukens (5,074 feet)

LARGEST STATE PARK WITHIN THE CITY LIMITS OF ANY AMERICAN CITY
Topanga State Park (9,000 acres), within L.A. city limits

THE REWARDS OF PUBLIC OFFICE
(Los Angeles County Supervisors with Parks Renamed for Them)
Otterbein County Park now (Pete) Schabarum Regional County Park;
Puddingstone Reservoir now Frank G. Bonelli Regional County Park; Baldwin
Hills State Recreation Area now Kenneth Hahn State Recreation Area

LOCATION OF L.A.'S FIRST TV TRANSMITTER
Mt. Lee, better known as the location of the Hollywood sign

FIRST NATIONAL FOREST SET ASIDE IN CALIFORNIA
San Gabriel Timberland Reserve (now Angeles National Forest), established 1892

WORST LOS ANGELES WILDFIRE IN TERMS OF LOSS OF LIFE
36 workmen perished in a 1933 brushfire in Griffith Park

BEST VIEWS OF EARTHQUAKE FAULTS
Santa Susana Fault from O'Melveny Park
Whittier Fault from Schabarum County Park
Newport-Inglewood Fault from Signal Hill

WORLD'S LARGEST COLLECTION OF NATIVE CEANOTHUS (CALIFORNIA LILAC)
Rancho Santa Ana Botanic Garden, Claremont

NAMES SHORTENED FROM THEIR 18TH-CENTURY USAGE
Mt. San Antonio, Old Baldy, De Valle, Santa Catalina de Bonia de los Encinos,
The Valley, Pueblo de la Reina de Los Angeles, L.A.

FIRST PARK IN AMERICA LOST TO FREEWAY CONSTRUCTION
Arroyo Seco Park to Pasadena Freeway, 1941

FIRST PARK IN AMERICA MADE POSSIBLE BY FREEWAY CONSTRUCTION
El Dorado Park, Long Beach by San Gabriel River Freeway, mid-1960s

MOST VISITED NATIONAL FOREST IN THE UNITED STATES
Angeles

LARGEST LOS ANGELES CITY PARK
Griffith, 4,100 acres (five times the size of New York's Central Park)

SECOND LARGEST
O'Melveny, 714 acres

WE'LL BE DEAD BEFORE IT'S DONE AWARD
To the Santa Monica Mountains' Backbone Trail; after more than 30 years,
this 65-mile-long trail has yet to be completed

MOST VISITED PARK
Griffith, with about 10 million visitors per year

LEAST VISITED PARK
Cold Creek Canyon Preserve with about 1,000 visitors per year

REPUBLICAN STRONGHOLDS
(President Ronald) Reagan Ranch, (Senator Frank) Flint Peak,
(Governor) George Deukmejian Wilderness Park

ONLY CITY IN U.S. BISECTED BY A MOUNTAIN RANGE
Los Angeles, by the Santa Monica Mountains

SPANISH OR ENGLISH, BUT NOT BOTH, PLEASE
Montecito Hills (Little Hills Hills); Rio Hondo River (Deep River River);
Arroyo Seco Canyon (Dry Canyon Canyon)

PARKS HONORING MOVIE COWBOYS
William S. Hart County Park in Newhall, (Ronald) Reagan Ranch—part of
Malibu Creek State Park—in Santa Monica Mountains, Wilacre (Will Acres)
Park in Hollywood Hills, Will Rogers State Historic Park in Santa Monica
Mountains, Leo Carrillo State Park in Santa Monica Mountains, Ray "Crash"
Corrigan, Corriganville Park, Simi Hills

Index

Cartographer Hélène Webb is an artist and cartographer for maps and illustrated marine charts. A USCG Captain, Hélène shares her expertise and love for the Santa Barbara Channel with charter sail trips and sailing lessons. Contact her at www.aquarelle.com

Editor Cheri Rae has a long background in lifestyle sports and served on the editorial staff of *Runner's World, Bicycle Sport,* and many other magazines. As a book editor, she's particularly fond of projects with California themes and subjects.

Book designer Jim Cook is a master typography with more 30 years of experience in designing fine books. A native with a deep appreciation for California and the natural world, he decided to evoke the Great Hiking Era in books designed for The Trailmaster.

Cover Artist Gwen Pentecost is a native Californian now living in Pinetop, Arizona. Her paintings capture the diverse landscape of the West and Southwest. Learn more about her work at www.artbypentecost.com.

Long-time Los Angeles Times hiking columnist John McKinney is the author of a dozen books about walking, hiking, and nature. McKinney writes articles and commentaries about walking for national publications, promotes hiking and conservation on radio and TV, and serves as a consultant for hiking tours and hiking-related businesses. Contact him at www.thetrailmaster.com